Protecting the Workforce

Protecting the Workforce

A Defense of Workers' Rights in Global Supply Chains

Marquita R. Walker

LEXINGTON BOOKS
Lanham • Boulder • New York • London

Published by Lexington Books
An imprint of The Rowman & Littlefield Publishing Group, Inc.
4501 Forbes Boulevard, Suite 200, Lanham, Maryland 20706
www.rowman.com

6 Tinworth Street, London SE11 5AL

British Library Cataloguing in Publication Information Available

Library of Congress Cataloging-in-Publication Data Available

ISBN 9781498586160 (hardback : alk. paper) | ISBN 9781498586177 (electronic)

∞™ The paper used in this publication meets the minimum requirements of American National Standard for Information Sciences Permanence of Paper for Printed Library Materials, ANSI/NISO Z39.48-1992.

Printed in the United States of America

Contents

Acknowledgments

My interest in the topic of global supply chains stems from my years in manufacturing as a worker and member of an organized labor union. Serving in several capacities within the union (steward, first female chief steward, bargaining agent member, executive board member, secretary/treasurer) with a membership of 1,200 allowed me to learn firsthand how difficult maneuvering the complexities of the labor-management relationship are and how little power workers have to effect change on their own without the power of the collective behind them. This efficacy is exacerbated within global supply chains because of the neoliberalism rampant in our current economic and political environments and the animus against organized labor and the collective in general. My belief is a shift toward worker protections in this unequal power differential which favors corporations must occur if workers worldwide are to survive and maintain any sort of living standard. I believe it is in the best long-term interest of all workers worldwide for the extreme dichotomies which now exist between corporations and labor to become more equitable. My hope is that this book, *Protecting the Workforce: A Defense of Workers' Rights in Global Supply Chains*, will contribute to this field of literature.

It is unlikely in our current political and economic climate that changes in "business as usual" will come from the top down. Our value system and our belief in the institutions which protect this country and its workers are under attack from a conservative neoliberal ideology which only values profits and not people. The hope for change lies in resisting the powerful corporate and institutional forces which create hostility toward the very workers who add value to a product, the collective which fortifies and represents workers through the bonds of solidarity, and the belief that all people have a right to decent work, a fair standard of living, and dignity in the workplace.

Throughout my life, I have primarily tried to do two things: provide for and take care of my family and represent workers to the best of my ability. My failures in these areas are my own. Having said that, I dedicate this book to my son, Shane, who died July 25, 2015, from an ethanol and fentanyl overdose. The opioid crisis is a real and constant danger. It is my hope that someday the social and economic stigma associated with drug and alcohol addiction is better understood and there are more successful ways to help those struggling with addictions. Clearly what we are doing now is not working.

Introduction

Global supply chains (GSCs) are networks of local, regional, national, and international firms who produce and distribute goods and services worldwide and affect our lives in a multitude of ways. Each product, good, or service we use is produced and distributed via a network of suppliers, producers, and distributors whose digital reach is global. Products made in Bangladesh may use inputs from South Africa and be assembled in the United States. The far-reaching tentacles of global production means we as consumers are unsure of where the goods we purchase are made, under what conditions they are produced, or who produces them. Even if consumers were able to track the trajectory of production, there is little recourse for consumers to take which doesn't involve costly litigation and long-term court battles. Societal influences spurred by status envy constantly encourage us to purchase products we don't need and bombard us with ads to buy certain products, consume more goods, or pledge loyalty to a brand. Our children want the latest sports shoes from Nike, our grandchildren want the newest robotic toys, and adults wish for bigger houses, faster cars, and the latest fashions. How did we get to a point in which our livelihoods and the very essence of our beings depended upon consumerism? Why are we so concerned with stuff?

PLANNED OBSOLESCENCE

The drive to consume hasn't always been the modus operandi of the world's population. During the Second Industrial Revolution, sometimes called the Technological Revolution and generally agreed to be between 1860 and 1910, in which increased technology witnessed economic progress and rapid changes in transportation, products were made to last. If one purchased a Model T Ford from Henry Ford's River Rouge automobile factory near Detroit, Michigan, in 1908, one could expect the vehicle to last for decades. There was no need to replace one's current vehicle because all Model T Fords were built to last, designed exactly alike, and only came in the color black. Consequently, it is little wonder Ford Motor Company's current tag line for advertising purposes, "Built to Last," reflects Ford's traditional long product history. The lasting value built into other products such as tools and furniture diminished the need for new product because goods and products were made of durable material and crafted for years of use.

This was a problem for all manufacturers in a capitalist economic society whose existence depended upon consumerism. In order to sell more product, whether cars, furniture, or fashion, the number of consumers had to increase. Enter Alfred P. Sloan in the 1930s, sometimes known as the savior of General Motors, who introduced into the automobile market the idea of *planned obsolescence*, the idea that products with shorter shelf lives required periodic newer purchases thus increasing sales. Planned obsolescence means producing goods and products which quickly become obsolete through design changes, use of non-durable inputs, or termination of replacement parts, requiring frequent replacement. Sloan borrowed this idea from women's fashions. He noted that women often purchased new seasonal dresses even though their older dresses were not threadbare. He simply applied this logic to vehicles by introducing yearly model changes. He also catered to various classes of consumers by introducing less expensive cars for the common man and more expensive cars for the elite. He also introduced the idea of credit for those who didn't have cash upfront.

One big problem in moving forward with model changes was the idea of *social wastefulness*, purchasing new product when one's current product still had value. Sloan responded to social wastefulness by introducing a market for used cars. Thus was born the idea of trade-ins, trading an existing or older car for credit toward a newer car. This transaction was designed to pacify the guilt a consumer might feel when purchasing a new vehicle when there was nothing wrong with the current vehicle.

Convincing consumers to purchase new product when their current product was still useful meant changing the mindset of a society who valued thrift and conservation as God-like qualities. The idea of planned obsolescence had to be gradually ingrained into the psyche of consumers so there was no guilt or remorse for purchasing replacement goods when value still existed in their current goods. This was no small feat for a US population just recovering from the Great Depression. The classical economic tenet encouraging consumerism was believed necessary to lift the United States from a depressed economy in which around 25 percent of the population was jobless. The shift in mindset was a resounding success. Increased spending and purchasing new vehicles or the latest greatest gadget became associated with amplified status. Consequently looking at the car one drove or the outfit one wore signaled one's wealth and social status. The desire for increased social status compelled people to work harder to earn more money to purchase more goods. The cycle continues today.

THE DRIVE TO PRODUCE MORE GOODS

The history of consumerism originates within a capitalist economic system based on producing and selling goods and services at the lowest cost per unit. Capitalism, by its nature, requires exploiting resource-rich regions and labor in order to produce low-cost product which is then sold to consumers in local, regional, national, and international markets; capitalism's goal has been and continues to be profit making for shareholders. This is achieved through competition between producers who fight for market share among consumers by producing a single unit of a good or service at the lowest cost. Efficiency drives competition, and competition drives capitalism. This circular continuation requires unlimited resources in the form of land, capital, and labor, so owners of production via corporations constantly need to shave production costs. Production costs include inputs into the production process: land, capital, and labor. Since land and capital are fixed costs, corporations look to labor as an avenue of easy cost reduction. Seeking cheap labor by outsourcing or offshoring production devalues workers by making them a disposable and exchangeable human component in the production process. Workers then become no more than interchangeable parts in a system seeking higher profits for its shareholders.

The push to produce, sell, and distribute goods and services globally in an efficient manner has divided the world into the Global North and the Global South, two distinct classifications separating developed nations from developing nations, producer nations from consumer nations, and richer nations from poorer nations. The search for cheaper resources drives corporations to regions in which labor and environmental laws are weak or unenforced, where populations are desperate for work because their standard of living is so low, and where untapped natural resources abound. This has created an international divide between the Global North, developed consumer countries whose populations are among the richest in the world, and the Global South, undeveloped and underdeveloped countries whose populations have been exploited and starved into submission through trade agreements and structural adjustment policies. These policies are touted as job creators for undeveloped and underdeveloped countries where few good paying jobs exist, so poorer nations have little choice but to accept these empty promises.

In reality, these poorer nations are offered an illusion of choice through the seduction of jobs and raised living standards. What they receive in return are low-paying, substandard, and hazardous jobs which suck resources from their land. They are held hostage by promises of capital infusion through interest-bearing loans to provide much-needed work. Forced to pay a high rate of return on the loans, poorer nations are consequently unable to sustain their own infrastructure or provide social transfer payments to their citizens. This exploitative and abusive way to do business is sustained through corporate greed and is a zero-sum gain for the Global South and a win-win for the Global North.

The interconnected nature of global communication, technology, and transportation means our world is getting smaller in terms of the production and distribution of goods. We easily now are able to buy product from anywhere in the world and have it delivered to our home in a few days (and sometimes by a drone), offshore capital anywhere around the globe, and employ labor in countries who skirt labor laws and worker protections through lax enforcement. One hundred years ago, these global maneuvers were not even a twinkle in the eye of entrepreneurs then just developing electricity, telephones, and talking boxes (televisions). The military foray into computers for purposes of protecting secure information to keep our country safe has morphed into artificial intelligence (AI) which can beat human intellect at *Jeopardy*. Computers can now take over many human jobs and do those jobs more efficiently. What does this mean for future human labor? Will AI replace the need for human workers?

SITUATING GSCS IN THEORY

There exist several lens through which we can look at GSCs to make sense of their origins, developments, and current status. Theories provided by social theorists help us make sense of historical social, political, and economic events which interact to create ways of knowing or looking at inequalities. A synthesis of these interactions provide general trends or patterns from which we make certain assumptions. During the mid-twentieth century, social theorists deemed structural-functionalism, a social system in which each "function" within the "structure" was dependent upon or related to another function, to provide stability to a culture. The structure changed as the functions changed. One such theorist was Talcott Parsons (Clark 1972) and another was Wilbert Moore (Moore 1974); both claimed social systems changed by adaptation to the environment. Critics of structural-functionalism couldn't square its naïve approach to more modern times in which the process of industrialization forced societies to change as the division of labor was altered due to technological changes. These theorists believed modernization was more a function of looking at societal differences resulting from specialized institutional and work roles. Modernization theory claimed societies embracing long-term, specialized industrial functions and stable governments would progress economically, and countries which did not conform would remain stagnant and poor as a result of "historical backwardness" (Shannon 2018, 6). Critics of modernization theory and structural-functionalism fault these theories for their insistence on orderliness and stability and a lack of acknowledgment that conflict begets change, differences of group identities, social status, and prowess exist within countries, and an assertion that industrialized nations had imposed on poorer countries an "'imposed backwardness' through exploitation and repression" (Shannon 2018, 8).

Influencing theoretical approaches to understanding GSCs' emergence are the writings of Marx, who emphasized power relationships between the owner of production and workers would eventually lead to class conflict and the overthrow of the bourgeois, Lenin, who believed imperialism would eventually result in the demise of capitalism, and Braudel, who foreshadows the idea of core and periphery countries as the economic dyad in which exploitation takes place and posits the historical evolution of capitalism since the 1500s (Shannon 2018). As an outgrowth of these influences, dependency theory reflects the difficulty peripheral countries have in achieving economic success (Amin 1976; Frank 1984). Both theorists agree corporate exploitation by rich core countries has kept periphery countries economically disadvantaged and decreased their living standards. Further analysis of interactions between core and periphery countries is the purview of Immanuel Wallerstein and world system theory.

A macro look at GSCs through world systems theory as propagated by Wallerstein and emerging from sociology suggests capitalism was accidently created as a result of conflict in feudalism during the eleventh through thirteenth centuries. Agricultural deficits like droughts fostered epidemics like plagues which fostered economic depressions. To recover, Europeans reached across borders to access raw materials through conquest or acquisition. World systems theory focuses on a power hierarchy between three categories of nations: core, those nations capable of independent self-control which dominate/exploit weaker nations, semi-peripheral, less developed countries acting as a buffer between rich and poor nations, and peripheral, the least economically developed and technologically orientated nations which house unskilled labor (Wallerstein 2011). Proponents of world systems theory study societies in relationship to one another as a "minimal requirement for the intelligent study of social change" (Chirot 1982, 102) while critics fault the theory for failing to take into account similar capitalist development in countries regardless of their position within the world system (Chirot 1982; Wallerstein 2011). One critic is Robinson (2011) who argues globalization is a recent phenomenon "associated with social change of the late 20th and early 21st centuries" (3) while others would argue globalization began around the 1500s or the dawn of history.

I situate this research in Robinson's global capital theory because I believe the current globalized environment has qualitatively and quantitative new dimensions unlike any seen in recorded history. Global capitalism theory views capitalism, which previously positioned production, income/wealth accumulations, class relations, and governance within nation-states during the Fordist era, as a flexible global system integrating nation-states and allowing corporations to freely dictate financial operations in a post-Fordist era. Robinson (2012) explains, "Globalization represents a new epoch in the ongoing evolution of world capitalism distinguished by the rise of a globally-integrated production and financial system, an emergent transnational capitalist class, and incipient transnational state apparatuses" (349).

WHAT THIS BOOK OFFERS

This book explores the nature and structure of GSCs, the corporate and institutional push for higher profits at all costs, the abuse, degradation, and exploitation workers face in their work lives, and the recommendations for remedy made by international collectives seeking to reinstate workers' rights and protections. GSCs are the primary production and delivery systems for the world's goods and services. They touch every facet of human life because populations are dependent on outsourcing almost every daily activity: food production, housing, healthcare, child and elder care, education, transportation, and communication. None of these activities take place within a vacuum; the production and delivery of each is interconnected to other state and international regions where these goods and services are placed in the hands of consumers as cheaply and quickly as possible. The story of GSCs is one of an international production and delivery system which seeks a competitive advantage within all markets to produce units at the lowest cost and extract maximum profits for shareholders.

Chapter 1, "How the Evolution of Global Supply Chains Exploits Workers," serves as an introduction to the history, organization, framework, and complexity of global supply chains and the theories of work organization which explain their proliferation. The focus is on worker exploitation and abuse as a consequence of corporate power over worker power. Multinational corporations (MNCs), controlled by large financial institutions, set the agenda for worldwide trade, investment, and coordination of operations of GSCs. MNCs employ lobbyists to encourage and secure legislation through political channels in order to sway governments toward neoliberal policies which favor corporations and weaken worker and environmental protections. Worker and environmental safeguards on an international scale have been so compromised by corporate power that workers, particularly in the Global South, now have little recourse for remedy through the courts, international tribunals, or trade unions. The international framework under which GSCs operate provides an opportunity for exploitation at each point along the supply chain where value is added to the product.

Chapter 2, "The Regulatory Framework," provides an overview of the regulatory framework, its evolution, the rule makers, the mechanism for dispute settlement, and the fallout to workers, workers' rights, social justice issues, and the environment. The corporation, whose goal is to make profits at all costs, is at odds with workers who seek protections against abuse through labor unions and legislation. The tension between these competing ideologies is known as cultural hegemony, the idea that powerbrokers in the form of corporations control the workforce through social and cultural values and norms instead of violence and threats. The pendulum for control of the workforce has swung to the right in recent decades because legislation and public opinion have favored corporations. The transnational nature of GSCs makes governing from an international standpoint difficult because various players in the supply chain seek to maintain autonomy within their own country, and currently no mechanism exists to fill those unregulated international spaces. This unregulated space in which no international authority exists allows corporations to run roughshod over workers. International organizations such as the G20 and the United Nations offer recommendations for worker protections, but, to date, there has been little movement to agree upon those suggestions.

Chapter 3, "The Development of Global Supply Chains," explores the drivers of GSCs and their impact on development. How necessary are components like forced and child labor, human trafficking, privatization, and deregulation to remain in place for GSCs to exist? Logic would suggest coupling sound investment practices with core labor standards should contribute to the eradication of these detrimental and negative components as well as positively affect global workers, increase worker protections, and ensure a clean environment. Establishing enforceable international regulations could go hand in hand with privatization and engage all workers in meaningful and profitable work while increasing corporate persona as reliable partners in the global manufacture of goods. When workers, the most valuable asset a corporation has, are treated with respect, paid a living wage, and provided safe and sanitary working conditions, the potential engines of economic growth via ingenuity and creativity are unleashed, and the longevity of the corporation as well as the economic good of the community increases. Respect for human rights is associated with uplifting the health, education, and security of all workers, fostering human capital development, and engendering economic security.

Chapter 4, "The Fragmentation of Work in the Global Supply Chains," looks at the continuum of inequity in GSCs and provides various examples of the realities of precarious work. Narratives include what constitutes decent work in the GSC, how labor is fragmented, and what effect that fragmentation has on workers and the environment. Fragmented work within GSCs is designed to solidify corporate power through weakened labor and employment laws, third parties acting as buffers for corporate liability, and the distribution of subsidiaries via supply chains in spaces where no international law exists. Corporations have used GSCs as a tool to facilitate corporate greed by organizational restructuring and flexibility in production processes which translates into strategies diminishing worker rights and protections. Consequently, workers in the formal and informal economy are disadvantaged when seeking restitution for physical injury or economic harm as a result of employer negligence.

Chapter 5, "How Industrial Tragedies Foster Policy," explains how tragedies can become focusing events which beget strategies to improve working conditions through policy changes, give impetus to workers' voice, and increase representation within the labor-management relationship. Multiple examples include the New York City Triangle Shirtwaist factory fire (1911) and the Bangladesh Rena Plaza collapse (2013). Tragedies, natural and manmade, sometimes galvanize public opinion in favor of workers when obvious corporate abuse is brought to light. Owners of production, often the financial institutions who fund corporations, have successfully distanced themselves from supply chains in which the actual work takes place, thus skirting culpability for industrial tragedies. This is the modus operandi through which MNCs transfer production costs to suppliers and avoid liability in case of workplace injuries. Though some legislative protections have been put in place, the track record for improving worker protections is dismal.

Chapter 6, "Corporate Social Responsibilities," explores how and why unilateral, voluntary, and non-binding corporate social responsibility (CSR) models have failed, the ineffectual auditing processes used in identifying and addressing the causes and barriers to success, examples of failed CSR efforts, and steps which could be taken to increase CSR within MNCs. The voluntary nature of CSR allows firms representing themselves as good corporate citizens to continue engaging in human rights and environmental abuses because to do otherwise would increase production and delivery costs and cut into corporate profits. Current self-regulation has proven to be ineffective. Global framework agreements (GFAs), instruments negotiated between multinational corporations and global union federations (GUFs) in which both parties agree to respect the labor and environmental standards of countries in which they do business, seems to be the best way forward. Yet the power to implement and enforce GFAs lies with MNCs who fear sharing power the GUFs will weaken their profit-making abilities.

Chapter 7, "Political and Legal Strategies to Regulate Global Supply Chains," describes the arguments and challenges employers face concerning regulations within the GSC and how employers attempt to mediate workers' concerns through voluntary measures. The international community agrees human slavery or environmental degradation should have no legal protections and should not be embedded as "business as usual" within MNCs' operations. Yet, efforts to curb industry initiatives through corporate responsibility codes or multilateral initiatives like the United Nations Global Compact, a corporate sustainability initiative encouraging firms to align strategies/operations with the universal principles on human rights, labor and environment laws, and take action again corruption and for advancing societal goals, have proven insufficient to curb corporate misbehavior. Current efforts to construct a top-down international framework under public, civic, and corporate governance is known as the Protect, Respect, and Remedy Framework, a set of practical ways to integrate human rights concerns with enterprise risk management. To date no international enforcement mechanism exists to police violations and apply remedies.

Chapter 8, "Strategies and Tools to Promote Workers' Rights in Global Supply Chains," demonstrates approaches to protecting workers' rights in GSCs through corporate research, soft laws, and technology. Workers are not without hope in resisting corporate power. Though the deck is very much slanted against workers, there are avenues of resistance which, when used strategically, can alter the power imbalance between workers and corporations in a free market capitalist economic system which seems to only favor and gives credence to corporate greed. Workers, fixating on long-term gains which advantage workers and the environment, must join together in solidarity through collectives, find common ground on which to build platforms of resistance, and work through an international framework which supports human and environmental rights for workers worldwide.

My rationale for writing this book is threefold: (1) to make students as workers and consumers of information, aware of the structural nature of GSCs, the intricate network of stakeholders involved in the production and distribution of goods and services, and how Global North and Global South workers are interconnected in unknown ways; (2) to explore how the slanted power dynamics involved in the worker/corporate dyad disadvantage workers through legislation, the courts, and international tribunals; and most importantly, (3) to provide hope to workers worldwide that there exist avenues of resistance through collective strength via trade unions and workers associations which can help shift the balance the power toward a more equitable dynamic which recognizes workers and their valuable contribution to GSCs.

Chapter One

How the Evolution of Global Supply Chains Exploits Workers

LEARNING OBJECTIVES

1. Students will be able to identify at least three hallmarks of global supply chains (GSCs) which violate workers' rights.
2. Students will be able to explain how the Fordist and post-Fordist frameworks of work organization operate.
3. Students will be able to outline three of the historical theories under which GSCs operate.
4. Students will be able to contrast the current methods multinational corporations (MNCs) use to protect workers' rights with the power of the collective to protect workers' rights.

Key terms: Global supply chain, Global value chain, Multinational corporation, Work organization, Worker exploitation

HOW SUPPLY CHAINS BECAME GLOBAL

GSCs are the current dominant production and distribution model for goods and services worldwide. Yet, supply chains, in some form, have existed ever since the first agricultural and household goods were produced and exchanged. A *supply chain* is simply a conduit through which goods and services are produced, distributed, bartered, traded, sold, transferred, or swapped in a *market*, a place where buyers and sellers come together. Early supply chains were local because transportation and communication outlets were poor; close proximity was necessary for the farmer/businessman to sell his goods and services to the nearby general population. Most goods and services were produced in the home and involved *craft production*, a specialized form of pre-industrialized work organization in which the producer of the good or service has total control of the work process. Entry into the craft profession was selective and usually involved long years of apprenticeship to learn the craft's trade and was often confined to relatives of the master craftsman. During this period the owners of production, as master craftsmen, owned and controlled their own work processes in a capitalist economy which placed high value on hard work and individualism. To be successful, one had to put in long hours and work hard.

As the *Industrial Revolution*, which most scholars agree was from 1820 to 1870, supplanted the agricultural era, the production of goods and services moved from the home to the factory and allowed local markets to broaden. The transition from home to factory is notable because it engendered the biggest advance in per capital earning ever, moved craft production to mass goods production, and logistically moved workers from the farm into cities. Because more consumers wanted more and different goods and services, new markets opened and more transactions could be facilitated though better methods of transportation and communication.

Broader distribution networks were made possible with the proliferation of steam technology during the late nineteenth and early twentieth centuries which allowed railroads and steamships to transport goods made in one part of the country to consumers in other parts of the country. This separation of production and consumption fostered the mass production of goods and services which allowed owners of production to take advantage of "scale economies and comparative advantage" (Baldwin 2012, 2). Around 1850, industrialization became rooted in northern geographies such as North America, Britain, and Europe, while agriculture was still predominant in southern geographies such as India and China. This dichotomy of northern industry, characterized by wage earners, innovation, economies of scale, and specialization, versus southern agriculture, characterized by slavery-like conditions and decreased incentives, created wage disparities still in existence today. Mass migration from southern lands to northern lands provided workers for this booming economy. Growth in northern industry fueled by two world wars and the Great Depression created spaces for industrialized sectors to cluster; close proximity for acquiring inputs such as raw materials and workers situated large factories nears rivers and lakes, manufacturing goods in large campus-like settings, and transporting outputs by rail or river reduced production costs and allowed northern geographies to flourish. This pattern of production and distribution continued until the digital revolution transformed the manufacturing landscape.

The expansion of operations meant the market for goods and services could be extended to broader communities who might produce different goods and services which increased consumers' choices of available products and services. Better forms of transportation and communication extended the supply chains which carried these goods and services from local markets to intra-state and interstate markets. Steam power, coupled with the inventions of the cotton gin, electricity, and the telegraph, stimulated a capitalist economy which was not without its problems. Mass production required hundreds of thousands of workers, including children, who were channeled into factory and mill settings in which working conditions were damp, polluted, and unsanitary. Workers, in the absence of safety and labor laws, found themselves in dangerous, unsafe, and contaminated workplaces which required unlimited work hours and schedules and inflicted mental, emotional, and physical anguish on their minds and bodies.

The production and distribution of goods and services in US markets has, from World War II to around 1970, been guided by the Fordist model of production, the legacy of Henry Ford who mass produced automobiles in an assembly-line fashion based on *Taylorism*, a strict adherence to efficient and sequenced motions in the production process. During this Fordist era, often known as the Golden Age of production, manufacturing became very standardized which led to increased productivity and economies of scale which birthed rising wages for workers and profits for firms. Federal laws during the New Deal era ensuring collective bargaining allowed workers to negotiate wages, benefits, and working conditions with employers who sought to maximize profits, and a middle class of people arose who could provide an increased standard of living for themselves and their families. These economic good times continued until 1970.

THE RE-ORGANIZATION OF WORK

Work organization plays a unique role in production and distribution within global supply chains. During the Fordist era, factory work on an assembly line required workers to remain fixed, devote time and motion to one specific action in the production process, and work in concert; workers remained at stationary posts while a conveyor belt brought the work to them via the assembly line. Each worker had one specialized skill he or she employed before the unit moved to the next worker. The goal was to make acceptable products with few defects and keep an acceptable inventory of goods at the ready for consumer purchase (Jha 2014). Shop floor bosses were then able to control the rate of production by slowing down or increasing the speed of the assembly line. This type of management tactic, known as the *speed up,* effectively allowed shop floor bosses to control the flow of production without accompanying pay increases. Workers were relegated to mind-numbing, repetitive motions in one specific task and often required to meet production quotas or lose their jobs. Known as *Fordism,* this system of mass production effectively wrested control of the work process away from the worker and into the hands of management. Workers, like the products they produced, became little more than interchangeable parts in a production process which now considered them as expendable commodities.

The 1970s witnessed the reorganization of work. A shift in the locus of control of production and delivery of goods and services moved from heavy industry-specific manufacturing firms in automobiles, aircrafts, and other durable goods to transnational retailers and marketers who designed images and "brands" and produced light manufactured goods such as clothing and electronics in multinational locations. This post-Fordist era introduced a new organizational work model into American production known as the Japanese Toyota *Just in Time* (JIT) model. Touted as "lean" manufacturing, the JIT model "sought perfection in the production process which meant no defects, flexibility in model changes, and no inventory buildup. Engaging in lean production means creating a multi-skilled workforce capable of using increased technology to produce 'products in enormous variety'" (Jha 2014, 5). The goal of JIT work organization was to produce product on demand and deliver product to the consumer in a short span of time. The mantra used during the introduction of JIT production was to work smarter, not harder. This new model of work organization utilized a team approach which meant that several workers were usually responsible for producing a module containing several parts; the modules were then assembled to produce some product. Each team member was trained on each task and became skilled in multi-tasking in order to produce the module; decisions were team based rather than individually based. Inventory was kept at a minimum thus reducing the cost of storing product which took up warehouse space and retrieval time in packing and shipping the product. This would result in increased profits for the firm by saving warehousing costs and increase consumer demand by delivering product on an as needed basis.

Enter the age of globalization. As technology continued to replace workers in the production process, a new invention revolutionized the manufacturing landscape and changed the way humans and work interacted. The transistor, a small silicon-based semi-conductor device which allows electrons to flow through solid matter reliably, cheaply, and quickly, "enabled a rich array of new products and services" (Ross 1998, 7). The transistor revolution kick-started the electronics industry and allowed for the production of radios, televisions, calculators, and microwave ovens. This one small invention revolutionized an entire economy "to one in which an organized system for management resources reflect digitized technologies, upgraded skill levels, flexible work arrangement, globalized markets, new managerial controls, lateral workflows, and an emphasis on service work rather than manufacturing work" (Walker 2015, 28–29).

The transistor spurred digital technology and birthed a digital revolution which allowed for more efficient transportation and communication and faster and easier production, preservation, transfer, and shipping of goods and services to expanding markets which now reach consumers in local, regional, national, or international markets. Computerized technology made possible the digitization of countless jobs which could be performed worldwide and increased competition for those jobs between workers in industrialized countries, who made decent wages, and workers in deindustrialized countries, who were paid poverty wages. Any job that could be digitized could be offshored or outsourced. The implications for the employment relationship between management and labor became more polarized as more and more manufacturing jobs were shipped abroad in search of cheaper labor.

This digital revolution requires firms to adjust to technological changes within a global context. Globalized firms increase the power of consumption by opening new markets to more consumers via the elimination of trade barriers through trade agreements. As consumption and production needs arise, firms look for ways to reduce costs by seeking the best and brightest, most productive, and most innovative workers in order to maintain their market shares. They seek out countries with fewer governmental and environmental regulations which allows them to further reduce input costs and increase profit margins. Always looking for cheaper inputs, firms look to undeveloped and underdeveloped countries whose natural resources are plentiful and who need to sell those resources in order to meet state financial obligations and provide social welfare for their citizens.

The introduction of technology in "information, communication and electronics, made it possible to globalize the production process" (Jha 2014, 3) and the ability of global actors to connect with each other worldwide ushered in an era of lowered wages for American workers who saw production outsourced and offshored so firms could capitalize on lower labor costs. This shifting production and distribution system resulted in a new transnational production paradigm focused on producing goods at the lowest cost while disregarding the toll on workers. The age of state interventions gave way to global interventions governed by the *World Trade Organization* (WTO) which effectively decentered production processes by moving them from the Global North to the Global South in search of cheaper raw materials and labor surpluses. This new more flexible approach to production which takes advantage of economies of scale and scope powered by the free flow of information, communication, and transportation led to the emergence of GSCs.

Globalization via the digital revolution allowed the new sheriffs in town, corporations such as Nike, Walmart, and Home Depot, to replace and control GSCs by shifting the production and distribution of goods and services from a producer-driven economy to a buyer-driven economy through marketing, price setting, and *branding*, the development of an image or design which represents the corporation. No longer do industry-specific production firms dictate production and commodity flows, but rather corporations control the image and design of their products and outsource the product's manufacture through some contractual arrangement with a supplier in a decentralized location; this, in turn, has shifted the governance of production and distribution from the "state, the corporations, and the union" during the Fordist era to corporations, NGOs, and "contract factories in Asia and Central America" during the post-Fordist era, making buyer-driven commodity chains the driving force in transnational capitalism (Appelbaum 2006, 3).

According to the ILO, GSCs

> have profoundly transformed the nature of cross-border production, investment, trade and employment. Key factors enabling the growth of global supply chains include, first the development of telecommunications, financial services and information technologies, which have enabled real-time coordination and logistics of fragmented production in various parts of the globe. Second, improvements in infrastructure, logistics and transport services have enabled more reliable and speedy delivery of inputs and final goods and have reduced their cost. Third, trade agreements have played a role in facilitating and reducing the costs of trade, including through tariff reduction, harmonization of institutional frameworks and liberalization of services under the General Agreement on Tariffs and Trade and subsequently the World Trade Organization (WTO) as well as bilateral and plurilateral trade agreements. Lastly, the emergence of China and India and their participation in global supply chains, has doubled the supply of labour to the global economy. (Decent work 2016, 5)

Lead firms, primarily based in developed countries and whose businesses control the GSCs, set the boundaries for compliance among the firms under their control, are responsible for the final sales of their products, and coordinate production and consumption flows through intra- (outsourcing) and inter- (offshoring) relationships. Originally MNCs engaged in local labor/consumer markets with the intent of distributing to regional/national markets. The developments in communication, transportation, infrastructure, trade agreements, and logistics made possible, on an international scale, the expansion of development, production, and distribution to new markets, particularly in Asia and Latin America. So MNCs were able to tap into developing countries' resources through outsourcing and offshoring of production "without investing in their own production facility with directly hired employees" (Decent work 2016, 6). This strategy fostered a weakened infrastructure (less enforcement of regulatory, labor, and environmental laws) in developing countries which sought *federal direct investment* (FDI), monies from other countries with which to pay their obligations, which led to lower wages and hazardous working conditions for workers.

MNCs in developing countries face challenges to lower production costs in GSCs as the number of export-related industries and global production capabilities increase. They, in turn, look to labor costs as an easy fix because it is not a fixed cost as is land or capital. In labor-intensive industries such as garments and textiles, where global buyers can easily shift production, lowered wages, hazardous working conditions, shifts in production location, shifts in product demand, and/or temporary employment provide insecure incomes and few job prospects for employees (UNCTAD 2013). For example, the disparate wage gap between US workers and Asian workers is significant and contributes to the push of MNCs to locate production work in the Global South. According to the Bureau of Labor Statistics, in 2005 American workers made $21 per hour while their Chinese counterparts made $0.67 per hour for the same work. Developing countries' average income, already greatly lagging behind developed countries' average income by half, "increased approximately 30 percent in 2008 according to ILO statistics" (Jha 2014, 2). Supplementing the role of GSCs are governments who encourage and give tax breaks to and foster weakened environmental regulations for corporations to ensure increased investment in their country.

CORPORATIONS MAINTAIN POWER

History documents the ill treatment of workers prior to legislation which instituted protections for some workers. In the United States, these protections were mainly enacted during the New Deal era in the 1930s. During the Golden Age of Labor, 1935–1947, power shifted to organized labor, and around 25 percent of the workforce was unionized. Corporations feared labor was becoming too powerful and pushed for legislation to curtail worker power. The Taft-Hartley Act of 1947 was passed which shifted the balance of power back toward business. Beginning in the 1970s, the continual weakening of labor laws protecting workers increased because governments shifted their focus toward property rights of employers and away from workers' rights. This consolidated effort to shift the balance of economic power to management, which has always been the goal of owners of production, is almost complete and is exacerbated under the framework of GSCs.

The power of GSCs is deeply rooted in the factors of production and distribution in an interconnected world. Several factors contribute to this shift in power. The persistent repression of workers' rights, according to Anner (2015), begins with the ability of firms to set prices paid to supplies and to set the time frame in which supplies must produce products. The following factors have contributed to the ability of lead firms in GSCs to set lower production prices and shorter lead time for the production of goods and services. First is the issue of trade agreements which allow governments to eliminate barriers to trade through tariff reductions. Second, technological advances allow major retailers to advance control over supplies worldwide, so soliciting cheaper supplies from the lowest cost producer is as simple as clicking a mouse. Third, the entry of countries such as China, India, and Vietnam into the world market has increased the potential low-wage labor pool not represented by a collective. Fourth, developing countries are producing/exporting similar products which creates a glut of these products for the market. These factors particularly play out in the technology, garment, and agriculture industries (Anner 2017).

ENTER THE MIDDLE MANAGERS

The old system of capitalism under craft manufacturing which relied on owners of production to manage their own transactions wasn't robust enough to handle the burgeoning network of production and distribution necessary to serve consumers in these broader markers. As consumer demands grew, these networks continued to expand and required massive investments and complicated operations necessary to handle myriad transactions. A new group of workers, middle managers, emerged to handle these operations.

Salaried or middle managers filled the space created by increased consumer demands and further separated the owners of production from their work processes by handling the jobs of production, distribution, transportation, and communication. The introduction of an intermediary to handle operations not only effectively further separated the owners of production from their work processes but also acted as a buffer for liabilities low-level workers incurred in the actual production of the product. Managers now handled all operation decisions. The volume of goods and services produced at less cost by large manufacturing firms rather than small facilities allowed for "substantial economics of scale and scope" (Chandler 1990). Owners of production, in order to take advantage of low cost/high volume production, made investments in three arenas: facilities, national/international marketing and distribution networks, and management.

New managerial models of control evolved as digitization allowed global markets to prosper. Hierarchical work flows, known as *vertical integration*, were flattened to lateral work flows which fostered teamwork (Vallas 2003) and participatory decision making (Bolman 2013) which theoretically gave greater decision making to lower-level workers in the production chain. In actuality, the lateral workflows required less labor and more management thus reducing the number of workers required to produce the same quantity of goods and services. This hegemonic concept gives workers a false sense of control and aligned workers with management who undermine workers' ability to act collectively (Graham 1995; Grenier 1988).

Lateral workflows, fewer regulations, and the inability of workers to act collectively allowed for corporations to gain a greater market share, intensify production, and increase profits. The picture for workers isn't so rosy. The additional challenges and burdens workers face in the global marketplace is lowered wages, nonexistent benefits, inflexible work arrangements, and lowered living standards. For many workers in the digitized economy, life is frustrating, difficult, dangerous, and disheartening.

The digital revolution, which fostered the transition from an industrial economy to an information economy, has been as difficult for twenty-first-century workers as was the transition from an agrarian economy to an industrial economy for nineteenth-century workers. In both cases, workers must learn new skills, acquire new knowledge, develop new abilities, and embrace new ways of thinking about the world. This is particularly true for workers in the digitized economy who find themselves unable to compete in a global marketplace because they do not have the greater technological skills learned through science, technology, engineering, and math (STEM). Without these new skills, workers underperform and are unprepared for future high-tech and green jobs of the future. Older workers who had industry-specific skills are disadvantaged and must seek training and education in order to compete with younger workers more attuned to new technology as well as global workers who work for lower wages.

THE FRAMEWORK FOR GSCS

The framework under which GSCs exist and operate has implications for the workers who produce the goods and services worldwide. Forced overtime, low wages, unsafe working conditions, and multiple violations of workers' rights including workers' inability to form collectives and engage in strike activity are hallmarks of GSCs. Why is this the case? What is it about global supply chains, their structure, framework, and interconnectedness that increases the persistence of worker rights' violations?

To understand how global supply chains operate, it is necessary to understand how this vast network of firms, small and large, local and global, is structured. Assumptions generally held by scholars, the media, governments, and non-governmental organizations (NGOs) about transnational corporations' ownership and control was the catalyst for a complex network analysis to determine exactly who were major players in GSCs and how those players influence trade, production, credit, stock prices, products, and boards of directors (Vitali 2011). This multifaceted quantitative study involved "43,060 TNCs . . . and the ownership pathways originating from and pointing to TNCs. The resulting TNC network includes 600,508 nodes and 1,006,987 ownership ties" (Vitali 2011, 2) These research findings reflect a worldwide structure of control dominated by "737 top holders [who] accumulate 80 percent of the control over the value of all TNCs" (Vitali 2011, 4). This accounts for 147 TNCs at the core of the network known as the "'super-entity'" (Vitali 2011, 4) three-fourths of which are financial conglomerates such as Prudential Financial, Morgan Stanley, Citigroup, Bank of America Corporation, JP Morgan Chase and Co., Goldman Sachs, Bear Stearns, Lehman Brothers, T. Rowe Price, USB Ag, Barclays PLC, Deutsche Bank Ag, Credit Suisse, Commerzbank AG, and Franklin Resources. The core of this global network then has "a control ten times bigger than what could be expected based on their wealth" (Vitali 2011, 4).

It is little wonder that most of the financial firms who control the global marketplace are primarily based in the United States. It is the ability of financial institutions to engage in speculative and risky investments supported through trade agreements which established "supply linkages between U.S. parent corporations and their emerging foreign subsidiaries and subcontractors" (Cox 2013, 21). This relationship between global financial investors and policy makers allowed the United States to become one of "the recipients of the largest financial bailout in U.S. history—on terms highly favorable to the profit margins of the biggest financial holding corporations left standing" (Johnson 2009 in Cox 2013, 22) after the Great Recession of 2007–2008.[1]

According to Cox (2013), around the 1970s, the United States' shift toward conservative neoliberal policies "resulted in lower taxation, deregulation, weakened labor laws and weakened antitrust laws" (1). US corporations sought to be competitive in a global market by reducing costs through restructuring their work organization from one of vertical integration to one of subcontracting work to independent contractors who took on the risks of owners of production, creating an "arms-length relationship with independent supply networks" (Cox 2013, 2). As fewer corporations control more market share by taking advantage of new trade agreements and investment strategies, shedding unprofitable suppliers, offshoring and outsourcing production and distribution, shifting profits to shareholders and decreasing wages for workers, and seeking less costly inputs from suppliers in the Global South, an oligarchy of transnational corporations has risen to the top. The latest US efforts to position US corporations in competitive global business circles are the new tax cuts signed into law by the Trump administration in 2017 effectively cutting the corporate tax rate from 35 percent to 21 percent.

This is important because the control of global supply chains resides in the hands of a few financial institutions (which Cox [2013] calls transnational interest blocs), and the policies they influence have implications for how work is structured, how products are produced and distributed, and how workers fare in the process. This historical shift from industry and manufacturing to retail and service, from distribution chains to supply chains, from producer-driven commodity chains to consumer-driven commodity chains, and from centralized power structures to decentralized power structures was made possible by

> two conjoined phenomena: first the logistical integration made possible and necessary by the revolution in information/transportation technology (bar codes, data storage, containerization, global communications), and second, the neoliberal transformation of the worldwide political economy, which in the US has facilitated the massive expansion of a low-wage, import dependent retail sectors while in China it has generated a huge export-manufacturing boom. (Appelbaum 2006, 106)

Logistical integration is based on instantaneous communication. When a product is sold at a market in the United States, a bar code is scanned which sends information to a supplier/distributor who replenishes the sold product by immediately shipping it to the seller. This point-of-sale (POS) data collection method, made efficient by the Walmart Corporation, replaced an outdated system of sellers vying for shelf space and slow methods of delivery. Equally important is the push by conservative capitalists for a neoliberal political ideology based on classical economic theory which values deregulation, competition, cost-cutting measures, and de-unionization. Decision makers and policy wonks in governments and corporate board rooms promote tearing down all barriers to free trade which includes getting rid of governmental and environmental regulations which impede profit making, promoting property rights over workers' rights by dismantling protective labor laws such as collective bargaining and minimum wage legislation, and pushing for trade agreements which favor the Global North over the Global South (Appelbaum 2006). Instant POS data combined with a conservative political ideology allowed for discount retailing to become a predominant production and distribution strategy.

THE COMPLEXITY OF GSCS

GSCs are "complex, diverse, fragmented, dynamic and evolving organizational structures" (Decent work 2016, 1). Terms used interchangeably for GSCs are global production networks and *global value chains*, although global value chains have a more specific meaning involving an interrelated set of activities a firm uses to create a competitive advantage (Porter 2011). When using these terms, we are referring to the cross-border production and trade activities which develop, produce, and deliver goods and services to consumers worldwide. These networks include MNCs who contract and subcontract work to various suppliers under precarious arrangements to procure raw inputs at the lowest cost. This arrangement often depends on FDI made attractive by cheap and lowest cost available workers and raw materials, the flexibility of moving development, production, and distribution easily and quickly from one venue to another, the ease of capital fluidity, and lax environmental and regulatory legislation and enforcement (Decent work 2016). The goal for employees is to enable business to flourish without sacrificing labor rights. The International Labor Organization, in Report IV, provides guidance on how to secure this goal. Though GSCs organize investment, production, and trade which creates employment and social development, GSCs also can have negative implications for workers.

The specific meaning associated with global value chains within the context of global supply chains refers to the value added to a product or service which makes it more attractive to consumers so the consumer will purchase one firm's product/service over a competing firm's product/service. The competition for market share in a globalized economy is fierce and leads to the "reshaping [of] global production and trade and thereby alters the organization of industries" (Gereffi 2012, 25). The firms' abilities to move production and assembly offshore in search of cheap labor has been labeled a shift from "'trade in goods' to 'trade in value added'" (OCED 2011; WTO & IDE-JETRO 2011 in Gereffi 2012, 25). The concept of value-added means that all points along the supply chain, including *upstream and downstream suppliers*, potentially add value to the product by increasing the product's *competitive advantage*, the superiority or leverage of a firm over its competitor by adding value to its product or service which makes the product or service more attractive to its customers. No longer is competitive advantage limited to one firm's ability to effectively compete with another firm, but rather the concept has broadened to mean a supply chain's ability to compete with another supply chain.

More trade generally means more employment, but the quality of the employment varies greatly. Firms within the supply chain compete on "price-cost, quality, delivery, and flexibility" (Suhong 2006), so there are multiple opportunities to increase competitive advantage at many points along the supply chains. Each of these points increases the chances of worker exploitation. Labor-intensive industries within GSCs, such as garment, textiles, electronics, food processing, and agriculture, often provide low-quality, low-wage work which is often seasonal. More value-added to the production process increases the need for higher skilled labor who may command higher wages.

The production cycles of firms have tighter windows in which to produce new lines of goods, so firms can't predict production shifts and/or costs. To accommodate shorter turnaround times, firms hire few workers and demand a faster work pace in order to meet production deadlines. GSCs are a

> dominant feature of world trade and investment encompassing developing, emerging, and developed economies. The whole process of producing goods, from raw materials to finished products, is increasingly carried out wherever the necessary skills and materials are available at competitive cost and quality. The international fragmentation of production is driven by changes in the business and regulatory environment, new technologies, shifts in corporate thinking and firm strategies, and the systematic liberalization of trade and investment over the past two decades. (ILO 2013, 8)

Because this new global landscape for developing, producing, and distributing goods and services is fragmented across national boundaries it is necessary for these countries to have "open, predictable and transparent trade and investment regimes as tariffs and other unnecessarily restrictive non-tariff measures impact foreign suppliers, international investors, and domestic producers" (ILO 2013, 8).

The International Trade Union Confederation (ITUC) reports the "repression of workers' rights goes hand in hand with increased government control over freedom of expression, assembly and other fundamental civil liberties, with too many governments seeking to consolidate their own power and frequently doing the bidding of big business, which often see fundamental rights as incompatible with its quest for profit at any expense" (ITUC 2016). The framework of GSCs provides a conduit through which business seeks to restrict workers' rights using neoliberal practices such as deregulation, deunionization, privatization, and dehumanization. This allows businesses to compete in a laissez-faire environment to produce goods and services at the lowest cost per unit at the expense of the human component, their workers. The direct and indirect cost of this management style leads to low wages, unsafe working conditions, physical violence against workers, and increased worker dissatisfaction.

THEORIES OF WORK ORGANIZATION ASSOCIATED WITH GSCS

The move from a Fordist framework to a post-Fordist transnational framework is predicated on three theories: *regulation theory, long wave theory, and flexible specialization theory*. Regulation theory suggests capitalism, inherently unstable by its nature, must have rules, norms, and institutions to "stabilize" its function. Originating in France during the early 1970s and sometimes referred to as the *regulation approach*, regulation theory finds is footing in regulations or the "'conscious and active intervention by the *state* or other collective organizations'" (Boyer 1990, 20 in Painter 1995, 277). Controlling or regulating the economic cycles of capitalism during "regime[s] of accumulation" (Painter 1995, 277) means periods of boom and bust are created by the imbalances in production, consumption, and investment as a result of supply and demand. Social and political activities and cultural and moral mores may contribute to long periods of market stability but also contribute to instability in the market when challenged within economic, social, and political arenas. Relaxed regulations during regimes of accumulation lead to boom cycles but too few regulations also contribute to bust cycles as evidenced by the Great Depression in the 1930s and the Great Recession in 2007–2008. Regulation theory then contends that stabilization with a capitalist economic system is dependent on rules, social and political acumen, and cultural and social mores.

Fordism had such rules based in Keynesian economics which said state interventions were necessary for capitalism to sustain itself and for the human component in the production process to maintain value. The term Fordism, generally attributed to Antonio Gramsci during the 1930s, refers to the period between the 1940s and the 1970s when markets in Western culture were stable. The stability of markets was attributed to a regime of accumulation, mass production techniques involving assembly line work, worker protections in the form of New Deal legislation, and a labor process which gave workers standing in the labor-management dyad (Walker 2015). Around 1970, the period of post-Fordism emerged primarily characterized by changes in the labor process which shifted more power to corporations, instituted laws which undermined workers' rights, and increased flexibility in production and distribution attributed to the digital revolution.

Long wave theory emphasizes that economic conditions as cyclic developments are ruled by technology and is based on Russian Professor Nikolai Kondratieff's ideas that economic cycles of accumulation and consumption, which last around fifty to sixty years, are fueled by the cheap accumulation of goods and services necessary to maintain a standard of living (Kondratieff theory 2002; McDonough 2003). But as those prices increase and production and consumption fall, a new period of economic decline sets in which leads to a period of depression. Kondratieff's theory has a great deal to do with debt accumulation and collapse which is historically represented by boom and bust cycles. Economic analysts represent these boom and bust cycles as seasons with spring representing expansion periods, summer representing recession periods, autumn representing plateau periods, and winter representing depression periods. According to Kondratieff scholars, the current cycle began after WWII and lasted until 1966 (spring: expansion), a period which saw economic growth, stable employment, and the buildup of the middle class. From 1966 to 1982, during the summer recession period and characterized by the Vietnam War, the world experienced inflationary prices resulting from an oil crisis and went into a recessionary period. The autumn plateau period followed from 1982 to 2000 measured by a new world order which witnessed real estate bubbles, a collapse in commodity prices, low inflation, and extreme debt buildup. Unsustainable debt recovery led to the winter depression period beginning in 2001 and continuing currently. The collapse of the tech market, plummeting stock markets, and financial crises led to the Great Recession of 2007–2008 which saw manufacturing lose 15 million jobs, huge numbers of home foreclosures, and millions of individuals thrown into poverty.

Interesting enough Kondratieff theory posits that during the winter depression period there is a buildup of "sinister forces that are religious in nature." In the 1930s, Nazism rose and led to WWII. Today, terrorism, led by fanatic extremist groups hijacking the Muslim faith to pursue their own narrowly conservative interests, has forced retaliation from world leaders. Evangelistically conservative world leaders have marshaled their own bases to counter terrorism threats in the name of religion and created yet another schism between conservative and liberals across the world. Proponents of Kondratieff theory believe these boom and bust periods are generational and occur every two to three generations after the first generation to experience the wave dies. Consequently the newer generations believe the historical situations which happened to their grandfather/mothers could never happen to them.

Flexible specialization theory is based on the need for flexibility in production centered on the changing needs of the firm. Flexible specialization is "defined as the manufacture of a wide and changing array of customized products using flexible, general-purpose machinery and skilled, adaptable workers" (Hirst 1991, 2). Around 1980, firms in the current marketplace began exploring a more flexible business model in order to compete in a highly volatile world of consumer demands and rising prices of inputs. The traditional Fordist model of work organization, with its Taylorist tendencies, was considered too rigid and inflexible. A work organization model which allowed for product to be produced and delivered on demand was necessary. A *second industrial divide* (Piore 1984) focused on economies of scope rather than economies of scale, smaller-scale production to increase the firms' competitive edge, and devolved control overseen by human resource management and would position firms once again as players in the global marketplace.

The move toward flexible specialization theory is a push against what is considered to be inflexibility in the labor market and impediments to employment growth. Neoliberalists contend fewer state interventions would allow the market to self-correct. They believe a *contract at will*, an unwritten agreement between a worker and his/her employer which allows the worker to be terminated without cause or warning, is a better policy than a *collective bargaining agreement*, a contract between employers and the employees' bargaining representatives. Additionally neoliberalists believe (1) wages are too high and workers are priced out of jobs which creates unemployment, (2) labor rights are too extensive and expensive which creates higher labor costs and creates barriers to managements' ability to control their own workforce, and (3) social welfare policies such as unemployment and social security create disincentives.

WORKER EXPLOITATION WITHIN GSCS

The countless examples of workers exploitation, devaluation, and abuse within GSCs has to originate from somewhere and identifying the cause can take different tracks. Several factors dictate how workers in various industries are reimbursed for their labor and treated at their workplace. In today's world in which production is geographically dispersed and decentralized, corporations and governments fear compliance with worker protections via labor laws, labor advocacy, and labor unions "may negatively impact their comparative advantage in low production costs" (Anner 2013, 3). Profits reign supreme at all points along the GSC. In efforts to keep costs low and the supply chain filled with product, suppliers and retailers constantly seek cost-cutting measures. Fixed costs such as raw material have little wiggle room for cost reduction, but labor costs can easily be manipulated through a contingent workforce who serve at the pleasure of the corporations. Since brand retailers, such as Walmart and Nike, have the power to set prices in an economic environment masterminded by proponents of trade liberalization and retailer consolidation, a downward pressure is exerted on workers' wages by holding hostage manufacturing suppliers. Workers' ability to influence their wages and working conditions are compromised without the protection of labor laws or the power of a collective to speak in their behalf. Consequently, workers are also held hostage through poverty wages by transnational corporations who remain in powerhouse positions within the GSC.

The slavery-like conditions experienced by millions of workers worldwide is not a new phenomenon but one which could be addressed through cooperation between MNCs, governments, policy makers, and labor unions. When MNCs and governments turn a blind eye to worker abuse or are simply unwilling to orchestrate enforcement of binding rules which would protect workers from sweatshop and slavery-like conditions, the long-term success of global economies is at peril. According to Anner, Bair, and Blasi (2013), "the root cause of sweatshop conditions in international subcontracting networks is to be found in the sourcing practices of the brands and retailers that coordinate these supply chains" (3). This is, of course, not a new phenomenon and efforts to decrease this exploitation have ebbed and flowed throughout history. Often it takes manufacturing tragedies such as building collapses and factory fires in which human life is lost, such as the well-documented Triangle Shirtwaist Fire in 1911 or the Rena Plaza building collapse in 2013, to bring public attention to the atrocious conditions under which workers suffer; sometimes these tragedies result in some legislative policy to prevent future damage, but as a whole, the policies are ineffective and provide few worker protections. A fuller discussion of workplace tragedies as focusing events to change workplace protective policies takes place in chapter 5.

CONCLUSION

It doesn't have to be this way. Global supply chains are made possible by the influence of global actors in the form of MNCs who set the agenda for worldwide trade, investment, and control and coordination of operations. The concentrated power and money of MNCs is beholden to large "financial institutions such as The Goldman Sachs Group, JPMorgan Chase & Company, and Barclays Bank" (Fichter 2016, 1; Vitali 2011). These actors engage in political activities via governments which secure their market positions. Lobbyists of MNCs not only secure legitimacy for their firms and processes but conduct public relations campaigns which shore up the experience of buying a product whether the actual product is good for the purchaser, society, or the environment. Historically, the responsibility for firms' ethical action was safeguarded by "state regulations, collective bargaining and civil society activism" (Utting 2000, 1). These safeguards have all but disappeared due to the confluence of neoliberal policies based on conservative ideology which promote property rights over worker rights, privatization and deregulation over state intervention and the collective, and profit seeking through low-wage, import dependent retail sectors and logistical integration made possible by information and transportation technology.

Global supply chains are described as complex, diverse, and fragmented networks of production and distribution. Scholars posit various theoretical explanations for the proliferation of GSCs which include the move during the 1970s from a Fordist model of work organization based on state interventions to a transnational framework including long wave or flexible specialization theories of work organization based on economic boom and bust cycles fueled by political ideology and social and cultural mores. The development of this transnational framework and the encouragement of a value-added component to production and distribution in order to gain a competitive advantage within the market increases the opportunities for worker exploitation and abuse at many points along the supply chain. If workers worldwide are to (re)gain standing within GSCs, a reversal of current neoliberal policies including worker protections in the form of collectives or legislation will be necessary.

NOTE

1. The Glass-Steagall Act of 1933, signed into law by Roosevelt to restore confidence in the banking system after the Stock Market Crash of 1929, separated commercial and investment banking and created the Federal Deposit Insurance Corporation (FDIC). Its main purpose was to restrict bank credit for speculative purposes and divert more investment into industry, agriculture, and commerce. The Gramm-Leach-Bliley Act of 1999 repealed the Banking Act of 1933 that restricted affiliations between banks and securities firms.

Chapter Two

The Regulatory Framework

LEARNING OUTCOMES

By the end of the chapter, students will be able to:

1. Identify the goal of a corporation.
2. Identify at least three organizations attempting to influence regulatory policy.
3. Restate Gramsci's theory of cultural hegemony.
4. Contrast the MNC viewpoint on regulatory reform with that of environmental groups, non-governmental organizations, and consumer protectionists.

Key terms: Cultural hegemony, Value chain governance, Fair trade, Classical liberalism, Embedded liberalism, International framework agreements

This chapter provides an overview of the regulatory framework, its evolution, who makes the rules, the mechanism for dispute settlement, and the fallout to workers, workers' rights, social justice issues, and the environment.

THE RELATIONSHIP OF MULTINATIONAL CORPORATIONS WITH WORKERS

Global supply chains (GSCs) are international collections of corporations who control production and distribution of goods and services worldwide and operate under a regulatory framework which allows, encourages, and protects them from liabilities. All corporations have the common goal of seeking profits for their shareholders. If corporations are unable to make profits and distribute them to shareholder actors, the corporations exit the market. The existence of corporations depends on their ability to produce profits. That is their only goal.

Without workers, corporations couldn't exist. Corporations need workers to function and thrive, and workers need corporations to function and thrive. Since neither corporations nor workers could survive without each other, there should be reciprocity within the corporation/worker relationship. Corporations rely on workers to provide the labor which adds value to their products at all points along the GSC. Since corporations must seek profits to exist, they employ workers at the least cost possible. Corporations believe in *at-will employment* which means they have total control over workers who they can hire and fire for any reason. This gives corporations a great advantage over workers who often have few to no choices about for whom they work. Corporations have leverage in deciding where to put facilities, how and when to schedule production, and who to hire. They also can utilize capital fluidity, the ability to infuse or withdraw monies from one facility to another with ease, to maximize production where needed.

On the other hand, workers employed by corporations are at a disadvantage in at-will employment. One reason is the fallacy of an at-will employment contract or the idea that workers can leave and find employment elsewhere if they are unhappy with their current job. Workers are generally *tied to the soil*, which means they have roots in a family and a community and cannot relocate easily. Workers then become a captive audience for a particular corporation which may be the only assessable nearby employer. Lack of transportation to and from distant worksites, child and elder care issues, and lack of training and education contribute to the workers' inability to command higher wages. Workers simply have less mobility than do corporations in relocation and availably of opportunities. The at-will contract for workers is more of an illusion of choice than a real option of choice.

Workers obviously have a relationship with the corporation as a wage earner, but workers have multiple relationships with other entities and organizations at the same time. Workers are also members of sports teams, grocery store customers, patients of doctors, or union members. The list of competing relationships the worker has is endless. So why does the relationship the worker has with the corporation receive more attention and have more gravity than do the relationships the workers have with other groups? In other words, why is the membership in the corporation so much more powerful for the worker than other memberships?

Antonio Gramsci, a political theorist and historian in the early twentieth century and considered one of the most important Marxist thinkers, had an idea about this which he called the theory of *cultural hegemony*. Cultural hegemony, a worldview domination, describes how wealthy powerbrokers use ideology (instead of violence or coercion) to maintain certain values and norms which then become so embedded in the psyche of the populace, they become the status quo. The perpetual reinforcement and reproduction of these norms is propagated through the dominant cultural institutions of society, the church, school, government, media, and the market, and promote a certain way of thinking about ethical and moral beliefs. In other words, populations identify their own working lives with that of the power elites and not with other workers. He believed the powerful engage in a sort of passive revolution by allowing small tokens of resistance to rise and be given some accommodation to pacify their anger in order to mollify the larger population. Gramsci termed this *domination by consent* because the population is, in essence, agreeing to be oppressed by cultural institutions. In other words, workers vote for their own oppression.

This relationship between workers and the corporation is all the more powerful when corporations gain power through legal means. Corporations, under national and international law, are granted citizenship status which allows them to manage their businesses in a most efficient manner as long as they comply with the law.

> The Supreme court ruled in 1886 that corporations were "natural persons" under the US Constitution and thereby "entitled to the pretentions of the Bill of Rights, including the right to free speech and other constitutional protections extended to individuals." This ruling overturned the concept that corporations were simply legal entities whose right to make profit was granted only on condition that they served the public interest. Instead "corporations finally claimed full rights enjoyed by citizens while being exempted from many of the responsibilities and liabilities of citizenship." (Korten 1995, 59 in Richter 2001, 7)

Corporations can sue and be sued, only pay fines for breaking the law, and never go to jail or serve in national service (Scherrer 2016a, 43). The laws differ in various countries. For instance, in Germany, trade unionists are required to sit on corporate boards which govern how the business is run. No such laws exist in the Unites States. Internally, domestic law "regulates how corporations interact with others, with their suppliers, [and] customers, . . . [and] to what degree they are allowed or not allowed to collude on prices together" (Scherrer 2016a).

The legal status of corporations calls into question the ways in which they can be held accountable in their relationships with workers, consumers, and society. Most governments regulate worker protections through legislative means such as minimum wage laws or health and safety regulations. These regulations have strengthened and weakened as national governments sway from conservative to liberal worker protections. Environmental regulations also have an impact on workers as environmental activists and governments debate this newest social policy. As multinational corporations (MNCs) expand operations, individual governments face difficulties in holding corporations accountable because of the lack of international regulation (Richter 2001, 8).

CALLS FOR REGULATION

The citizenship status of corporations and the requirements to only follow national and international law allows corporations great leeway in the management of their businesses. Because GSCs are doing business in multiple countries, they must comply with varying domestic laws which are often at odds with one another; the lack of an international governing body to provide macro-rules dealing with these transactions creates a vacuum which gives corporations space to act on their own. Corporations, given these loopholes, fight to maintain this power because it gives them more control over their transactions.

> Though there has always been international trade in earlier centuries, the era of globalization is said to begin around 1970. One of the premier elements for truly global trade, the ability to move monies into and out of a country quickly, didn't exist until the 1970s when, under the Nixon administration, the US currency base was moved from the gold standard to one of capital fluidity. This gave the US an edge in investment opportunities in countries that had cheap natural resources which could be exploited through *structural adjustment policies*, credit extended to developing and underdeveloped countries by the International Monetary Fund (IMF) and the World Bank which helps them become economically self-sufficient. In reality, these policies allow developed nations like the United States to hold hostage the debtor nations by infusing money into their economy in exchange for products which exploit the developing countries' natural resources because it is cheaper for the United States to buy cheap imported goods than to produce the goods. This puts the developing country in the position of not only producing cheap goods for developed nations but paying interest on the debt owned which leaves little or no money to infuse into their economies for infrastructure building and social programs. (Walker 2015, 146)

The push in the 1970s to regulate corporations was a call to regulate international regimes because nations perceived there to be an unfair and unjust economic order. For instance, in 1973, Chile's President Salvador Allende met a "violent death at the hand of a CIA-supported military coup" after he had alerted the United Nations "to plans of the International Telegraph and Telephone company (ITT) and the Kenneth Copper Corporation to overthrow his government with the help of the U.S. government" (Richter 2001, 9). This death contributed to the gravity of the need for MNCs to be regulated and the United Nations (UN) to push for codes of conduct to monitor MNCs, strengthen developing countries' capacity to deal with MNCs, and propose frameworks for MNCs' activity. The herculean task was slow because of its magnitude and the diversity of views on its construct.

The elections of Reagan in the United States and Thatcher in the United Kingdom (UK) in the 1980s gave way to neoliberal economic policy which favored deregulation of MNCs. As the primary investor in *federal direct investment* (FDI), the United States opposed interventionist regulation and espoused a free market approach to MNCs which maximized profits and reduced global welfare. Known as the *Washington Consensus*, this approach pushed for trade and investment liberalization and UN efforts to produce a code of conduct for transnational regulation of MNCs was abandoned.

Further gutting the UN's efforts for international corporate regulation, Western industrialized states vented opposition to environmental regulations which were eventually removed from Agenda 21, the UN's global action plan. The recommendations were deleted from the proposal with the caveat that industry would and could self-regulate in a socially responsible manner by means of best practices, voluntary initiatives, and standard guidelines. This was a win for MNCs who argued it was more economically profitable to self-regulate than to comply with external regulations. Some *non-governmental organizations* (NGOs) continue to demand regulations while others work in a co-regulatory mode believing corporations will keep their promise to be more socially responsible.

The World Trade Organization (WTO) was organized in 1995 to implement and deal with rules of international trade based on agreements between member nations, settle trade disputes, and "'harmonize' standards for products that are traded internationally" (Richter 2001, 12). Complains about the WTO, which is not a member of the UN and makes its ruling in private, revolve around minimum enforcement of health, environmental, and labor standards, the excessive influence of MNCs in their decision-making processes, and their power to issue sanctions against countries who violate trade agreements.

The financial crisis in Latin America in the 1980s hastened rule changes by the International Monetary Fund (IMF) to more freely allow transfers of money between countries. This has great implications for corporations because "it allows them also to control their subsidiaries, and to a certain extent also the other suppliers by establishing profitability benchmarks because they control the flow of money within the GSC" (Scherrer 2016b, 2). The West holds the balance of economic power within GSCs which creates an unequal playing field for developing countries. Africa's government, for instance, has less ability to negotiate beneficial trade deals because they structurally don't act as one trading partner, but rather each African nation acts as its own trading partner, weakening the ability to compete on a global scale (Mote 2016). Rich in minerals, Africa is seen as a treasure trove of raw materials which can be exported, and developed countries, like the United States, take every advantage of this.

As the Mexican (1994) and Asian (1997) economics floundered in the late 1990s, *transnational corporations* (TNCs) became increasing concerned about an unregulated international market affecting financial and social environments, so the *International Chamber of Commerce* (ICC) argued for better regulation to create a more stable business environment while advocating for "de-regulation of national rules governing trade and other areas so as to minimize interference with companies' ability to maximize shareholder value" (Richter 2001, 14). The UN-ICC Global Compact resulted which calls for "a set of core values in the areas of human rights, labour standards, and environmental practices" (Richter 2001, 14), a document wholly voluntary through corporate compliance. Following the UN-ICC Global Compact, the UN Human Development Report (UNDP) proposed the establishment of a more "'coherent and democratic architecture for global governance in the 21st century' which would include a more binding code of conduct for multinational corporations" (Richter 2001, 15) through criminal sanctions against MNCs who are convicted of human rights abuses.

The current environment in which MNCs operate trends toward the new liberalized free market approach. Privatization and deregulation, hallmarks of laissez-faire economic theory, predominate at the expense of socially and environmentally friendly policy. The debates now center on how to attract corporate money and often regulations are traded away in return for voluntary corporate responsibility. These intentions overlook (or totally dismiss) the significance of an unbalanced economic power relationship between corporations and workers.

PAST EFFORTS TO REGULATE INTERNATIONAL TRADE

Regulatory frameworks have not always been so corporate-centric. From the late 1880s to the early 1900s, regulation was enacted to prevent the economic concentration of power within newly emerging industries. President Cleveland signed legislation known as the *Interstate Commerce Act* (1887), and Congress created the *Interstate Commerce Commission*, a five-member enforcement board, to regulate railroads in charging for the transportation of goods. The *Sherman Act* (1890) was enacted to deal with monopoly power and price fixing, the *Pure Food and Drug Act* (1906) was the result of consumer outcry against unsanitary and violent practices in slaughterhouses, and *public utility commissions* regulated private gas, electricity, and telephone companies. Labor laws against the exploitation of child and forced labor were also passed.

Even with some regulations in effect, *classical liberalism*, the ideology which emphasizes freedom from government intervention, during the late 1880s and early 1920s, led to the Great Depression of the 1930s. A New Deal regulatory framework instituted interventionist protections which limited corporations' power to exploit workers with the goal of stabilizing the economy. Worker protections in the form of minimum wages, hours of work, and working conditions lifted the country out of an economic depression and ceded some power to collectives in order to level the playing field between management and labor. The *Golden Age of Labor*, from 1935 to 1947, was short-lived as labor's power once again waned, and corporations gained ground through *welfare capitalism*, the idea that management could better look out for the needs of its labor force than could newly elected representative bargaining agents in labor unions.

Around 1960, new voices emerged calling again for consumer protections. Ralph Nadar, a consumer protectionist, and Rachel Carson, author of *Silent Spring,* roused public sentiment which forced Congress to pass regulations governing "occupational health and safety, consumer product safety, clean air, clean water and toxic waste, and created an elaborate regime for assessing environmental impacts and regulating the financial system" (Richter 2001, 19).

During the late 1970s, corporations cited burdensome regulations as detrimental to their ability to maximize profits. Instead of renegotiating these regulations to fix current situations, calls for total deregulation were sounded, none more loudly than by the new Chicago School economists including Milton Friedman. The conservative movement and businesses embraced the neoliberal agenda and calls for deregulation followed. The idea behind deregulation was that society and government could no longer be depended upon to enforce rules for its own benefit and the only way for society to function was the free market which would police itself. This belief is supported by two approaches. The first is that corporations are responsible enough to regulate themselves through codes of conduct so society no longer needs to oversee that conduct through some legally binding international regulation. The second approach is that MNCs have so much power they are currently impossible to regulate by any external agency or organization and that voluntary agreement is more practical than forcing them into international regulatory agreements (Utting 2000).

Although the free market drum continues to beat, industrialized countries do need (and want) some regulation in the operation of their businesses but this desire doesn't extend to international markets. Currently, scholars report that left to their own devices, MNCs "are likely to fulfil their responsibility in a minimalist and fragmented fashion. Their strategies may be conducive to economic growth and the stability of their operating environments, but not necessarily to sustainable human development. They still need strong and effective regulation and a coherent response from civil society" (UNRISD 2000a, 90 in Richter 2001, 22). The trend toward "'voluntary' self-regulation or co-regulation between industry, citizen groups and governments" is now "considered the most appropriate way to set global rules" (Utting 2000, 1).

THE INTRICACY OF GSCS

The framework under which GSCs operate is complex. Scholars agree the framework should act as a vehicle for "promoting predictability and stability in an integrated global economy and international production systems" (Birkbeck 2015, 3), but they often disagree on how that vehicle should operate. Some believe the framework should be "seen as a tool for supporting robust, well-functioning markets and addressing the practical constraints that firms can face when conducting business internationally" (Birkbeck 2015, 3). Others want the vehicle to operate as a mechanism which "facilitates and harnesses trade and investment in ways that foster sustainable development while preserving national political autonomy" (Birkbeck2015, 3) while still others wish to see a more inclusive leveling of trade and investment relationships between countries. Though various methods exist, all agree the final framework should incorporate a "system of shared values: a sense of common purpose" (Lamy 2012).

The changing landscape of international trade demands taking a look at varying patterns and trends in trade and investment flows which engender policy debates. In the last three decades, the global economy has tripled while trade has grown sixfold (UNEP 2015). Trade is a major contributor to a nation's *gross domestic product* (GDP) and encompasses tangible and digital goods, services, and financial transactions. These transactions have implications for international as well as domestic trade and shape policies for production and consumption. This changing landscape reflects the emergence of China as a major economic power since China is now the leading goods exporter moving from thirtieth position to first position in 2011 (UNCTAD 2015b), the growth of South-South trade (primarily involving the extractive industries such as mineral fuels, ores, metals, precious stones, and non-monetary gold) (UNCTAD 2015a), and the influx of trade in developing countries (UNCTAD 2015b). Manufactured goods have taken a back seat to trade in commodities and services while agricultural products, though still important, have slowed, and extractive industry trade increased (WTO 2014, 2015). The burgeoning knowledge-based and digital economy command ever-increasing attention while trade governance and protections concerning their consumption and distribution woefully lag behind. All areas of production and consumption have the potential for black market interference with the possibility of harm to a global community (Efrat 2012; Stuckler 2012).

The Rise of China as an International Branded Marketer

As GSCs fragmented and outsourcing and offshoring promoted exports, the intertwined networks in developed and developing countries pulsed with "recurrent wages of foreign direct investment (FDI) and global sourcing" (Gereffi 2013, 330). As trade barriers fell during the 1990s and the WTO was established to monitor trade agreements, markets in Brazil, Russia, India, and China opened and doubled the pool of available workers for globalized manufacturing as well as the pool of potential consumers for products and served as mecca for raw material (Gereffi 2013). European and US firms took advantage of these new resources and became more adept at outsourcing production to Asian countries, Africa, Latin America, and East Europe; anything digital that could be outsourced and offshored was. Over the next two decades, expansion continued in many countries, but the greatest surge in exports was in China now known as "the factory of the world" (Gereffi 2013, 331). China, taking advantage of its huge population which serves both as a manufacturing base and a consumer base, is able to reorient their production capacity if necessary to expand or contract production needs from international to domestic.

Capitalist profit seeking, neoliberal trade policies, capital fluidity, surplus labor, and advances in technology, communication, and transportation set the stage for locus-of-power changes in GSC governance structure from the tripartite state, corporations, and labor union/workers to retailers/brands, NGOs, and suppliers. The move from producer-driven commodity chains to buyer-driven commodity chains shifted to retailers and branded merchandisers the ability to set production and distribution standards which forces end-suppliers to control production schedules, hiring, and wage determination to meet retailers' constraints (Chan 2011; Lichtenstein 2009). Major retailers such as Walmart create their brand by conscripting suppliers to produce goods and services under the Walmart name without actually producing a single product themselves (Lichenstein 2005). Retailers, seeking low-cost labor and lax regulations for supplier opportunities, expanded into Asia during the 1990s and 2000s (Arrighi 2009). Laying the groundwork for China's rise was the assistance of US firms and government during the 1960s and 1970s by moving production to Japan and then to Taiwan in search of cheap labor during and after the Cold War to stop the spread of communism and secure an economic foothold in the Asian region. Taiwan and South Korea opened their markets to Japan at the insistence of the United States and solidified an Asian economic trading region which catapulted Japan into the role of leading manufacturer and exporter of all things electronic. Joining Japan were Taiwan, South Korea, Singapore, Hong Kong, Malaysia, Thailand, Indonesia, and India which fostered an electronic tsunami of products into the United States and European markets (Chan 2013). Taiwan, South

Korea, and Hong Kong also began exporting apparel (Chan 2013). The availability of cheaper labor in Asian economies spurred other US firms to offshore production, and Asian markets responded by creating massive factories hiring low-wage, mostly rural female workers in both electronics and textiles (Appelbaum 2008). Examples of mammoth factories responding to retailers demands are Hong Kong–based Yeu Yuen, producer for Nike, and Taiwanese-based Foxconn, the largest electronic manufacturers of iPhone products for Apple (Appelbaum 2008).

The Chinese economy underwent an economic transformation in the imposition of a capitalist economic model onto an authoritarian regime. Heavy industry and manufacturing, which carried guaranteed life employment and social transfer payments for state employees, was replaced with private firms, which rely on FDI and cheap labor in light manufacturing. By situating itself as a special economic zone attractive to FDI which fostered China's prominence as a technology powerhouse, China moved into the position of leading exporter to become an international branded marketer. China solidified relationships with suppliers Yeu Yuen and Foxconn among others using its vast producer power in the form of low-cost labor and its vast consumer power of 1.6 billion people. Consequently, Foxconn, also known a Hon Hai Precision Industry Company, became and remains the leading world supplier/contract maker of electronics with factories throughout China (Chan 2013).

Changes in the reorganization of industrial and national economies created winners and losers. China has now stepped away from manufacturing and moved into the roles of designing, imaging, marketing, and customer service (Appelbaum 2006) by taking advantage of resources in less developed countries and has clearly become a major branding leader. Clearly China is a winner in the new industrial economy. The ability of developed industrialized nations to infiltrate China's working population through cut-throat leadership and a take-no-prisoners production model created a new Chinese working class of rural migrant workers seeking a way out of rural poverty. Though factory work at Foxconn, and other electronic and apparel factories, provides workers some benefits, it also is reminiscent of historical sweatshops in which workers toiled fourteen hours a day in unsafe conditions. These workers, primarily young and rural, often live in dormitories on or near the factories at which they work and lose any right to public assistance because Chinese law only provides public services to those who live on the site of their birth. The intensive nature of production scheduling requires longer hours and faster assembly line paces with attention to minute details of intricate electronic components (Chan 2013). Workers' safety and health is compromised as are their labor rights. As industry needs are confronted with worker shortages and increased pressure from external stakeholders, some opportunities for worker pushback are getting some attention, but clearly workers are the losers in the new industrial economy.

Assumptions about GSCs International Framework

The debate concerning what an international framework for GSCs should look like involves different assumptions. One is the assumption that free trade and open markets in a capitalist economic system are the best way for competition to thrive and produce the most goods at the lowest cost per unit. Under this assumption, governments who push trade liberalization, often known as neoliberalism, believe it is in their best interest to push trade deals which lessen or eliminate trade barriers such as tariffs worldwide, take advantage of economies of scale and scope, and utilize comparative advantage. This belief encourages economic development, offers a wider selection of products, promotes better living standards, and is welfare enhancing. Another assumption concerning an international framework is more protectionist in nature and underlies the belief governments should protect their own market share through tariffs and protectionist measures because this helps ensure the social welfare of the citizenry and promotes social justice. Known as "*embedded liberalism*" (italics mine) (Birkbeck 2015, 5), this way of thinking was exacerbated after the 2007–2008 Great Recession which almost brought the United States to the brink of a financial disaster. The global economic instability following the Great Recession called into question the viability of laissez-faire capitalism and reengaged the debate between neoliberalism and embedded liberalism.

The establishment of "rules-based regimes" (Richter 2001, 6) or regulation has a long history of government oversight and self-regulation. Even classical economics believe the free market performs best when prerequisites such as rules and regulations enforce civil rights such as "the right to own property, to enter into private contracts, and engage in market activity" (Scherer 2006, 505), guarantee participation in the political process via representative democracy, and provide social rights to education, healthcare, and a social safety net are in place to enforce compliance. According to Scherer (2006), the state maintains this regulatory compliance to induce a peaceful economic climate in which divisions between the public sphere and the private sphere maintain balance. Even classical economics like Milton Friedman know the nonexistence of regulations lends itself to anarchy, and strong economic communities need a regulatory regime in order to thrive. The argument then becomes how much regulation is necessary to maximize profits yet maintain order when regulatory regimes are broadened to include other communities in other nations.

Other actors also influence the framework of GSCs. Nations always want what is in their own best interests and, depending on their perspective, may disagree internally about the best way to structure GSCs. Often the dominant interests groups within a state carry more power and influence and are able to dictate tax and investment policy. "With the reality of a highly interconnected world, the rise of transnational alliances—whether of civil society, business, cities, or regions—on a range of global issues further complicates the prospect of discerning discrete 'national interests'" (Birkbeck 2015; Hale 2011). Non-state actors, such as unions, businesses (large and small), social movements, non-governmental organizations, think tanks, and private foundations, also try to influence the structure of GSCs and "offer a growing range of examples of how actions and initiatives of non-state actors can complement, challenge and alter the evolution of formal inter-governmental arrangements" (Weiss 2014). The push/pull of non-state actors over issues such as sustainable consumption and production is based on the non-state actors' principles to resolve issues through the collective versus market-based solutions. The multilayered approaches to resolving how to structure a workable, beneficial, and sustainable framework for GSCs showcases the difficulty in creating a structural architecture which serves civil society and the international community. The question then becomes should the framework be predicated on efficiency and effectiveness as the primary benchmark for assessing the quality of governance arrangements and their performance or should the framework prioritize principles such as inclusiveness and transparency, which foster legitimacy, "good outcomes," and the spirit of democracy (Birkbeck 2015, 7).

Most countries are in favor of some sort of nuanced openness as a general principle. *Multilateralism*, the principle of alliances between three or more governments, seems to offer the most potential for universal rules coverage. Multilateral negotiations, perceived to be fair and inclusive, allow smaller countries to form alliances and wield more power than they would in bilateral agreements or alone. The idea of inclusiveness in a global trading system is thought of as a public good which produces a fairer outcome and provides stability in global trade relations (Birkbeck 2015). Trade agreements are thought to have more legitimacy when all actors have a part in "consensus-based decision-making" (Birkbeck 2015, 43). This brings into the conversation the idea of *fair trade*, a social movement which came into prominence about forty years ago as a way to improve the lives of agricultural producers in the Global South through improved prices for products, improved market access and methods for sustainable farming, and human rights protections through social justice and economic security (Moore 2004).

Fair trade as a social movement helps agricultural producers in underdeveloped and underdeveloped countries receive better prices for their products while promoting sustainable farming and better trading conditions. The fair trade movement consists of producer organizations in the Global South who supply the product, buyer organizations in the Global North, umbrella organizations who enforce fair trade rules and act as connectors between buyers and sellers, and retailers who sell products (Moore 2004).

Tensions exist between what constitutes free trade and fair trade. Some opponents of fair trade see it as an impediment to free trade because it acts as a protectionist measure for some producers in the market. Birkbeck (2015) writes, "Fair trade schemes that aim to boost protections for developing country workers and producers may be viewed by others as posing unfair constraints on their access to markets" (43). Free traders says fair traders seek an undue advantage in the market by demanding labor and environmental standards be met as a way to protect their own jobs. Free traders claim a more appropriate way to compensate Global South producers would be through a donation program from the Global North. Global South producers contend donations depend on the largess of the Global North and do not constitute social justice.

The concept of social justice embedded in the fair trade movement suggests there is an inherent injustice embedded in free trade. After all, free trade is based on the premise of producing the most units at the lowest cost. Free traders say it makes little sense to purchase what they perceive to be a substandard product at a higher price and are only now taking into consideration the impact of fair trade since fair trade sales have risen. To account for these increased sales, one has to consider which consumers are buying fair trade produced products and why. Consumers under the age of thirty-five are interested in ethically and socially responsibly produced goods and are the primary market for fair trade products. The consumer base must be broadened if fair trade is to remain viable. It is difficult to see how the fair trade movement can be perpetually sustained within the capitalist system without altering the social and cultural ways in which consumers purchase products. If price continues to be the only criteria by which consumers make purchases, fair trade loses. If consumers choose to incorporate quality and social responsibility into their purchase decisions, fair trade could gain momentum.

GOVERNANCE FRAMEWORKS

The term *governance* has different meanings dependent upon its analysis and geography within GSCs. *Governance*, in general, is the power to allow or constrain the behavior or activity of stakeholders to make and/or enforce implicit or explicate rules. *Corporate governance* speaks to the internal rules and policies which guide and direct the firm's day-to-day operations. *Market governance* speaks to external institutions which dictate the firm's economic behaviors. As corporations morph into streamlined global supply chains and their production and distribution activities take on an international flavor, an *industrial governance* structure is required to coordinate production, distribution, finances, and trade and investment activities (Bair 2013). The job of regulating international activities was given in 1945 to the *World Bank* and the *International Monetary Fund*, international organizations created at Bretton Woods, New Hampshire, to provide economic and financial stability to a world reeling from the aftermath of the destruction and devastation of WWII. This regulatory regime sufficed to control the governance of international firms until the early 1970s when its requirements were no longer adequate for an interconnected, globalized world in which private sector corporations gained great power. This created a space or gap of contested governance between the private and public sectors which has yet to be filled by a regulatory system satisfactory to corporations, governments of different countries, non-governmental organizations, social and environmental groups, labor unions, and political operatives.

The actors who helped to create this void, MNCs, are also the ones stepping in to fill the void by asserting their own form of private governance through *corporate social responsibility*. Corporate social responsibility is a form of internal policing, voluntary in nature, which outlines the ethical and social parameters of behavior and activity for the firm. It is not enforceable by any outside actors such as governments. This "fox guarding the henhouse mentality" sets up a tension between corporations who wish to maximize profits by assuring consumers their products are ethically produced in environmentally protected and worker-friendly safe places and non-governmental stakeholders who want to replace corporate greed with corporate responsibility and protect workers' rights.

It is worth noting there are two competing perspectives concerning governing GSCs depending on whether the focus is on *global value chains* (GVCs) or *global production networks* (GPNs). Global value chains (GVCs) consist of various points within the production process at which value is added to the product. At each of these points, opportunities for worker exploitation and environmental degradation is possible, so the industrial governance of GVCs encompasses notions of who has the power to control interactions between stakeholders within the chain and what are the consequences for stakeholders associated with the risks of those activities. This perspective speaks to internal processes or the intra-dynamics within GVCs whether the chain is vertically integrated as in the production of durable goods such as automobiles and major appliances or horizontally integrated such as in the production of clothing, textiles, and electronics. The complexity within the production process of coordinating global stakeholders and organizing activities at each point to add value to the product is the purview of lead firms who currently "are *the* power brokers" (Horner 2017).

Proponents of the term GPNs suggest solely focusing on the activities within the chain is a misrepresentation of the power dynamics affectively controlling stakeholders. They, instead, suggest a non-linear look (hence the term network instead of chain) at external forces such as non-governmental organizations, labor unions, social movements, and the state who exert pressure on GPNs to behave in certain ways (Bair 2015; Horner 2017). Horner (2017) suggests "strategic coupling" (3) between local, regional, and global territories could be further developed to more evenly distribute power within the networks.

INTERNATIONAL ORGANIZATIONS SEEKING WORKER PROTECTIONS

Two international organizations are important to discuss concerning the global governance of trade and investment: the G20 (Group of 20), a political forum for global economic governance founded in 1999 to study, review, and promote policy discussions concerning the promotion of international financial stability, and the United Nation's 2030 Agenda for Sustainable Development, an action plan to eradicate poverty worldwide in order to bring peace and prosperity to the world. The membership in the G20 includes "85 percent of the global economy, 76 percent of international trade, and two-thirds of the world's population" (Birkbeck 2015, 56). Though the G20 is a powerful venue for policy discussion, there is disagreement on exactly how, whether, and to what extent the G20 should actually influence trade and investment policy.

The G20 generally underperforms as an actor influencing trade and investment policy. Appeals from the G20 for restraint in using protectionist measures to curb imports and keep multilateral trade agreements alive have "only marginally served as a space for coordination among governments on trade" (Birkbeck 2015, 56). The UN's 2030 Agenda for Sustainable Development suggests a stronger need for coordination among all actors to facilitate sustainable development and better coordinate the work of all agencies charged with those activities. The challenges include the unwillingness of governments to allocate their resources in ways which do not benefit them. Since governments vote with financial resources and developed countries have more financial resources, it is unlikely developed countries will vote for policies detrimental to themselves. This exacerbates the role of the UN in attempting to influence trade and investment policies worldwide. This leaves many unanswered questions concerning the scope and functions of governments and actors with roles and responsibilities in international institutional processes which affect GSCs. How should international agencies, economic, political, and social, better coordinate their activities in order for workers' rights to be protected? How could trade treaties be constructed to foster trade and investment while encouraging sustainable development in which workers could also thrive?

The slow pace of top-down "international negotiations and global governance" (Birkbeck 2015, 7), which involve treaty-based commitments relying on multi-stakeholders' agreements, is moving the needle for resolution toward bottom-up local governance and the private sector which involve public-private partnerships, best practices, self-regulation, and corporate social responsibility. A fuller discussion about these approaches takes place in chapter 6 when we discuss corporate social responsibility and its impact. Should the framework for GSCs be an either or approach or should the best practices from multiple stakeholders be considered? Can existing formal models of international alliances be mediated by new and informal models of alliances to produce sustainable and efficient outcomes for all involved parties? These important questions will continue to be discussed during chapter 3 when we talk about the development of GSCs.

CONCLUSION

It doesn't have to be this way. The complexity of GSCs, GVCs, and GPNs complicates cooperation between MNCs, states, NGOs, and labor unions because of competing ideologies associated with neoliberalism and embedded liberalism and what constitutes best practices. The corporation, whose goal is to make a profit and views workers as an input into a system of global production which seeks unfettered restraint in control of the workforce, is at odds with workers who seek protections against exploitation and abuse through labor unions and legislation. This polarization of competing ideologies results in cultural hegemony, a worldview in which powerbrokers, namely MNCs, control the workforce through cultural and social values and mores instead of violence and results in workers contributing to their own exploitation. Past efforts to reconcile the gap between corporate power and worker power have ebbed and flowed depending on the economic power of global stakeholders garnered via public opinion and legislation. Currently the vast majority of economic power resides with the corporations leaving workers with little recourse but to accept jobs for low wages, no benefits, and few worker protections.

The framework for the governance of GSCs is difficult because its transnational nature crosses local, regional, and international boundaries which have different labor and environmental protections, sometimes enforced and sometimes not. The unregulated space in which MNC activities takes place is then filled by private corporations who seek to police themselves through corporate social responsibility, a voluntary method of compliance which discounts state intervention. International organizations such as the G20 and the United Nations Agenda on Sustainable Development offer recommendations for worker protections through sustainable economic and environmental recommendations such as the eradication of extreme poverty. To date, there is very little movement from corporations in the direction of harmonizing relationships with workers if it means corporations must cede some of their power.

Chapter Three

The Development of Global Supply Chains

LEARNING OBJECTIVES

By the end of the chapter, students will be able to:

1. Identify the ways in which investors have a responsibility to their shareholders.
2. Indicate the role investors play in pumping monies into developing countries.
3. Identify three to five indicators of forced labor.
4. Define the term "hyperglobalist."
5. Differentiate the position on deregulation taken by corporations/investors with the position on deregulation taken by labor unions, environmental groups, non-governmental agencies, consumer protectionists, and human rights organizations.

Key terms: Hyperglobalist, Investment, Forced labor, Human trafficking, Privatization, Deregulation, Collective good

This chapter explores the drivers of global supply chains (GSCs) and their impact on development. What components must remain in place for GSCs to exist? Investment? Forced and child labor? Human trafficking? Privatization? Deregulation?

DRIVERS OF GSCS AND THEIR IMPACT ON DEVELOPMENT

All humans who consume goods and services are in some way connected to GSCs as owners, managers, workers, or consumers. This means it is the responsibility of all people to understand the impact GSCs have on the lives of those who own and produce the goods and services we consume. There is no doubt that global supply chains and global production networks "are the most critical organizational platforms through which production in primary, manufacturing, and service sectors is coordinated and organized on a global basis" and now "constitute the long-term structural architecture of the global economy" (Yeung 2015, 30). Yet the stability of GSCs relies on the maintenance of unregulated institutional structures, lax worker and environment protections, and neglect of enforcement mechanisms to monitor and correct deficiencies in the market which create multiple venues of unmitigated human exploitation and suffering particularly in the Global South. Exploring the components necessary for GSCs to exist in their current state brings to light the deficits and deficiencies in their structure and maintenance and suggests some alternatives for improvement in their operation. We first turn to investment, a necessary component for the existence and longevity of GSCs.

COMPONENTS OF GSCS

Investment

GSCs could not exist without investors. Investors are often individuals, conglomerates, and public or private financial institutions whose sole motivation for investing is to seek profits for themselves or other stakeholders. Economic systems raise investment to an elevated status particularly in capitalist nations. Investors have a responsibility to their shareholders to make profits in ethical ways which respect the dignity and self-worth of their workers and to "identify, monitor, and prevent the use of forced labour in their supply chains and operations" (St-Onge 2016, 1). Because investors are at financial risk for a firm's operations, it is increasingly important for them to require transparency in the firm's policies and practices involving nefarious activities such as forced and child labor and human trafficking. When reports of migrant workers being beaten and forced to work against their will come to light, the international community has an obligation to investigate, and investors have a responsibility to require companies to "respect human rights within their operations and wider areas of impact" (St-Onge 2016, 1) and improve these workers' conditions.

There exists an innate tension between investment and human rights' abuses. Conventional wisdom suggests firms seeking to maximize profits move to developing countries where labor is cheap, natural resources abound, and populations can be controlled and exploited through investment, legislation, and social conventions. Keeping the poorest populations in peripheral societies dependent on elite populations in capitalist's developed countries creates a win-lose scenario in which the Global North takes advantage of the Global South. The use of militant intervention to tamp down workers' rights to protest and collectively bargain is a popular way to introduce and ensure certainty in the market and reduce investor risk due to political and economic instability. Consequently, developing countries then become harbors for potential investors because of tight labor market controls, low labor costs, manageable populations, and compliant host governments. This tightly controlled labor arena also breeds opportunities for human and environmental exploitation, especially in the informal economy, and is often touted as the cost of doing business.

There is an assumption made by stakeholders that a country's entrance into a GSC will promote economic expansion, stimulate physical and social infrastructure, encourage foreign direct investment (FDI), and allow countries to compete more fairly in a global marketplace. And yet the data presented by the global labor picture don't provide evidence of greater expansion but rather promote static or small incremental growth (Jha 2016). For instance, according to the United Nations Conference on Trade and Development (UNCTAD) (2013), emerging markets reported a 30 percent growth in gross domestic product (GDP) and developing countries like China and India reported trade-related activity increased five to six times. Yet the bulk of these gains channeled to only a few stakeholders while the vast majority of workers remained in precarious work in the informal economy. Part of the accumulation of capital for developing countries like China, Japan, South Korea, and Taiwan has more to do with domestic restructuring in land reforms and agricultural production which allowed them to increase their "home markets" (Jha 2016, 1) and less to do with their entry into GSCs.

The 2007–2008 Recession had investors skittish, so many investors took a wait and see approach to pumping money into the economies of developed and developing nations. From 2007 to 2014, FDI devoted more to developing countries (52 percent) than developed countries (42 percent). The reasons for this are twofold: *offshore financial centers* (OFCs) and *special purpose entities* (SPEs) probably attracted investments because of favorable tax conditions, and the reinvestment of earnings as a long-term investment is higher in developing countries than in developed countries (UNCTAD 2013). This trend shifted in 2015 and, according to UNCTAD (2017), FDI was erratic during 2016 with 2 percent less investment in developing countries such as Asia, Africa, Latin America, and the Caribbean while investments to developed economics rose by 5 percent. Investments in *least developed countries* (LDCs) such as Angola, Haiti, and the Democratic Republic of the Congo fell by 13 percent. Reasons for declining investment in developing countries was attributed to weak economic growth and policy risks as perceived by MNCs. LDCs are perceived as structurally weak for sustainable development and vulnerable to economic and environmental shock and have low levels of assets. Policy in 2016 trended toward "*investment promotion, facilitation and liberalization*" (UNCTAD 2017, xi) in countries which liberalized economic policies. Projections for increased investments remain cautiously optimistic as uncertainty in geopolitical circles is affected by the United Kingdom's exit from the European Union, the United States's withdrawal from the Trans-Pacific Partnership, potential renegotiation of the North American Free Trade Agreement (NAFTA), and new tax laws signed into law by the Trump administration (UNCTAD 2017).

Policy trends in national investment policy making are changing and favoring investments in new development strategies because governments wish to "attract and facilitate foreign investments as a means for productive capacity-building and sustainable development" (UNCTAD 2013, x). The expansion of GSCs is impacted by FDI as evidenced by the correlation between FDI stocks and GSC participation. Clearly, FDI is more robust in developing countries prior to 2015 than in developed countries. *International investment agreements* (IIAs), specific laws that address cross-border investment, use strategies of international investment in order to diversify their products, spread risk among firms, and shore up their investment portfolios to protect, promote, and liberalize their investments. In 2017 there were 3,324 IIAs reflecting (re)adjustments due to the liberalizing of economic policies (UNCTAD 2017). As hundreds of IIAs reach their end date, renegotiation opportunities are trending toward self-protection in regional blocks instead of global spaces. This means more countries are seeking assurances their investments are protected and safe.

Several factors affect the decision of developed countries to invest in developing countries. The domestic political stability within a country makes it more attractive to investors because political stability means less unpredictability in policy changes. In the past, it was believed autocratic regimes were attractive to FDI because of the ability of autocrats to tamp down "labor demands and by the absence of election-induced policy uncertainty" (Büthe 2008, 743). That no longer seems to be the case as evidenced by increased flows of FDI in politically stable developing countries. A second factor affecting the decision of developed countries to invest in developing countries is the naturally occurring power shift to developing countries, sometimes called host countries. FDI suggests a long-term commitment in capturing a *return on investment* (ROI) because an infusion of cash into a host country goes into establishing brick and mortar structures and equipment not easily retracted. Host countries have an economic incentive to comply with the long-term strategies of their investors, but as resource-starved countries, they have a greater incentive to changes the terms of the agreement to recoup short-term gains (Büthe 2008). A third factor influencing investors is the digital economy. Digital technologies can have a profound effect on international production as investors seek to enter markets with domestic digital capabilities, a narrow digital divide, and the potential for increased digital technology. The concern is that digital technology will decrease employment as MNCs shift their corporate value from "labor to capital" (UNCTAD 2017, 162).

The investing country is interested in fluidity in its transactions so they prefer investing in countries which promote liberal economic policies with little government intervention. Host countries interested in attracting FDI look for ways to ensure establishing and protecting liberal economic policies. Costs occur if either party breaches the IIA. One type of IIA is a *trade agreement*, a pact between two countries which sets the terms for the exchange of goods and services. A trade agreement has several purposes. The trade agreement enshrines an apparatus through which foreign investors commit monies in exchange for assurance their assets are protected, encourages increasing investments, and ensures stability in economic and political circles for some specified period of time. In other words, trade agreements "institutionalize commitments to liberal economic policies" (Büthe 2008, 745) and make publicly visible parties who fail to comply with the agreement thus triggering economic or social retribution.

Types of Investments

Two types of FDI exist: *horizontal FDI* and *vertical FDI*. Horizontal FDI means a firm duplicates production efforts in two or more countries, and sales occur domestically. Profits from horizontal FDI are affected through tariff changes and transportation, labor, and raw input costs. Vertical FDI means firms invest in upstream or downstream suppliers and/or distributors, often in different locations, for efficiency in logistics, wages, skill levels, or availability of inputs. Vertical FDI lends itself to GSCs which often use the product of one firm in one country to add value to another product made at another firm in another country. FDI into host countries tend to be vertical investments (Büthe 2008).

Some evidence exists that IIAs do increase FDI in developing countries as measured by increased GDP and trade-related activities (Moran 2002; Oman 2000). It is also true that developing countries move toward liberal economic policies in order to solicit and accept FDI because the infusion of capital translates into much needed jobs. But these econometric measures do not necessarily reflect or take into account the effect FDI has on workers, their standards of living, or their chances of success in achieving gains in wages, worker protections, or worker mobility. Developing countries, particularly in the Global South, may have no other choice but to engage in trade agreements and accept FDI because the alternative for their populations is too bleak: no jobs for workers, no chance of success, and no future hope. Though some would suggest that FDI in host countries considers the issue of human rights abuses because not doing so focuses a "spotlight" (Blanton 2007, 145) on their corporate activities and paints them as human rights' violators, there exists mounting evidence to the contrary.

One such example of how FDI in a host country violates human rights is the case of *extractavism*, "the largescale withdrawal of natural resources . . . [in] agriculture, commercial farms, forests, plantation growing and fishing" (Cottle 2016, 1) in Africa. Extractavism depletes Africa's natural resources and repatriates profits to the Global North instead of using the profits for the benefit of the African population. Though extractive industries in Africa provide potential development opportunities, they are very skill and capital intensive and account for 75 percent of all exports while manufacturing accounts for 14 percent. Yet the industry remains a marginal employer and doesn't produce large-scale employment or lift people out of poverty (Cottle 2016). The detrimental effects of extractavism leave African citizens without access to large swaths of land, clean water, and social services.

Adding Transparency to the Mix

Investors can help in policing human rights abuses by requiring transparency within GSCs and pushing for firms to improve policies and practices. They must be aware of pending legislation and requirements in various countries and how that legislation will impact workers. Three current pieces of key legislation which help promote transparency are the California Transparency in Supply Chains Act (2010), the UK's Modern Slavery Act (2015), and the EU Non-Financial Reporting Directive (2014) (St-Onge 2016).

The California Transparency in Supply Chains Act (2012) requires California's large retailers and manufacturers to disclose on their websites their "efforts to eradicate slavery and human trafficking from [their] direct supply chain for tangible goods offered for sale" (Harris 2015, i). The act does not mandate the firm to implement actions ensuring their supply chains do not engage in abusive activities related to forced labor or human trafficking, but it does offer recommendations on how to implement such policies and provide best practices which comply with the law and improve consumers' understanding of anti-trafficking and anti-forced labor efforts.

The UK Modern Slavery Act (2015) applies (after March 31, 2016) to all large businesses with a turnover of 35 million pounds in the United Kingdom. "These businesses are required to publish an annual slavery and human trafficking statement of the steps they have taken to ensure that slavery and human trafficking are not taking place in their business or in any of their supply chains" (St-Onge 2016, 5). (See below for more info on the UK Modern Slavery Act.)

The EU Non-Financial Reporting Directive (2016) is required to include in strategic annual reports specific details on human rights in order to improve transparency in eligible EU companies (more than 500 employees) in terms of non-financial information. The impetus for investors is that corporate social responsibility goes hand in hand with long-term sustainability.

Though businesses and not investors are sanctioned if human trafficking or forced labor is found in supply chains, the exposure of human rights violations carries reputational and branding risks and may be detrimental to the company's profits, causing investors to pull funding from the firm. Also, in some cases, victims of forced labor can seek redress for their exploitation through a country's court system. Though most lawsuits filed have been dismissed, these actions do highlight the growing interest of consumers about human rights' violations in supply chains.

FORCED AND CHILD LABOR AND HUMAN TRAFFICKING

Forced labor in global supply chains is a global problem. According to the International Labor Organization (ILO), about 20.9 million people are forced to work under slave-like conditions in the informal and illegal economies. The number of humans in forced labor is astounding with the bulk of forced labor in the Global South. Private agents in labor-intensive industries such as "manufacturing, fishing, agriculture and food processing, domestic work and construction" account for 90 percent of that forced labor (Caught at sea 2013; 2016). Forced and child labor is particularly prevalent in the lower tiers of GSCs, in home-based business, and in the informal economy (Andrees 2016).

Traditionally, workers enter into a labor relationship at a port of entry. This suggests a choice is involved at the beginning of the labor-management relationship in which workers consciously provide their labor in exchange for compensation. Forced labor, on the other hand, suggests workers are conscripted or enslaved through some involuntary manner into the labor relationship. Child labor is certainly characterized as forced labor because children do not have the ability to consent. Working adults, though, are often compelled to work under dire working conditions for weak wages because the opportunities for better wages and working conditions are unavailable to them. O'Neill refers to this illusion of choice as "*compulsion by necessity*" (italics mine) (Barrientos 2007, 1039 in O'Neill, 2011). Workers are shunted into bondage employment through poverty, "continual and chronic conditions of need," and forced to stay there "by the constraint[s] that are imposed on a person's ability to leave a particular arrangement—unfreedom at the point of exit" (Barrientos 2013, 1039).

Myriad constraints prevent workers from leaving compulsory work arrangements. *Economic debt bondage*, sometimes called *bonded labor*, is the most common form of slave labor currently in existence; it is the usually unwritten contract between a laborer and an employer in which the worker is compelled to work for some period of time in exchange for debt repayment, job security, and his/her release; it is commonly used for temporary or contract labor. Seasonal workers and short-term contract workers are attractive to employers who are not obligated to provide benefits as required in long-term contract arrangements. Other forms of financial bondage include fees and charges for procuring employment, "'run-away' insurance to prevent [workers] from absconding," and "'circular obligation,'" in which debt is owed to a third party who procured the work position, yet the worker is obligated to the employer for repayment (Barrientos 2013, 1040). Other constraints include confiscation of passports, intimidation and violence against workers or their families, threats against deportation for immigrants, and physical and social isolation. Turning a blind eye to these atrocities is not in the long-term best interest of the development of GSCs and certainly does nothing to protect workers' rights and safety.

The ILO works toward creating overall standards governing forced and child labor and human trafficking but is hindered by various countries' cultures and the absence of legislation concerning freedom of association and collective bargaining. The ILO's definition of forced labor refers to working involuntarily under the threat of penalty. "Forced labour, modern slavery, debt bondage and human trafficking are closely related forms of exploitation though not identical in the legal sense" (St-Onge 2016, 2). This means all situations in which a human is forced to work by means of violence, accumulated debt, retention of identity papers, or threats of denunciation to immigration authorities (St-Onge 2016). According to the ILO, forced labor nets industry $150 billion USD per year, $99 billion of which results from commercial sexual exploitation and $51 billion USD from forced economic exploitation (Organization 2017).

The ILO lists indicators of forced labor as follows:

- Abuse of workers' vulnerability, e.g., disabilities, language barrier
- Deceptive recruitment practices
- Isolation, e.g., held in remote locations
- Intimidation and threats
- Withholding of wages
- Excessive overtime
- Abusive working and living conditions
- Restriction of movement

- Physical and sexual violence
- Retention of identity documents, e.g., passports
- Debt bondage

Global supply chains are multilayered, offer multiple points for human rights abuses, and are difficult to police, but that does not absolve MNCs from their obligation for transparency. Major abuses seem to take place in labor-intensive sectors at the commodity and raw materials levels where oversight is weak. Higher-risk industries include construction, agriculture, food and beverage, manufacturing, mining, electronics, and apparel and footwear. The ILO is pushing for standardized ways in which to measure child and forced labor globally.

Human Bondage in the Fishing Industry

The ILO investigated human bondage in the fishing industries which provide food security and employment globally. This report was presented in Turin, Italy, in 2012 and answered questions concerning the scope of forced labor and human trafficking in fishing industries, the institutional and legal frameworks in existence to combat the problems, and the main issues that inform discussions on how to move forward (Caught at sea 2013). The nature of fishing requires workers to spend long months or years at sea in isolation. Often these workers, mostly migrants, are coerced or deceived into debt bondage by intimidation, threat, or deceit. Intense work, long hours, and hazardous conditions put these workers at risk for physical injury, psychological and sexual abuse, and death. Known as *capture fisheries*, these industries have the "highest occupational fatality rates in the world" (Caught at sea 2013, v). The shift of sourcing fish from developed countries to developing countries allows the solicitation of more migrant workers and the opportunity for further exploitation.

Flag ships, those fishing vessels operating under a country's flag, have the primary responsibility for combatting forced labor and human trafficking as members of the ILO and ratifying parties to the "IOL Forced Labour Convention or the United Nations Trafficking in Persons Protocol" (Caught at sea 2013, vi). But these ships and their sponsoring countries often breach their obligations. The ILO and other organizations have developed and presented legal binding and non-binding safety and labor instruments to improve worker safety and working conditions, but none have been approved. This contributes to the lack of transparency concerning workers and their working conditions and "undermines effective investigation and prosecution of crimes committed on board fishing vessels" (Caught at sea 2013, vi). Atrocities exacted against workers on fishing vessels are documented in Thailand, Myanmar, the United Kingdom, and Indonesia. Illegal measures taken against Taiwanese fisheries are also documented as is precarious work in the Asian seafood global value chain.

The international community is taking note of forced and child labor and human trafficking and encouraging non-governmental organizations (NGOs), such as corporations, to respect human rights through their business practices. Recognizing the global power of global supply chains, many national governments have taken action to move the needle toward respect for human dignity by addressing forced labor issues. The creation of the United Nations Global Compact, an "initiative to encourage corporations to commit to human rights principles [and] . . . The effective abolition of forced labour" and the Guiding Principles on Business and Human Rights which "provide an authoritative global standard for business conduct related to human rights" (Feasley 2015, 2) are steps in the right direction but have little enforcement authority. Some corporations are making efforts to create voluntary ethical codes in supply chains in attempts to be more socially responsible, and some states are addressing the issue through transparency and disclosure regulations.

The global consensus is that slavery in any form is a serious human rights violation and no one should benefit from the crime of forced labor "directly or from forced labour exacted by a third party in a global supply chain" (Burrow 2017, 10). In an effort to combat forced and child labor in supply chains, transparency engendered by national and international legislation to force MNCs to comply with labor standards and promote human dignity is necessary. The United Kingdom took a step toward this goal in 2015 with the passage of the UK Modern Slavery Act (MSA) in an effort to "establish legal tools to combat the scourge of forced labor—not only in its territory but also in the supply chains of UK-based technologies" (Burrow 2017, 3). Their recommendations include (1) supply chain transparency which requires all firms making more than 36 million pounds per year (which in the UK is around 12,000 firms) to publicly furnish in an easily assessable central repository (such as a website) their efforts to combat forced labor punishable by sanctions should the firm provide false or misleading information; (2) extraterritoriality which holds all UK firms liable under UK law for forced labor or human trafficking within their supply chains wherever the crime was committed; and (3) due diligence and civil remedies mandated in the firm's home jurisdiction for supply chain violations (Burrow 2017, 5–8).

The United States passed the Trade Facilitation and Trade Enforcement Act of 2015 (TFTEA) which prohibits entry of goods, subject to seizure, made by forced or conscripted labor into any US port. President Obama signed this legislation into law on February 24, 2016. It is the first comprehensive authorization of US Customs and Border Protection (CBP) since the Department of Homeland Security was formed in 2003. The goal is to protect US economic security, strengthen enforcement capabilities, collaborate with the private sector to ensure the provision of benefits to the commercial sector, modernize/streamline paperwork for trade processes, education about trade laws, create preclearance programs for US bound travelers, and raise the value of shipments from $200 to $800. This law can now be used as a human rights tool as well.

Verbiage against forced and child labor was included in the Transpacific Partnership (TPP) legislation, though that legislation is now dead after President Trump withdrew the United States from participation in 2017. The TPP was a trade agreement among twelve countries, Brunei, Chile, New Zealand, Singapore, Japan, Malaysia, Mexico, Peru, Vietnam, the United States, Canada, and Australia, which would lower tariff and non-tariff barriers to trade and establish an investor-state dispute settlement mechanism. Included in the legislation was language which prohibited exploitative child labor and forced labor, ensured the right to collective bargaining, and prohibited employment discrimination. These tenets are also included in the International Labor Organization's Universal Declaration of Human Rights and the Declaration on Fundamental Principles and Rights at Work.

The International Union of Food, Agricultural, Hotel, Restaurant, Catering, Tobacco and Allied Workers' Associations (IUF) is an international federation of 424 affiliated trade unions in 127 countries representing over 10 million workers employed in agriculture and plantations, the preparation and manufacture of food and beverages, hotels, restaurants and catering services, and all stage of tobacco processing and publishes stories about the victimization and exploitation of workers in various industries (IUF 2017). Countless cases of abuse, illegal discipline and termination, and unfair treatment are rampant.

PRIVATIZATION

The principles of the free market, market liberalization, and laissez-faire capitalism based on competition have been around for decades and have been embraced by heads of state worldwide. Margaret Thatcher and Tony Blair, prime ministers of the United Kingdom, promoted the free market as the only economic system which worked, as did Presidents Ronald Reagan and Bill Clinton in the United States. The idea behind the free market analysis is based on private ownership and private allocation of all goods and services exchanged in the market whether the market is local, state, national, or international. Individuals who support unfettered free market capitalism are known as *hyperglobalists* and believe the states have ceded power to the global market and their role is now to facilitate a smooth transition to a globalized economy in which market forces now dictate economic, social, and political policy.

Counter points to the hyperglobalists' prediction of powerless states include states as major actors in maintaining state sovereignty by "sharing sovereignty with each other in order to retain it as well as non-state actors such as global companies that are themselves agents of the transformation underway" (Mikler 2013, 5). This then becomes a battle between market forces and political forces. MNCs are now being seen as political and social actors and not just economic actors who can drive economic, political, and social policy. Consequently it makes sense to then look at MNCs and states as sharing/merging their interests rather than as factors competing over power relationships between public and private interests.

Private Versus Public Control

Wainwright (2014) makes the argument that mass privatization efforts have failed to produce the necessary efficient predicted outcomes at least in the public sector. She writes that applying the logic of privatization to the "management of shared resources, natural and social and the meeting of social needs" . . . has turned "on its head '*the tragedy of the commons*' [italics mine] which was an attack on the idea that people can effectively manage common resources together for the shared benefit, if they have suitable conditions" (4). The benefit of the commons is a shared interest in sustainable development and growth predicated on insourcing work to local communities who can then return their investments into service improvements instead of sending them to corporate stockholders. The term "remunicipalisation" (Wainwright 2014, 4) is coined to reflect returning services to public management because service quality is improved and greater efficiencies are gained from a public value perspective. "'Remunicipalisation' has meant more control and oversight from the elected authority and representatives" (Wainwright 2014, 1) and less authority from the WTO, IMF, and the European Union (EU).

The shop floor, the home, or the local utility company are the places where services interact with consumers so it makes sense for resistance actions against privatization to begin locally. "The significance of U.S.-dominated international bodies as institutions through which free market ideology, especially as personified in the governments of Reagan and Bush, has driven, spread and reinforced the process of privatization" (Wainwright 2014, 7). This top-down approach by international bodies to reinforce neoliberal policies filters down through our elected legislative bodies as a premier regulatory regime backed by treaties or imposed as financial conditions imposed on countries with the threat of monetary withdrawal. At the WTO meeting in Seattle, Washington, in 1999, an anti-globalization movement took form. Sometimes called the Battle in Seattle, representatives from labor unions, environmental and consumer protection groups, and others concerned with labor rights protested the WTO Ministerial Conference. Interestingly enough, these protestors, who faced tear gas and rubber bullets, were driven by the same concerns as the recent 2011 Occupy Wall Street or the 99% Movement which protested economic inequality worldwide after the devastating 2007–2008 Great Recession in which 15 million workers in the United States alone lost their jobs.

The United States has, over the course of the last two decades, used its power to impose neoliberal market policies on international bodies (Wainwright 2014). The idea that privatization is the best possible approach to the provision of all services everywhere counters the idea of the commons, the effective management of common resources for a shared benefit under suitable conditions. The tragedy of the commons is built on the narrative that individuals only act in their own self-interest and have no interest in collaborating over shared problems. The commons then begins at a local level with individuals who are aware of similar struggles and work together to fix their problems.

Proponents of bottom-up approaches view as valuable the concept of *public value* or *public good or collective good,* that which is best for the majority of the group not just those who can afford to pay for a service (Olson 1971). The concept of public good is not new and stems from the idea that a good or service must be both non-excludable and non-rivalrous in that individuals cannot be excluded from its use and where its use by one individual does not affect its use by another individual. Wainwright (2014) cautions the need for resistance to privatization at all levels in the face of national and international privatization and "challenge[s] unelected and secretive international bodies such as the World Trade Organization, the International Monetary Fund and increasingly the European Union" (6). Wainwright (2014) explores several bottom-up approaches to combat the push for privatization at any cost by citing examples from several countries in which public service workers have successfully formed public-public or public-civic partnerships to manage public services in lieu of privatizing public services.

The idea that privatization of firms within GSCs will foster growth, production, and profits has its detractors. Yeung (2015) recognizes the interplay of interfirm relationships often leads to fractions and disruptions between and among firms, their upstream suppliers, and their downstream outlets. He takes exception to the idea that the existing model of global value chain (GVC) governance is the only way interfirm or intrafirm collaborations arrive at cost-containment measures and suggests looking at "The role non-firm actors, such as the state, international organizations, labor groups, consumers, and civil society organizations" (Yeung 2015, 50) who influence such things as fair and ethical trade initiatives and the privatization of regulatory standards play a role in inter- and intra-governance. For instance credit rating agencies affect a firm's ability to obtain financial capital, and high-tech industries set industrial standards that influence stakeholders' value activities (Yeung 2015). Non-firm actors also play a role in helping firms establish legitimacy as responsible partners in different economic markets and geopolitical territories. Firms perceived as having a socially and environmentally responsible conscience realize greater economic gains.

DEREGULATION

Deregulation is the removal of government barriers

> such as environmental and financial restrictions on industries and opens the door for participation, thus increasing competition. The argument for deregulation is that business can operate more efficiently and at a lower cost if not required to comply with costly regulations such as safe disposal of hazardous waste or consumer protection. Arguments against deregulation are that is causes wide volatility in markets and provides an unreliable product source. (Walker 2015, 84)

As free trade and flexible labor have become part of the global landscape and structural adjustment policies in developing countries are touted as the most efficient way to increase corporate profits, deregulation in labor markets has proliferated. In order to produce goods and services cheaply, the regulation of worker and environmental protections are under assault. Though public awareness of the abusive labor and environmental conditions under which many workers suffer leads to campaigns by civil society to force corporations' compliance with minimum labor standards, few strides have been made (Barrientos 2007).

The debate is between organizations like the World Bank and the IMF who use their leverage through loan programs to "demand domestic labor market flexibility" and the International Labor Organization's Core Labor Standards (CLS) which champion "freedom of association and collective bargaining" which, as collective rights, "enable the exercise of other rights" (Anner 2010, 151). The ILO is the UN body which sets recommendations for a global floor of labor rights in consultation with NGOs, governments, corporations, and workers; the ILO produces non-binding guidelines. Participating countries can sign onto and ratify ILO recommendations at which point the recommendations become *conventions*, legally binding international treaties. Since the ILO has no enforcement power over recommendations, many countries choose to only comply with recommendations and fail to engage in conventions which the ILO does have power to enforce. The hesitancy of the World Bank and the IMF to embrace CLSs is "related to economic theorizing about the effects of unions and labor standards on economic outcomes" (Anner 2010, 156) such as the CLS impact on international trade and investment and the effect of the collective on economic efficiency and growth. The IMF and the World Bank were reluctant to embrace the CLSs of freedom of association and collective bargaining which they considered an impediment to efficiency and protectionist in nature. Their opposition softened during the Clinton administration's push for the ILO Declaration of Human Rights in 1996 shored up by the US's agreement to provide one-quarter of the funding for the ILO's budget and the assessment of several studies conducted by the World Bank and the IMF reporting improved labor standards "enhanced rather than harmed economic efficiency" (Martin & Maskus 1999, 3 in Anner 2010, 159).

The World Bank and the IMF have greater enforcement power than does the ILO. The IMF's goal is to "ensure international monetary stability in order to facilitate international trade and thus contribute to 'high levels of employment and real income'" and their "mechanism for achieving monetary stability is temporary financial assistance to member countries facing balance of payment difficulties" (Anner 2010, 160). The World Bank is charged with eliminating poverty worldwide through reconstruction and low-interest loans to developing countries. Both organizations have the power to infuse, withhold, or withdraw loans if certain performance criteria are not met by recipients of the loans. The poorer the country, the less able they are to meet these criteria, and the more likely it is they will face imposed penalties.

Though some change has occurred over the course of the last two decades with respect to the World Bank and IMF embracing CLS as suggested by the ILO, there is still work to be done. In 1996, the *Doing Business Report* published by the World Bank included "a chapter on 'Hiring and Firing Workers' that defined a wide variety of labour regulations as obstacles to investment" (Bakvis 2006, 1). These deregulations include setting low minimum wages, maximum weekly hours to prevent reaching overtime, and no advance warning for termination or lay-off. Corporations claim these labor deregulations are a must have for them to remain flexible in a rapidly changing market environment. The report explains, "In a competitive and integrated world, jobs need to move flexibly from less productive to more productive sectors to take advantage of new market opportunities. Reforms to reduce labor market rigidity . . . can have positive effects on job creation and growth" (De Rato 2006 in Anner 2010, 161). So the tension between CLSs as promoted by the ILO and the need for market flexibility pushed by the World Bank and IMF continues.

The trade policies of a country greatly affect the way GSCs are structured and operationalized in other countries. Because multiple suppliers from various countries frequently trade across borders in the production of a single product, exacting tariffs on exported and imported goods significantly impacts the cost of the final product. Though the general trend has been toward lower tariffs, the cumulative effect of cross-border tariffs leans toward protectionism in some countries. For instance, downstream suppliers may pay tariffs on "imported inputs and then face tariffs again on the full value of their exports, including on those same inputs. Tariffs can add up to a significant level by the time the finished good reaches customers, dampening demand and affecting production and investment at all stages of a value chain" (Implications 2013, 13). The Office of Economic and Cooperative Development (OECD) suggests comprehensive trade facilitation is more effective than piecemeal facilitation.

Increases in costs also arise from meeting compliance regulations for safety, technical, and environmental standards. Tracing defects through multiple countries who have varying requirements for food safety and environmental protections is difficult. "Promoting the convergence of standards and certification requirements and encouraging mutual recognition agreements can go a long way to alleviating the burden of compliance and enhancing the competitiveness of small-scale exports" (Implications 2013, 16). GVCs can have a positive impact on a country's GDP per capita growth rate if the value added contribution within the GSC is not limited to low-skill/low-value added employment.

Spurred by the suggestion of sustainable development requirements or social clauses in trade agreements, the European Union Commission, hoping to avoid binding and legal rules concerning environmental and worker protections, preempted negotiations by offering a European Corporate Social Responsibility Framework, a non-binding self-policing approach to managing environmental and working conditions. The argument was the complexity of international social and business interests could not be addressed through legislation. Instead, the EU Commission proposed a profit-maximizing, private international effort to regulate the working conditions within global supply chains to be driven by the Business for Social Compliance Initiative (BSCI). Developed in 2003 by European retailers who wished to "audit and monitor the social performance of their suppliers world-wide by utilizing a common system" (Knudsen 2013, 390) to ensure an ethical approach to securing inputs, improving social relationships with suppliers, and engendering transparency and accountability in transactions, the BSCI rests on and adopts the ILO conventions concerning workers' rights. Voluntary membership in the BSCI requires signing the BSCI Code of Conduct and then complying with the code in supply chains. The idea is threefold: to monitor social compliance, to empower member/suppliers through capacity building, and to engage with stakeholders within supply chains (Knudsen 2013).

MNCs demand large, medium, and small suppliers adhere to the principles of BSCI as a way to self-police firms' activities concerning environmental and worker safety concerns (Knudsen 2013). In the absence of international regulatory compliance, MNCs energetically embrace corporate codes of ethics to fill a void created by the lack of control over international regulation and state deregulation. MNCs largely handle this through international compliance attempts. Medium and small firms who do not do business abroad create their own corporate ethical codes in order to provide a public projection the firm is concerned about its workers' welfare and the environmental impact of their production processes and parameters for employee behavior and activity within and outside the firm.

Three groups of stakeholders drive corporations toward private policing: those who demand standards, those who supply standards, and those who employ the standards. Organizations external to the firm, such as labor unions, consumer groups, social activists, NGOs, and governments, may demand private regulation in order to lower transaction costs, legitimize the functions of the firm, create efficiencies in production processes, and stabilize the market in which transactions are made. These political and economic actors function in the place of state control. Knudsen (2013) calls these external organizations "rule-demanders" (389). Firms will create their own codes of conduct in order to increase monetary gains by supplying internal standards which preempt state standards, in which compliance might be costly, and/or filling a void in which state standards do not exist. Knudsen calls these firms "rule-suppliers" (39). Firms supplying and policing their own standards may create legitimacy within the buying public reinforcing the idea the firm is environmentally conscious and worker-friendly. These rule suppliers are generally MNCs and not medium or small firms. Lastly, those who employ or engage with corporate standards are generally SMEs within domestic markets in Western cultures who interact with downstream suppliers in less developed countries and not SMEs who interact with upstream suppliers in international markets. These "rule-takers" (Knudsen 2013, 389), primarily SMEs often forced by MNCs into compliance with international codes of conduct, are unable to meet the costs of MNCs requirements. So SMEs find themselves in a catch-22 situation in which they cannot afford to comply with MNCs requirements but must comply in order to do business with MNCs.

The result of MNCs' push for SMEs to join and comply with BSCI requirements creates a gulf between MNCs and SMEs which can only be bridged if MNCs are involved with helping SMEs meet regulatory demands. It is unlikely MNCs will seek to rectify this situation unless there is some profit motive for them which leaves us once again with the fox guarding the hen house. The existence of a code of conduct does not necessarily equate with code of conduct compliance. A fuller discussion of corporate codes of conduct appears in chapter 6.

CONCLUSION

It doesn't have to be this way. Coupling sound investment practices with the eradication of forced labor, child labor, and human trafficking in developing and developed countries could positively affect the lives of millions of global workers, increase worker protections, and ensure the continuation of a clean environment. Establishing international enforceable regulations in compliance with core labor standards should not disparage privatization, but rather strengthen the ability of all workers to engage in meaningful and profitable work while shoring up the branding and public persona of corporations. Establishing regulations which support workers' abilities to participate in GSCs even in the face of fluctuating markets increases employment stability and stabilizes labor markets. The pressures to lower costs for goods and services from global buyers would benefit from a floor under which prices could not sink and mean more stable employment, better working conditions, and stronger occupational safety and health concerns. When workers win, corporations win.

Workers are the most valuable asset MNCs have. When workers are repressed, abused, and exploited, vast potential for ingenuity and creativity, the engines that drive economic growth, are stifled. Workers who can collectively join together to better themselves, their working conditions, and their communities contribute to the longevity of the firm and the economic good of the country. Workers who have job security, decent wages and benefits, and decent working conditions are better able to participate in higher levels of training and education in order to attain the knowledge, skills, and abilities to further position themselves and their countries as leading economic players. In sum, greater respect for human rights is associated with uplifting the health, education, and security of all workers by "fostering the development of human capital and engendering economic benefits" (Blanton 2007, 146 in Jensen 2003; Kucera 2002).

Chapter Four

The Fragmentation of Work in the Global Supply Chains

LEARNING OBJECTIVES

At the conclusion of the chapter, students will be able to:

1. Identify the difference in the formal and the informal economy.
2. Analyze the International Trade Union Confederation's position on workers in the informal economy.
3. Identify the three types of value chain governance.
4. Discuss how power is maintained in the informal economy.

Key terms: Soft law, Informal economy, Formal economy, Value chain governance, Flexibility

This chapter looks at the fragmentation of work in global supply chains (GSCs) as the result of global outsourcing and the restructuring of businesses, external organizations, and the employment relationship. The continuum of inequality between the Global North and the Global South in GSCs is fueled by a business model driven by corporate greed which promotes worker exploitation and abuse in the name of shareholders' profits. The push for flexibility increases management's control of inputs in the production process, especially labor, a corporate lobby which seeks to undermine and overturn workers' rights, safety, and environmental laws, and the strength of multinational corporations (MNCs) who hold hostage the governments of developing countries through financial exploitation. This march toward corporate domination leads to precarious work for millions of workers in the formal and informal economies and disrupts stability for workers worldwide.

Understanding what constitutes decent work in GSCs, how labor is fragmented, and what effect that fragmentation has on workers and the environment will help explain the current status of precariat workers, the changing environment in which they work, and how restructuring the employment relationships disturbs workers in their everyday lives.

The momentum to accommodate "flexibility and lower costs" (Flecker 2010, 9) in the workforce has led to a dispersion, fragmentation, and restructuring of the workforce through outsourcing, unstable employment, and weakened workers' rights. This fragmentation is facilitated by deregulation in the form of weaker laws protecting workers, their safety, and the environment, and privatization which seeks profits over people. Consequently, workers take the brunt of this reorganization through employment insecurity in the form of lowered wages, weaker benefits, fewer or no worker protections, and job insecurity. There are also indirect consequences suffered by workers in the form of increased issues of physical and mental health, social instability through affordable home ownership, and the inability to move upward in social and economic strata. The reorganizational structure of national employment laws affect how GSCs operate and impact the opportunities and challenges workers face in their employment relationship.

Proponents of restructuring national employment laws which filter down to reshape the terms and conditions of employment argue restructuring from the top down frees "workers from bureaucratic subordination, empower[s] them and provide[s] space for self-development" (Flecker 2010, 9). Their argument is based on the philosophical idea of laissez-faire markets in which all impediments to the free market are eradicated leaving control of the workforce and all work processes in the hand of the owners of production. The basis for the free market is competition between producers who will strive to lower production costs in efforts to provide low-cost goods and services which are attractive to consumers. They believe leaving all decisions about work in the hands of management allows workers to perform their work tasks free from the complicated morass of decision making allowing them more free time to pursue their own interests. This approach adheres to the adage that management is the head and workers are the hands in any production process.

Opponents of restructuring national employment laws argue these efforts are simply attempts to produce the lowest cost per unit product by shifting much of the insecurity and risk away from corporations and onto the worker. According to Flecker (2010), "the main driver is the attempt to cut costs, and wage costs in particular, in order to circumvent company or sector-level wage regulation or benefit from lower wages in other locations" (10). Shifting the onus of risk to workers has a deleterious effect on supplier and service providers who are often at the end of the GSC. When corporations outsource and subcontract work in order to cut costs and improve flexibility they are essentially integrating an intermediary in the supply chain to distance themselves from issues of liability and employment concerns such as hiring/firing/maintaining the workforce (Holdcroft 2016). This includes rationalizing human resource strategies which favor covert discrimination, undercut equal pay for equal work, and prefer temporary and part-time employees to full-time employees. Workers often cannot determine for whom they work in these "insecurity-and-risk-transfer chains" (Frade/Darmon 2005, 116 in Flecker 2010, 11).

Take, for example, workers in call centers, customer service, or information technology (IT) who may physically work on the premises of one employer but be subcontracted to that employer by an outside firm, such as a private IT service provider or subcontracted by a temporary agency, either of which may be a subsidiary of a national firm which works at the pleasure of an international corporation. Often the workers remain stationary or on site while the risk and insecurity associated with their performance, which should be borne by the actual corporation, is transferred further and further down the risk chain to the worker. The differences the worker may perceive in this risk-transfer chain are a heavier workload, increased surveillance, and a more strenuous standardization of their work.

These polarized viewpoints reflect an overall unawareness of the ways restructuring national employment laws influence the way workers and their rights in GSCs are viewed and managed: Is the buying public unmindful of worker abuse and exploitation involved in the manufacture of electronics, vehicles, and apparel? Are consumers oblivious to ways in which their food is sourced, prepared, and made ready for the market? How can consumers be made mindful of worker abuse and what can they do about it? Understanding how work is organized and restructured can enlighten consumers, workers, and employers about helpful and harmful practices in the employment relationship and best practices in alleviating worker suffering while being mindful of employer-side drivers to which workers must react and interact.

THE FORMAL ECONOMY VERSUS THE INFORMAL ECONOMY

All workers function in either the formal or the informal economies. The formal and informal economies employ around 3 billion workers, 60 percent of which are in the formal economy and 40 percent of which are in the informal economy (Burrow 2016), so it would be important to distinguish between what constitutes formal and informal economies. The formal economy is that sector of the economy which has an organized system of employment, rules for recruitment, agreement, and job responsibilities, a standard employment relationship maintained through some sort of formal contract (written or unwritten), has fixed hours and wages and a decent working environment, is entitled to benefits, has recognized sources of income on which taxes are paid, may have an organized association where grievances are discussed and settled, and is covered by some social protections such as life insurance, health insurance, and pensions. Individuals working in the formal economy work in the public sector, civil service, defense, multinational/national/private firms, and social organizations such as schools, churches, non-governmental organization, and so forth.

The informal economy, sometimes called the hidden economy or the gray economy, is that sector of the economy which has no written rules or agreements, in which the employment relationship is based on verbal contracts, does not have fixed hours of work or wages, has an unsanitary and cluttered working environment, has no mechanism by which the collective can air grievances, is unable to save because of low wages, and has a low or nonexistent level of understanding social protections or the necessity of insuring themselves. Individuals who work in the informal economy work as home-based workers, laborers, artists, micro-entrepreneurs, small farmers, street vendors, hawkers, or small traders. The International Labour Organization (ILO) defines the informal economy as follows:

> The informal economy thrives in a context of high unemployment, underemployment, poverty, gender inequality and precarious work. It plays a significant role in such circumstances, especially in income generation, because of the relative ease of entry and low requirements for education, skills, technology and capital. But most people enter the informal economy not by choice, but out of a need to survive and to have access to basic income-generating activities. The informal economy is marked by acute decent work deficits and a disproportionate share of the working poor. (Conference 2014, 3)

The ILO goes on to explain that empirical research shows workers in the informal economy face greater risks of poverty, are exposed to unsafe working conditions, have high illiteracy levels and few opportunities for advancement, are physically and financially vulnerable, and have low skill levels. The informal economy operates outside the formal reach of the law or operates within reach of the formal law, but the application of the law isn't enforced because of the high cost of compliance (Conference 2014). In some countries the informal economy operates in the private sphere while in other countries, it operates in a shadowy realm or underground. Though these workers may produce goods and services legally, they may not be in compliance with legal requirements such as immigration laws or registration requirements.

Serrano (2016) describes the informal economy as multi-faceted and includes "the total number of informal jobs whether carried out in formal sector enterprises, informal sector enterprises or households, during a given reference period" (1). It would also be important at this point to distinguish between working legally and illegally in the informal economy. Workers in the informal economy produce goods and services through informal processes such as home-based businesses which are perfectly legal, while workers who deal in illicit drug activity, though part of the informal economy, are covered by criminal law and certainly are not going to be protected under labor or commercial law. There are also gray areas in the informal economy where formal workers are paid "under the table," skirting tax liabilities, or when formal workers' wages and working conditions are subpar (Conference 2014).

Workers in the informal economy are creative, entrepreneurial, and skillful, but barriers such as opportunities for educational qualifications or work credentials often get in the way of their upward mobility. Workers gravitate toward the informal economy because of need and not choice. Countries experiencing high unemployment or underemployment and jobs requiring entry level skills attract workers who otherwise would not find work, but these jobs often don't provide decent work. The informal economy could serve as an "incubator for business potential and an opportunity for on-the-job-skills acquisition. In this sense, it can be a transitional base for accessibility and graduation to the formal economy, if effective strategies are put in place" (Conference 2014, 69). Yet, the work deficits far outweigh the work benefits in the informal economy because workers are not protected under labor or social safeguards. As unrecognized workers, they cannot exercise their fundamental right to collectively withhold their labor, seek redress for grievances, or protest for better wages and working conditions. They have no social protections such as unemployment benefits or social security and few chances to upgrade their skills through education, workforce training, or apprenticeships. There is no healthcare or child care for these informal workers which contributes to and represents the social exclusion of workers in the informal economy (Conference 2014).

The ILO states:

> While some people in the informal economy earn incomes that are higher than those of workers in the formal economy, workers and economic units in the informal economy are generally characterized by poverty, leading to powerlessness, exclusion, and vulnerability. Most workers and economic units in the informal economy do not enjoy secure property rights, which thus deprives them access to both capital and credit. They have difficulty accessing the legal and judicial system to enforce contracts, and have limited or no access to public infrastructure and benefits. They are vulnerable to harassment, including sexual harassment, and other forms of exploitation and abuse, including corruption and bribery. Women, young persons, migrants and older workers are especially vulnerable to the most serious decent work deficits in the informal economy. Characteristically, child workers and bonded laborers are found in the informal economy. (Conference 2014, 69)

According to the International Trade Union Confederation (ITUC) (2016), "corporations command 60 percent of global production, transport and services through their supply chains" (3). Major corporations employ only 6 percent of their workforce through direct means and the other 94 percent through the informal or hidden economy. This business model supports profits over people and is based on corporations' abilities to pay low wages, lobby against minimum worker protections, and disregard slavery conditions within their workforce. Fueled by corporate greed, major firms have lost their moral compass and function as if labor is simply a disposable input in a production process for the purpose of increasing shareholder profits. This business model damages all of society because it is not in the long-term best interests of the world's population to encourage wealth and income inequality which gives to the top 1 percent of the population almost 99 percent of the wealth.

The top 50 companies in the world have a combined revenue of 3.4 trillion dollars yet the global reality for workers is that "58 percent of countries exclude groups of workers from labour law, 70 percent of countries have workers who have no right to strike, 60 percent of countries deny or restrict workers collective bargaining and 52 percent of countries deny workers access to the rule of law" (Frontlines 2016, 7).

Soft approaches to correct worker injustices through voluntary campaigns for corporate social responsibility have, for the most part, failed, so other measures must be used to shore up and strengthen workers' rights. The ITUC suggests the following:

- Supply chain transparency so firms know their suppliers and make this info publicly available
- Safe work in which work sites are inspected, hazards corrected, and workers' rights are recognized through safety committees
- Secure work which ends short-term or temporary contracts
- Minimum living wages so workers can maintain a decent standard of living and dignity in their workplace
- Collective bargaining so workers can collectively seek living wages and decent working conditions (Frontlines 2016, 7)

WORKER DEMOGRAPHICS IN THE INFORMAL ECONOMY

Workers in the informal economy are diverse in terms of ethnicity, "income (level, regularity, seasonality), employment status (employees, employers, own-account workers, casual workers, domestic workers), sector (trade, agriculture, industry), enterprise type and size, location (urban or rural), social protection (social security contributions) and employment protections (contract type and duration, leave protections)" (Conference 2014, 4). This diversity complicates interventions to help workers transition into the formal economy in GSCs which function on multiple levels, department, firm, local, state, national, and international, and in different countries which operate under various labor and environmental laws. On each of these levels and in each of these countries, workers interact with management as full-time, temporary, part-time, freelance, self-employed, or subcontracted employees in a contractual or a free-will relationship. The organization of GSCs and the organization of work within each of these different venues means workers are constantly at a disadvantage depending on the worker's relationship with the employer, who is often at a disadvantage because of his/her relationship with the owners of production. In order for owners of production to maximize profits and pacify shareholders and investors, they act as a detriment to workers as well as middle management, through non-standard work/employment arrangements including the transfer of risk to the worker, the insecurity of the work arrangement, tiered-wage structures, and precarious employment. Known as "contested terrain" (Fichter 2016a, 1), "*The fissured workplace*" (Weil 2014),[1] or "*The daily grind*" (Walker 2015),[2] this unleveled playing field between labor versus management, workers versus employers, and property rights versus workers' rights heavily slants toward the owners of production.

The restructuring of the workplace has undergone changes in the last several decades. In the 1980s and 1990s corporations began distancing or subcontracting their non-profit making operations such as maintenance, security, and custodial care to external firms (Flecker 2010; Weil 2014). Outsourcing their responsibility to directly engage with workers, corporations continued to separate themselves from directly dealing with workers in other arenas such as distribution, customer service, and production. New technologies allowed this separation to continue and pitted suppliers of these goods and services to compete with each other for the privilege of working for the corporation which, in essence, meant continuing employment. This means suppliers fiercely fight to reduce labor costs often in violation of federal and state labor laws. The diffusion of this work fragments or splinters the responsibility for workers' safety and health and allows corporations to disavow accountability for exploitation, injury, or harm to workers. The division of allegiance among workers in a single workplace might go to many different subcontractors who actually have the employer-employee relationship with the worker, so workers working alongside each other in the same work environment may command different wage scales depending on their job, skill, and employer (Walker 2015; Weil 2014). This type of employer-employee arrangement is often known as *triangular employment* because the worker is actually contracted to different multiple employers at various points along the GSC. As one moves from the top of the GSC toward the bottom, working conditions usually worsen.

THE BOTTOM OF THE GSC

One sector of the informal economy which receives little attention is homeworkers, those individuals who are subcontracted to produce garment embellishments, assemble electrical parts, or package goods, usually by piece-rate (Kilbourne 2013). Kilbourne (2013) suggests there are more than fifty millions homeworkers in India and China alone who have no legal status as employees, no assurance they will receive compensation for the goods they produce, and no access to training, entitlements, or social protections. They have no direct relationship with their employer so they are not considered workers which means they have no standing in the employment relationship, no social security rights or health coverage, no worker protections under the law, and no platform on which to negotiate grievances.

Primarily women, these homeworkers at the end of the GSC are prime examples of the insecurity and risk transfer chain. Homeworkers incur all the overhead costs usually borne by a factory or mill (electricity, infrastructure cost, building rent) and will experience deficit costs if enough product isn't sold to cover those costs which include transporting their product back to the supplier (Barrett 2016). The ILO works to bring these vulnerable workers who feed into the manufacturing supply chain into the employment relationship through ILO *conventions*, an agreement or pact between countries stipulating rules or policies, which extend to homeworkers' legislation regulating working wages and conditions. For instance, some countries have laws covering specific categories of informal workers such as "[T]he Domestic Workers Act of 2013" which establishes rights and protections for Philippine workers and the "Home Workers Protection Act of 2010" which requires written contracts between Thailand's employers and homeworkers (Conference 2014, 33). These agreements are the exception rather than the rule, and even when agreements are in place, there is little monitoring or enforcement of the agreements.

MOVING FROM THE INFORMAL ECONOMY TO THE FORMAL ECONOMY

The actual scope, size, and composition of the informal labor market is difficult to assess because of many countries' hesitancy and/or inability to collect, estimate, produce, and disseminate good statistics (Conference 2014). Good data is necessary to formulate policy frameworks, so the paucity of data is a hindrance to creating useful and cogent strategies and procedures which must be considered preliminary; the assumption is the informal economy is more robust than current data suggests. Estimates of non-agricultural workers in informal economies range from 30 percent to 85 percent and that percentage grows if agricultural workers are included. The population in the informal economy, women, who outnumber men, migrants, children, and the old and disabled find themselves in an economic environment in which they are unprotected by law, vulnerable to exploitation, violence, and abuse, and are not recognized as workers in employment relationships. This means "the most vulnerable and marginalized groups tend to end up in the informal economy" (Conference 2014, 7) and their path into the formal economy is fraught with barriers.

There is a recognition that if the status quo concerning the informal economy continues, poverty, inequality, and vulnerability will increase. According to the ILO, "the informal economy will remain the most serious obstacle to the goal of decent work for all" (Conference 2014, 12). Workers in the informal economy experience tension and frustration about their circumstances. One striking example of tension and frustration against poverty and injustice erupted in 2010 when Mohamed Bouaziz, a young Tunisian man, set himself on fire in an open protest against his government which arrested him for selling fruit to earn a living. Bouaziz's actions resulted from decades of economic frustration with weak government policies of authoritarian regimes which failed to alleviate poverty and unemployment for millions of citizens, stifled opposition voices to human rights abuses, and consolidated political power among ruling religious elites.

This demonstration set off a wave of violent and non-violent protests across the Middle East and North Africa which came to be known as the Arab Spring, a movement which pitted religious elites against pro-democracy supporters in an attempt to increase greater economic equity into their countries. The violence lasted until 2012 when military intervention in many of the countries restored power to the religious elites; currently Tunisia is the only government to move toward a constitutional democracy. The intensity of the fervor by citizens, especially young educated millennials, in repressed regimes who often must pay bribes to police and political leaders in order to work, is reflective of political and social unrest which drives an informal economy. Moving workers from the informal to the formal economy is in the long-term best interests of all workers and has a twofold advantage: one for workers and one for corporations. The first advantage is for workers.

The necessity of bringing all workers under the protection of the law is a major step in moving workers from the informal to the formal economy. The formal economy provides some measure of stability in the employment relationship because the status of worker confers on an individual the recognition of certain rights. Approaches facilitating this transition differ in various countries; most labor legislation in most countries applies in theory to all workers, but some countries exclude categories of workers from labor and social protections. Domestic workers are particularly vulnerable to exclusion: global estimates suggest 52.6 million domestic workers, mostly women and including children under the age of fifteen, account for one half of workers omitted from national labor law protection (ILO 2013). Consequently these workers are not covered by minimum wage laws or other worker protections such as unemployment or worker's compensation, safety and health provisions, or pension and disability benefits. In order to change these work deficits, governments, collectives, and corporations must collaborate legislative changes and enforcement mechanisms to provide a framework which include international labor standards or social protections, regulations, and practices extending labor law for domestic workers.

The second advantage is for corporations. Corporations exist in all sizes, so the size of the business and its ability to exploit economies of scale limits opportunities to access skilled labor, credit markets, and trade activities. Medium and small enterprises (MSEs) which operate in the informal economy as unregistered businesses are likely to experience slower economic growth because they aren't able to complete with larger firms. According to the ILO, "high rates of informality drive countries towards the lower more vulnerable end of global production chains and attract capital flows related to the existence of a large low-wage labour pool" (Conference 2014, 9). Unregulated businesses in the informal economy often do not pay taxes or provide benefits to workers because the institutional structures governing them are weak and lack enforcement monies or power. So registered businesses then must incur the cost of providing their own enforcement through private agencies which is costly and is passed to the consumer in higher product cost. This also disadvantages registered businesses and governments in the formal economy who must compensate for the tax shortfall by constricting social services to their citizens and engaging in fewer infrastructure, health, education, and development projects. Compensating for lost tax revenue through a reduction in services opens businesses and governments to corrupt and illegal practices because the lack of money to legally enforce worker protections and safety and environmental laws doesn't mean the absence of enforcement; it simply means a more costly form of enforcement through a private firm, an underground apparatus, or vigilante justice. The weakened institutional apparatus of corporations and governments relegates firms and workers in the informal economy to unstable employment relationships which have a detrimental effect on job security, mobility, and living standards.

RESTRUCTURING THE REGULATORY ENVIRONMENT

The informal economy is sustained through badly designed and implemented macroeconomic policy such as structural adjustment and privatization which seek to replace jobs in the formal economy with lower paying jobs in the informal economy. Structured by developed countries, these misguided macro-policies facilitate the informal economies growth by seeking low cost labor in vulnerable populations and tax and environmental regulatory avoidance, so quality jobs are sacrificed for quantity jobs. The current globalization processes expose the difficulties in structuring a fair and equitable macro-economic landscape beneficial to all workers. Labor legislation, trade policies, and worker protections are distorted and weakened in efforts to shore up lucrative business practices. The ILO reports that "Informality is principally a governance issue" (Conference 2014, 70). Restructuring the way business is conducted in globalized arenas would go a long way in changing the protocols for governance which dominates GSCs. Let's take a look at the ways governance is constructed in GSCs.

Value Chain Governance

There are various types of value chain governance which impact the ways in which products are produced and eventually arrive in the consumers' hands. These ways involve a continuum which extends on one end of the market through a hierarchical value chain characterized by direct ownership of the production process by lead firms who develop and manufacture products in house, "provide regular employment, guarantee quality and build producer capacity" (Connections 2016). Market governance in hierarchical value chains is relatively simple. Transactions are concluded when a buyer and seller in a market decide on a transaction for some good or service at some price. This price point is known as the *point of equilibrium*; these "arms-length" transactions require "little to no formal cooperation between participants and the cost of switching to new partners is low for both producers and buyers" (Connections 2016). The social benefits associated with market-based hierarchical relationships are dependent on the firms' profits. Owners of production may offer some benefits to local communities when profits are robust by providing educational or health facilities or consumer credit which are helpful to vulnerable populations. But when profits drop, these socially conscious benefits can be lost, and vulnerable populations harmed.

The disintegration of hierarchical governance, also known as vertical integration, "the process by which steps in the production and distribution of goods and services are owned/run by a single owner/employer" (Walker 2015, 239) and the move toward lengthening value chains and the reorganization of work across regional and national borders, sometimes called the *new international division of labor*, has led to three distinct forms of global chain governance "'modular,' 'relational' and 'captive'" (Flecker 2010, 12).

Modular value chains, which produce modules constructed with standardized parts for flexibility and can be combined or connected in different ways and used for a variety of purposes, make bespoke goods or goods to customers' specifications. Modular value chains are closely related to hierarchical value chains in that firms take responsibility for the production processes and use generic machinery thus spreading investments across a wide consumer base (Connections 2016). Complex relationships between suppliers and owners of production are codified to keep interactions less difficult to manage. Most durable goods manufacturing is done within a modular value chain.

Relational value chains involve complex interactions between buyers and sellers and are often managed through reputations and family and ethnic ties (Connections 2016; Flecker 2010). Buyers and sellers mutually depend on the character of each other to supply products which have over time built a quality reputation. Because reputation building takes times, changing partners in relational value chains is costly and seldom occurs. Cultural preferences play a role in relational value chains. For instance, Japanese auto makers may prefer to maintain relationships with other Japanese suppliers because they trust them more than suppliers from the United States who may exercise more control in their supplier chain through captive value chains.

Captive value chains include smaller suppliers who are dependent on larger buyers who face fixed costs, so smaller suppliers are held "captive" to the buyers' control. In labor-intensive production such as garments and textiles or agriculture, producers are sensitive to wage costs, which is the main driver of outsourcing. Tax, environmental, and regulatory policies have major effects on a firm's decision to outsource. In captive value chains, lead firms carefully monitor and control suppliers, but also contribute by helping their suppliers through investments and process upgrading which increases efficiency in the supply chain. An ethical fair leadership is an important component in this process. For instance, small farmers who contractually sell chickens to large agribusiness processers constantly feel pressure to lower their costs against other competing small farmers in order to offer the lowest bid to agribusiness (Connections 2016). Another example is

> the sandblasting of jeans in informal clothing companies in Turkey where it is reported that young workers contract fatal silicosis because of the lack of health and safety measures (Cimrin et al. 2003). According to newspaper reports, thousands of people are expected to die in Turkey as a consequence of doing these jobs (Der Tagesspiegel 12.1.2009). Meanwhile, the Turkish government has issued a ban on sandblasting factories but the effect may be limited because they are part of the informal economy. (Flecker 2010, 13)

All types of governance share one thing in common: the ability to exploit workers for the attainment of higher profits, so giving workers protected status in the formal economy is one way to give workers a platform for equity. The primary vehicle to enable workers in the informal economy to move to protected status in the formal economy and stanch the hemorrhaging of jobs into the informal economy is the trade union and the capacity to move is known as the "*positive transition effect*" (italics mine) (Serrano 2016, 47). The positive transition effect incorporates the utilization of various power forms available to trade unions through coalition building, association with social movements, organizing and bargaining collectively, disrupting the production process to affect profit margins, using social media for communication and mobilizing, and creating ad hoc collectives to deal with specific issues arising from work, social, or community issues. By strategically joining with organizations who share the same goal of improving working conditions for those in precarious work, trade unions leverage power above and beyond their own efficacy. Using available tools and resources to educate stakeholders about the value of formal worker protections, communicate concerns about the long-term well-being of precariat workers, and build support among broader communities who seek/share similar outcomes strengthens chances for change from an agency and an institutional standpoint.

CRACK IN THE CORPORATE ARMOR

The fragmentation in GSCs, though pervasive throughout, may be showing some cracks in their ability to sustain low cost and flexibility at every level. Observations in various industries suggest some current employment practices may not be as beneficial to corporations as originally believed. High turnover in call centers and customer service representatives requires continued hiring and training costs and is detrimental to the quality of service workers provide to customers. Information technology industries which need highly skilled and trained workers to carry out the firm's functions may be voluntarily "harmoniz[ing] employment relations" (Flecker 2010, 21) when dealing with workers from various companies and countries. Though these examples are few and far between, they do provide a window into addressing issues of fragmentation and restructuring within GSCs. The more likely solution to solving problems of fragmentation and corporate greed lies in a collective response by workers.

HOW TRADE UNIONS ARE BENEFICIAL

Trade unions are in a unique position. As representatives of exploited workers, trade unions use their strategic and associational power to challenge existing structural, organizational, and governance approaches to controlling work and workers. Trade unions are imbued with power from workers who collectively join together to affect some change in their wages and working conditions. This solidarity bond is necessary if trade unions are to effectively shift the balance of power from management to labor. Rather than acting as passive agents who simply react to management's edicts, trade unions aggressively engage as active agents who make strategic choices using "workplace bargaining power, marketplace bargaining power, institutional power, social power, moral power, discursive power or communicative power, collaborative or coalitional power, organizational capacity power, strategic or logistical power and others" (Serrano 2016, 3). The analytical framework in which these power strategies are constructed is

> 1) The legal framework (i.e. labour laws and regulations); 2) economic and social protection measures beyond the labour law (minimum or living wage policy, universal income floor, universal health care coverage, universal social security, etc.); 3) union's organization structures and processes; and 4) trade union's strategies and measures in a given political economy and institutional context. (Serrano 2016, 4)

Serrano (2016) groups these power resources into four categories: structural, associational, institutional, and social. *Structural power*, the capacity to effect change from a position with an institution, comes from marketplace bargaining power in which skilled workers have competencies which are difficult and costly for the employer to replace. Skilled workers are then in a strategic position to engage in disruptive action in the production process and can use that ability as leverage against management. Instances of strategic disruption would include the strike (ability to withhold labor), natural soldiering (slowing down on the job), or producing defective product.

Associational power, the capacity to effect change through connections among groups, includes building coalitions with other organizations, increasing membership, cultivating social capital so union members identify with the collective, institutional vitality, the "capacity to adjust to new contexts, internal enthusiasm to embrace new strategies, a sense of introducing something new and 'fresh' to the union" (Serrano 2016, 3), and organizational flexibility which refers to mobilizing new members, reallocating resources, grooming new leadership, participating in activism, and being involved.

Institutional power is the capacity to effect change in institutions such as governments, corporations, or other organizations through the creation and maintenance of political will via legislation, elections, regulations, and policy making. Changing laws and policies in favor of workers' rights and away from property rights is a premier challenge for trade unions everywhere. When workers' rights are backed up by law, workers win.

Social power, the capacity to effect change by framing discourse through expertise, skills, knowledge, and information, lies in the abilities of trade unions to communicate in different discursive communities. For instance, when trade unions are able to articulate and clearly define the power of the collective as beneficial for all society, then the public better understands how important unions are for their own long-term well-being. Being able to frame the argument in their own terms, trade unions can effectively counter the spin by those promoting the free market at all costs. Being able to form coalitions and collaborate with other organizations who share common interests solidifies power within the collective and allows reciprocation among the coalition which further strengthens worker power.

It is important that an international floor for employment and social policy exists which addresses workers' basic rights and dignity in the informal economy. Workers in the informal economy are often hesitant to engage in collective action for fear of losing the precarious job they have because other jobs don't exist. Trade unions can help communicate the importance of the collective in fashioning policy by providing information to workers about their rights, mobilizing workers to push for respect and decent wages and working conditions within their working environment, and building support through coalitions of other organizations who share common interests with the workers. According to Serrano (2016), the most important component in moving workers from the informal to the formal economy is "institutional vitality" (47), the ability of trade unions to organize, mobilize, communicate, and affect policy changes which move toward protecting workers.

There must be a commitment to provide decent work for all workers because it is the right of everyone to have "conditions of freedom and dignity, of economic security and equal opportunity" (Conference 2014, 68). This commitment requires an overarching strategy which includes fundamental principles and rights at work such as living wages and opportunities for advancement, social protections, and social communication. These principles and rights complement each other and provide a way for workers to rise from poverty. These challenges are greatest in the informal economy in which "all economic activities by workers and economic units that are—in law or in practice—not covered or insufficiently covered by formal arrangements" (Conference 2014, 68) and where a high percentage of wage and self-employed workers toil.

CONCLUSION

It doesn't have to be this way. The fragmentation of work within GSCs is designed to solidify power in the hand of corporations who run rough-shod over workers whose power is stripped through weakened employment and labor laws, intermediaries who act as buffers for corporate liability, and the geographical dispersion of subsidiaries for which no international regulation exists. Governments and MNCs, pushing an economic system of capitalism, have succeeded in corporatizing an agenda which seeks cost-cutting measures at the human expense of workers and have used GSCs as the conduit to facilitate corporate greed. MNCs, at the behest of investors and stockholders, push for more organizational restructuring and flexibility in production which translates into employment and human relations strategies diminishing workers' rights, standards of living, and dignity.

Workers in the formal economy, many of whom are paid low wages and work in unsafe conditions and have few social protections, are not much better off than workers in the informal economy who have no rights, no social protections, and no redress through the legal system. The hope for workers lies in resisting corporate greed though legislation and the mechanism of the collective. Securing employment laws and policies which protect workers' rights is essential if workers are to survive in a corporatized economy. Trade unions and workers' associations strengthen workers' position within the labor management relationship through collective representation.

NOTES

1. *The Fissured Workplace: Why Work Became So Bad for So Many and What Can Be Done to Improve It* (Weil 2014) is the work of David Weil, the Peter and Deborah Wexler Professor of Management at Boston University's Questrom School of Business. He was also the US Wage and Hour Administrator at the Department of Labor for the last three years of the Obama administration. He is a leading international expert on workplace and labor market policy and was a professor of economics and management at Boston University School of Management before taking office. The insights contained in *The Fissured Workplace* deliver a bold perspective on the fundamental restructuring of employment and its impacts on workers and businesses, and were the basis of much of the work Weil did at the bureau. One of Weil's last posts on the Department of Labor blog—removed almost immediately by the Trump administration—was this important piece on wages and the garment industry.

2. *The Daily Grind: How Workers Navigate the Employment Relationship* (Walker 2015) is my work on the unequal balance of economic power between labor and management.

Chapter Five

How Industrial Tragedies Foster Policy

LEARNING OBJECTIVES

By the end of the chapter, students will be able to:

1. Give at least three examples of industrial disasters which became focusing events for workers' rights.
2. Explain how corporations disavow culpability for the protection of workers' well-being and workers' rights.
3. Define corporate social responsibility.
4. Explain how the workplace environment creates potential for disasters to occur.
5. Explain how industrial tragedies become focusing events with the potential to affect policy changes in workers' protections.

Key words: Focusing event, Industrial policy, Transparency in supply chains, Non-culpability, Corporate social responsibility

This chapter explains how industrial disasters and tragedies can become focusing events which begat strategies to improve working conditions through policy changes, give impetus to workers' voices, and increase representation within the labor-management relationship. Disasters are defined as a sudden event, accident, or natural occurrence which causes enormous damage, injury, or loss of life. A tragedy is defined as a sudden event, accident, crime, or natural occurrence which causes enormous suffering, destruction, and pain. These terms are used interchangeably throughout the chapter. Multiple examples include the New York City Triangle Shirtwaist factory fire (1911) and the Bangladesh Rena Plaza collapse (2013).

The global landscape is littered with disasters resulting from business non-compliance with safety and health violations, disregard for worker safety, and the push for greater shareholder profits at the expense of workers. Corporations distance themselves from these industrial disasters because the work has often been outsourced or offshored, the actual locus of employment has been subcontracted to another firm in the global supplier chain, and the workers are often hidden in the informal economy, so corporations incur little or no responsibility for the tragedies which result from production speed ups, unsafe and hazardous working conditions, and lax regulations regarding workers' safety and health. These disasters, corporations claim, could have been avoided if only workers weren't careless, middle management did due diligence, and safety and health rules were followed. Yet, thousands of workers each year suffer physical and mental exhaustion and pain, and hundreds of workers lose their lives to workplace disasters resulting from hazardous and unsafe working conditions in workplaces.

What follows is an exploration of how these tragedies occur and what the consequences of these tragedies are in the realm of public policy for workers' safety and health. This is, of course, not a new phenomenon and will likely continue under the current proliferation of global supply chains (GSCs). First, the discussion revolves around the environment which proliferates these tragedies followed by some examples of tragedies, and lastly, a look at the policies which changed as a result of these tragedies. Presenting a timetable of all workers' tragedies is certainly beyond the scope of this chapter, but an examination of several of the most damaging events which harmed and took human life will complement the narrative.

THE WORKPLACE ENVIRONMENT CREATES POTENTIALS FOR DISASTERS TO OCCUR

Past decades have witnessed the diffusion of governance in GSCs and the distance owners of production put between themselves and the workers who actually produce the goods and services consumers purchase. The spatial void has allowed responsibility for workers' health and safety and environmental integrity to become a non-culpable issue for corporations who can slough off their obligation to protect and do no harm to their workers and the environment. This strategy of non-culpability has been codified in the "deregulation of finance and labour markets and liberalization of trade. [Multinational Enterprises] MNEs and their global value networks account for 80% of worldwide trade; it is these structures that facilitate the precarization of work through outsourcing, offshoring and whipsawing" (Pillay 2009 in Fichter 2015, 1). States have been unable to soften the social impact of precarious work so human rights and worker rights violations occur with increasing frequency. The trend is for corporations to practice self-governance through voluntary codes of conduct which, in theory, move them away from the business model of profits at all costs toward more of a human resource model which puts workers at the forefront (Bolman 2013). Self-governance comes in the form of *corporate social responsibility* (CSR) and is defined as the firm's effort to assess and take responsibility for the effects the firm has on society and the environment. The International Labor Organization (ILO), "the tri-partite organization charged with setting standards for the world of work" (Holdcroft 2016, 4), analyzes and disseminates information on how well self-governance is working.

Multinational corporations (MNCs) are responsible for working conditions in GSCs yet often claim they are unaware of overwork, health and safety violations, and human degradation within their supplier facilities (Holdcroft 2016). Yet MNCs have no problem demanding deadlines and specific production processes to meet consumer mandates. These ultimatums for high volume and just in time production at low cost are the drivers which create "impediments to improving workers' rights in global supply chains" (Holdcroft 2016, 1). The production decisions for short lead times and malleable design changes made by MNCs allows the accrual of billions of dollars of profits. For instance, Apple

> reported the biggest quarterly profit ever by a corporation: US $18.4 billion [and] is sitting on cash reserves of US $216 billion [yet] workers who make products responsible for generating these unprecedented profits receive [about] US $4 for making an iPhone 6 that retails in the US for US $649. (Holdcroft 2016, 1)

Voluntary efforts toward CSR have produced few good results because CSR focuses on individual companies who police their own violations and can produce their own public relations spin favorable to the corporation. The CSR model relies on self-auditing. This fox guarding the hen house façade allows MNCs to hide behind reports and websites which cloak the actual damage done to workers and their rights. The International Trade Union Confederation (ITUC) named and shamed fifty top MNCs for their workers' rights' violations within the hidden workforces embedded in GSCs. Though public exposure can be a powerful tool to help sway public opinion, it does not have the impact of the law to enable enforcement of sanctions/fines against these firms. Efforts are also underway in the United Nations Human Rights Council (UNHRC), Industriall, the International Labor Organization (ILO), and various unions to form international agreements on protecting workers' rights.

There exists a huge accountability gap between MNCs and their workers. Within GSCs no one takes responsibility for imperiling workers' health and safety. Governments distance themselves from suppliers in other countries, and firms don't enforce health and safety regulations in existence. Since GSCs are now the conduit for the production of goods and services, employers are unlikely and often unwilling to compromise profits at the expense of transparency, accountability, and improved working conditions (Holdcroft 2016).

As a result of noncompliance with existing safety and health regulations, production speed ups, and a blatant disregard for workers' well-being, tragedies occur with increasing frequency throughout GSCs. Each tragedy can be considered a *focusing event*, a sudden, unexpected, uncommon occurrence which is harmful, geographically concentrated, known as potentially hazardous, situated within some community of interest, and is attention grabbing for its obvious and immediate harm (Birkland 1998). Workplace disasters fit this criteria and highlight the dangerous and exploitive conditions under which millions of workers labor daily. The difference in workplace focusing events and natural disaster events is the diffusion of the event's source. The nature of workplace violations has become so commonplace for most global citizens that it takes a major focusing event such as multiple human deaths or dismemberment in a factory fire or building collapse to bring home the reality that millions of workers constantly face physical harm or death in order to simply earn a subsistence living. Common workplace injuries and deaths "are sometimes subtle, contested, and difficult to visualize and are less likely to be focal" (Birkland 1998, 55) than are natural disasters which are obvious, portrayed through media outlets with pictures of devastation, and have an immediate impact on a specific community.

WORKPLACE DISASTERS AND TRAGEDIES AS FOCUSING EVENTS

Triangle Shirtwaist Fire

One event which brought public attention to deplorable and unsafe working conditions in the textile industry and galvanized public support in favor of safer laws was the Triangle Shirtwaist Fire in Manhattan, New York (Center 2011). This major fire, considered to be one of the worst industrial accidents in US history since the beginning of the Industrial Revolution, broke out on a wintery Saturday afternoon, March 25, 1911, in the Ashe Building, an old nine-story structure, home to the Triangle Shirtwaist Company where 500 women, primarily Italian and European Jewish immigrant seamstresses, who belonged to the needle trades, sewed cotton shirts and worked twelve to fourteen hours per day in sweatshop conditions in a non-union factory which paid low wages. Some of the women were as young as fourteen years old and had come to America with their families to find a better life. Instead, they found poverty conditions in their home and work life. This system led to the exploitation of workers who had little choice but to continue working at the factory or face starvation.

The fire erupted on the top floors of the building, and many workers on the ninth floor were trapped in the building by exit doors which were locked because management said workers were stealing product. The fire escapes on lower floors collapsed under the weight of fleeing workers, and the fire department's ladders were too short to reach the upper floor. The subcontractors tried unsuccessfully to put out the fire while demanding the women continue to work. As the fire raged out of control, the women, with their escape routes blocked by locked doors and piled up inventory, jumped out of upper stories onto the pavement in lieu of being burned to death. Others were consumed by fire and smoke inhalation. Those that did survive were permanently scarred and disfigured, marring future chances of marriage and family life. In all, 146 out of 500 women died that day.

Witnesses and the city of Manhattan, horrified by the tragedy, mourned the dead and demanded justice and restitution which would prevent further such tragedies. Calls for improvements in safety and working conditions, stronger unions, and punishments for the company's owners ensued.

This tragedy stirred public sentiment against worker abuses. The International Ladies Garment Workers' Union (ILGWA) Local 25 and the Women's Trade Union League (WTUL), to which some of the women had belonged, not only organized relief efforts for the victims' families but petitioned New York's mayor to form safety committees to investigate workplaces to assure the safety of the workers. The fire emphasized the inadequacy of fire inspections, safety exits, and worker protections. Frances Perkins, who later became the Secretary of Labor in the Roosevelt administration, watched the fire that day, an event that influenced her decision to become a worker's advocate. She assisted in the forthcoming investigation of the Triangle Shirtwaist Fire while serving as executive secretary of the New York Committee on Safety. The tragedy is significant because it highlighted the inhumane working conditions to which industrial workers were subjected.

The owners of the Triangle Shirtwaist Company, Max Blanck and Isaac Harris, were unscrupulous owners who paid no attention to basic workers' rights and forced workers to endure unsafe and dangerous working conditions. They subcontracted the administration of the company to male supervisors as a tactic to pay low wages to the workers and divert more of the profits to themselves. After the fire, the owners were interviewed, and declared the Asch Building was fireproof because it had been inspected and approved by the New York Department of Buildings. Regardless, charges were brought against Blanck and Harris by the District Attorney of Manhattan, and a grand jury indicted them on April 27, 1911, on seven counts of second degree manslaughter under section 80 of the Labor code which mandates that exit doors cannot be locked during working hours. The trial lasted twenty-three days; a jury acquitted Blanck and Harris of any wrongdoing because Max Steuer, their attorney, convinced them his clients were not on site that day and had no way of knowing the exit doors were locked. Individual civil suits filed later resulted in Blanck and Harris paying 75 dollars for each lost life. Restitution took three years. Defiant attitudes from Blanck and Harris continued even though the Asch Building was found not to be fireproof, littered with trash and flammable material, and with locked exit doors. Fines rendered for these violations were minimal, and judges apologized to Blanck for the imposition of his court appearance.

Phillips 66 Petroleum Chemical Explosion in Pasadena, Texas

Twenty-three workers died, one is missing, and 314 workers (158 Phillips workers and 129 contract workers) were injured in a chemical explosion caused by an ethylene leak at the Phillips 66 Huston Chemical Complex situated on an 800 acre property near the Houston Ship Channel in Pasadena, Texas; the plant produced 15,000,000,000 pounds of high-density plastics used in toys and containers (Dole 1990). The facility was multi-level, reinforced with concrete and steel, had a fourteen-story tower, and resembled an oil refinery. The plant, which employed 1,500 workers, 905 of whom were company employees and 600 of whom were daily contract employees, engaged in regular maintenance activities and new construction and was a vital link in the national production chain for polyethylene.

In an effort to save money and increase profits, Phillips Petroleum subcontracted necessary maintenance work to Fish Engineering and Construction, a less than reputable primary subcontractor. On October 22, 1989, an employee of Fish Engineering and Construction incorrectly reconnected gas piping for maintenance without isolating the line which sent flammable solvents and gas into a working area; the solvents exploded, killing one worker and injuring four others. The next day maintenance work continued on the plant's polyethylene reactor. An improperly secured valve allowed 85,000 pounds of highly flammable ethylene-isobutane gas cloud into the plant. No detectors or warming systems were in place. Within 90 to 120 seconds, the gas cloud came into contact with an unknown ignition source, which could have been "ventilation fans, electrical switches, and gas burn-off flames" (Yates 1989, 2) and was followed by the explosion of a 20,000-gallon isobutene storage tank. Five other explosions followed. The explosion resulted in injury and death to workers, and the resulting fire caused $715.5 million dollars' worth of damage to the plant, destroyed buildings within a half mile radius, and took two years to rebuild. The blast had the force of two-and-one-half tons of dynamite and registered 3.5 on the Richter scale and 4.0 at the epicenter. The magnitude and intensity of the blast rendered any pre-conceived evacuation plans or in-house emergency response measures inoperable (Yates 1989).

Investigations conducted by the Federal Bureau of Investigation (FBI) found that human error incorrectly connecting the gas valve which allowed the gas cloud to form could have been prevented or at least minimized if corporate safety procedures have been followed (Allen 2011). OSHA confirmed that had any one of the three safety protocols been followed, reconnecting the value correctly, lock-out/tag-out device in place, or a blind flange inserted for backup, the explosion would have been prevented. OSHA recommends following Process Safety Management (PSM), a discipline that recommends how industries safely manage highly hazardous chemicals. PSM was a work in progress at the time of the Phillips 66 explosion.

The Phillips Petroleum Plant, although inside the Pasadena, Texas, city limits, operated as unincorporated in order to receive a lower tax rate. This means the plant was not eligible to receive all city services but opted to provide their own "security, fire department, water, and sanitation along with other amenities" (Yates 1989, 5). The company's fire brigade initially responded and was joined by the Channel Industries Mutual Aid Association (CIMA), a coalition of firefighting, rescue, and first aid staffing power and facilities which responds to natural, man-made, or war emergencies (Yates 1989). Other cooperating agencies included the Texas Air Control Board, the Harris County Pollution Control Board, the Federal Aviation Administration, the US Coast Guard, OSHA, and the Environmental Protection Agency (EPA).

OSHA had not done a comprehensive inspection of the plant since 1976, but had previously cited the plant for several serious safety violations. Their findings after the explosion cited the plant for "566 willful and 9 serious violations with a combined total proposed penalty of $5,666,200 to Phillips Company and 11 willful and 12 serious violations with a combined total proposed penalty of $729,600 to Fish Engineering and Construction" (Scannell 1991) which included inadequate maintenance permitting system, ventilation system to nearby buildings, and standard operating procedures, no fail-safe block value, lock-out/tag-out procedures, or combustible gas detection and alarm system, and no fire protection system in a state of readiness.

Even unincorporated plants within the city limits of Pasadena, Texas, were subject to inspection by the CIMA under the Superfund Amendments and Reauthorization Act (SARA Title III) to determine if hazardous substances were in house. SARA Title III was a change in the 1980 Comprehensive Environmental Response, Compensation, and Liability Act (CERCLA), enforced by the EPA, which establishes the Emergency Planning and Community Right-To-Know Act (EPCRA). SARA Title III sets requirements for local and state emergency planning around hazardous chemicals, the right of the public to access information on chemical hazards in their community, and the reporting responsibilities for facilities that use, store, and/or release hazardous chemicals. As a result of government intervention in the protection and prevention of future chemical disasters, several recommendations were made to improve safety conditions and issues within the Phillips 66 plant. Legislative updates were made to the Federal register (FR 29150) Process Safety Management of Highly Hazardous Chemicals, 29 CFR 1910.119 (US DOL 1996) to prevent/minimize the catastrophic consequences of toxic, reactive, flammable, or explosive chemical releases (Environmental Protection Agency 2000; Jeffress 2000; Tokarski 2013).

Lax Regulation Blamed on Pakistan's Worst Industrial Accident

The worst industrial accident in Pakistan's history, dubbed Pakistan's "industrial 9/11" (Shams 2017), was a factory fire in Ali Enterprises textile factory in Baldia Town, a northwestern industrial suburb of Karachi, Pakistan, which took the lives of 289 workers, primarily men, on September 11, 2012. Most of the workers died from smoke inhalation and third degree burns while thirty-two more were injured. Locked doors and bars on the windows prevented workers from escaping the fire so some workers jumped from fourth floor windows. Many of the workers were from Orangi Town, a poor working-class neighborhood in Karachi. Seventeen of the workers lived on the same street. The workers earned an average of $70 per month.

Pakistan's manufacturing sector is a major contributor to its textile industry and a vital source of foreign currency "accounting for 7.4 percent of its GDP and employing 3 percent of the manufacturing work force" (ur-Rehman 2012). Seventy percent of the denim, knitted, and hosiery garments produced in this factory were supplied to German KiK, a discount retailer whose name, Kunde ist Konig, means "Customer is King" (Shams 2017), and the remaining product supplied Italian RINA textile factories; the garments were also in high demand by elites in neighboring India. The factory brings in between $10 million and $50 million per year for the owner, Abdul Aziz (European Center 2015). Several weeks prior to the fire, RINA issued a SA8000 certificate to the factory guaranteeing the building passed workplace safety standards, yet a former electrical inspector, Wali Muhammad, reported most likely an electrical fire was the cause of the disaster. Since 2003 inspectors were forbidden by law from inspecting manufacturing factories in Karachi and Punjab, so that cause can't be confirmed. Workers' rights advocates claim weak regulation, lax oversight, and corruption, which put profits over people, are blamed for the fire while Geo News, the nation's largest news channel, suggests extortionists may be to blame because of a prior attempt to extort money from the owner, Aziz. They claim criminal negligence.

The four-story factory building was "flimsily built and had no emergency exits" (ur-Rehman 2012) according to Zohra Yusuf, chairwoman of the workers' rights group. All exit doors except one were locked. Survivors of the fire say the locked doors were to prevent workers from leaving early or to prevent break-ins. Though workplace safety is guaranteed by Pakistan's Constitution, the general decline in governance has contributed to lax government oversight. According to Sharafat Ali of the Pakistan Institute of Labor Education and Research, a labor rights group, "151 workers died in accidents in 2011. The state was partly responsible for the deaths . . . because its civil servants 'silently and criminally allow violation of laws and regulations established to ensure health and safety provision at work'" (ur-Rehman 2012).

Survivors and relatives of the victims formed the Baldia Factory Fire Affectees Association. On March 13, 2015, one survivor and three families of the victims filed a lawsuit at the Regional Court in Dortmund against German-owned KiK, the main customer of Ali Enterprises while the European Coalition for Corporate Justice (ECCJ) called for an examination of the role European retailors played in monitoring their supply chains. The European Center for Constitutional and Human Rights (ECCHR) submitted to the High Court of Sindh in Karachi a brief calling for a broader scope of criminal investigations against Ali Enterprises suggesting that "KiK and RINA contributed to the fire through their failure to take action on safety standards" (European Center 2015). Their claim is based on international human rights norms which infer "Pakistani authorities have a duty to examine the evidence and, where appropriate, to hold these international companies to account" (European Center 2015). Assisting with this case are Pakistan's Medico International and the National Trade Union Federation (NTUF); the attorney is Dr. Remo Klinger (European Center 2015).

The plaintiffs in this lawsuit seek compensation for their loss, but equally important is the need for transnational corporations to take responsibility for the working conditions in their supply chains. The firm KiK made short-term relief payments to families after the fire, but refused to make any long-term compensation for loss of income. Negotiations broke down after two years when KiK made it clear there would be no long-term compensation for loss, and negotiations were tabled in December 2014. RIMA has not yet provided any compensation packages.

In 2015, investigations reopened stalled negotiations as the cause of the fire was determined to be arson perpetrated by Hammad Siddiqui, former chief of the Muttahida Qaumi Movement's Karachi organizing committee, the main secular political party of Pakistan. Victims' families respond that remedy isn't about who or what caused the fire but is about holding multinational companies "responsible for what is happening down the chain. They must ensure the working conditions at their manufacturers are up to the standards approved by the ILO" (Shams 2017). They hold accountable a capitalist system which profits from worker exploitation. The Awami Workers Party and trade union activists report:

> Countries like Bangladesh and Pakistan face tough competition from other markets that provide cheap labor to international companies. They compromised on safety measures to reduce their services cost. It works well for international retailers as they are there to make a profit. But at the end of the day, it is the responsibility of the local governments to make sure that the labor laws are properly implemented in these factories. (Shams 2017)

As the court case continued, the plaintiffs sought remedy through civil society organizations, legislators, and trade unions. The National Trade Union Federation, international rights' groups, the ECCHR, the Clean Cloths Campaign, and Medico International sought compensation through media campaigns. As a result, on September 10, 2016, KiK released $5.15 million in compensation for the families of victims of the Karachi-based Baldia town factory fire because of an agreement between KiK and the Pakistan Institute of Labor Education and Research. The money was transferred to an intermediary, the International Labor Union in Geneva, for dispersal. An announcement of monthly pensions for the survivors and victim's families was made in January 2018 to supplement already existing social security payments. KiK claims no direct responsibility for the fire itself because the arson nature of the fire was not documented in auditor reports. A computer simulation of the fire conducted by Goldsmiths, University of London's Forensic Architecture project, revealed inadequate fire safety measures led to the deaths of the factory workers and "small changes in fire safety precautions would have drastically reduced the impact of the fire" (Centre 2017). The simulation was presented to the court case in Dortmund.

Rana Plaza Building Collapse in Dhaka, Bangladesh

The Rana Plaza building collapse in Savar, an industrial suburb of Dhaka, Bangladesh, on April 24, 2013, which killed 1,137 workers and injured over 2,000 more, is considered the worst accidental structural failure as well as the deadliest garment factory accident in modern human history. Two hundred of these workers are still missing. Around 3,639 workers worked in five factories in the eight-story commercial Savar building known as Rana Plaza. Eighty percent were young women under the age of twenty who worked thirteen to fifteen hour shifts, ninety to one hundred hours per week, with two days off each month (Rana Plaza 2014). Younger workers known as junior operators made $0.22 per hour while senior sewers made $0.24 per hour.

According to Global Labor Watch, Rana Plaza was owned by Sohel Rana, a member of the ruling Awami League political party; the building housed a bank and shops on the lower floor and five industrial factories above. An inspection of the building(s) by an engineer revealed huge cracks in the foundation and walls which made the building unsafe, so the lower floor was evacuated, but other administrative officers overrode the engineer's assessment and ordered factory workers back into the building under threat of a month's lost wages. Global Labor Watch reports Rana, the building owner, "paid gang members to beat the women and men workers, hitting them with sticks to force them to go into the factory" (Rana Plaza 2014). At around 8:45 am the building went dark, generators kicked on, and an explosion buckled the building from the top down.

The building collapsed during morning rush hour when workers, many of whom had children in nursery facilities in the building, were inside producing garments for US and Canadian clothing labels and retailers such as Walmart, the Children's Place, Mango, Primark, Joe Fresh, and others. The structural integrity of the building was compromised, and there was a blatant disregard for building codes when the upper four floors were built without a permit, substandard material was used in the construction, the original commercial use was changed to industrial use, and the building was situated over a filled-in pond. After the collapse, the Bangladesh government declined assistance by the United Nations whose assessment was the Bangladesh government didn't have the expertise or equipment to carry out such a large rescue and recovery effort. The Bangladesh government, wishing to ensure their national pride, mounted an ineffective rescue operation which consisted of inefficient and unprotected volunteers who dug through rubble to find workers.

The Bangladesh garment industry is the country's economic engine and wields political clout. Even the images of mutilated bodies pulled from rubble has little chance of altering the status quo of GSCs who deliver low cost clothing to Western consumers. The *New York Times* reports that from 1990 to 2012, over 1,000 workers died in hundreds of factory fires or accidents in Bangladesh, and no factory owner was ever charged with any crime. The Bangladesh legal system supports an archaic legal code which needs modernization. Many of the economic elite are also members of Parliament and give heavily to political campaigns. Yet, in the case of the Rana Plaza collapse, Sohel Rana was charged and convicted and is now in prison. This rare occurrence is probably the result of national and international public relations campaigns.

Apple Factory at Foxconn, Chengdu, China

An explosion, "an eruption of fire and noise that twisted metal pipes as if they were discarded straws" in the Foxconn Chengdu factory, building A5, Chengdu, China, killed three workers and injured sixteen others in March 2011. The explosion took place in a sanding area of the factory where iPad cases were polished. Aluminum dust that filled the air and settled on workers' clothing, hair, and skin was thought to clog duct work in the area and cause the explosion. Prior to the explosion,

> an advocacy group in Hong Kong published a report warning of unsafe conditions at the Chengdu plant, including problems with aluminum dust. The group, Students and Scholars Against Corporate Misbehavior, or Sacom, had videotaped workers covered with tiny aluminum particles. "Occupational health and safety issues in Chengdu are alarming," the report read. "Workers also highlight the problem of poor ventilation and inadequate personal protective equipment." (Duhigg 2012, 13)

The report, sent to Apple, garnered no response. Dust, a known safety hazard, caused another explosion later in 2011 at the Shanghai, China, Apple factory in which fifty-nine workers were injured. Nicholas Ashford, the occupational safety expert at Massachusetts Institute of Technology says,

> It's gross negligence, after an explosion occurs, not to realize that every factory should be inspected. . . . If it were terribly difficult to deal with aluminum dust, I would understand. But do you know how easy dust is to control? It's called ventilation. We solved this problem over a century ago. (Duhigg 2012, 15)

According to Chinese workers in the factories who assemble iPhones and iPads, working conditions are harsh because of excessive overtime, long periods of time standing, living in crowded dormitories, unauthorized use of child labor, improper disposal of hazardous waste, and deadly safety problems. Within GSCs, records are falsified, and, though monitors are sometimes present as reliable, independent third parties, they turn a blind eye to abuses which occur daily.

This is not the only explosion which happened in Chinese factories. In 2010,

> 137 workers at an Apple supplier in eastern China were injured after they were ordered to use a poisonous chemical to clean iPhone screens. Within seven months last year, two explosions at iPad factories, including in Chengdu, killed four people and injured 77. Before these blasts, Apple had been alerted to hazardous conditions inside the Chengdu plant, according to a Chinese group that published that warning. (Duhigg 2012, 2)

Apple isn't the only firm which violates workers' rights and workers' health and safety within their GSCs. Other violators include Dell, Hewlett-Packard, I.B.M., Lenovo, Motorola, Nokia, Sony, and Toshiba. Though Apple promotes a supplier code of conduct which sets standards on labor issues and safety protections and demands corrections from their suppliers when violations occur, significant violations in over half of the suppliers remain. According to one executive who left the Foxconn Chengdu factory, "Apple never cared about anything other than increasing product quantity and decreasing production cost. . . . Workers' welfare had nothing to do with their interests" (Duhigg 2012, 3).

The conditions at Apple suppliers in China such as Foxconn have a long history of distorting, reneging, and outright falsifying actual occurrences at their factories. Because Apple is primarily interested in profits, they give to their suppliers only the narrowest of profit margins, so suppliers attempt to cut costs where they can which is usually lower wages for fewer workers who must work longer hours.

The production of Apple products occurring in Chinese factories was assessed from 2010 to 2011 by Chinese Labor Watch, a New York–based firm concerned with worker abuses in Chinese factories. After the Foxconn tragedy, protests over the production of Apple products resulted in a call for boycotts of Apple products. Headlines in US papers noted the tragedy yet equally noted the impact on consumers that iPad production might be harmed. Apple has a long history of keeping its supplier lists covert. Suppliers are eager to provide to Apple their services because getting a contract with Apple can tremendously boost a firm's profits as well as the implied endorsement of providing quality parts to a worldwide product. But the lack of transparency Apple requires of its supplies also gives Apple an edge in the market of electronic devices and makes it more difficult to improve working conditions with supplier factories.

The negative public relations associated with the tragedies in Chinese factories producing Apple products spurred Apple to release some names of suppliers but names of smaller firms which supply suppliers were not included. Though the list doesn't include the location of the factories, watch/advocacy organizations have found some of the locations and were barred from entry on Apple's orders. The obstinacy of Apple to limit inspection of its suppler factories makes real change impossible and speaks to the difficulty in changing a firm's culture concerning transparency. If Apple, one of the largest manufacturers of electronics in the world, were to overhaul its business model, other firms would follow. It is unlikely that Apple will respond to these charges unless there is growing demand from consumers. Most customers give Apple high ratings for producing a quality product though customers sometimes complain about the cost. Unless and until consumers demand labor rights for the workers producing these products, little is likely to change (Duhigg 2012, 16–17).

Young Female Factory Worker Killed in Korean-Owned Ajin Auto Facility

On April 4, 2017, Bloomberg Business reported on an Alabama non-union auto plant which revealed safety violations resulting in injuries to workers including "burning flesh, crushed limbs, dismembered body parts, and a flailing fall into a vat of acid" (Cunningham 2017, 1). According to Cunningham (2017), the fast pace of the production lines, long overtime hours, low pay, no union, and little to no training or consideration for safety contribute to the high incidence of workplace injuries and deaths. The article resulted from the number and severity of injuries and loss of life at the Korean-owned Ajin USA auto facility in Cusetta, Alabama, population 123.

On June 18, 2016, one of the workstations on Robot 23 line malfunctioned because a bolt became stuck in a machine which mounted pillars for side-view mirrors onto dashboard frames at the Ajin auto plant. The plant is a stamping parts supplier for the Mercedes-Benz, Hyundai, and Kia firms which had negotiated with the town in 1997 for "a quarter-billion dollars in tax breaks and other public giveaways to land the first Mercedes factory outside Germany" (Waldman 2017). A worker, Elsea Ogle, a twenty-year-old bride-to-be who earned $8.75 per hour working for the temp agency, Alliance Total Solutions and Joynus Staffing, under pressure to meet daily piece quotas and receiving no response from maintenance requests, cleared the jam herself, and the robot reengaged, trapping Elsea in its grips (Briquelet 2017). Coworkers tried to get the robot to release her while one worker took a forklift and raced across the plant to procure a maintenance man who, upon arrival, didn't know what to do, was Korean, barely spoke English, and ran away. When emergency crews arrived, they locked out the machine's energy source, freed Elsea from the robot, and transported her to a hospital where she died the next day.

Ajin still hasn't admitted any wrongdoing for Elsea's death or any of the other countless injuries at their facility for which they received substantial OSHA fines. They sent one single artificial flower to her funeral. Ajin assured the public they were committed to safety within the facilities and did agree to (re)train all employees in safety procedures, something which had not been done previously. According the Waldman (2017), "after investigating Elsea's death, OSHA fined the company $2.5 million for four 'willful' citations, the agency's most severe sanction, reserved for violators that 'knowingly' disregard employee safety. Ajin is contesting the findings." The callousness with which Ajin and other MNCs disregard human life and limb is difficult to understand through a human relations lens, but viewed through a cost/benefit lens is simply the cost of doing business in a global environment.

The state of Alabama has attracted auto manufacturing because of the concentration of a low wage workforce, anti-union sentiment, and compliant legislators. The region employs 26,000 workers who earned $1.3 billion in wages last year from working long hours for little pay. High turnover, little training, and scant safety concerns are hallmarks of this "New Detroit," which epitomized the competition between US workers and Mexican and Asian workers within global supply chains (Waldman 2017).

The major auto plants in the South, some of whom are represented by the United Auto Workers (UAW), have a somewhat better safety record than do the suppliers to these plants. OSHA reported higher incidents of traumatic injuries in Alabama's auto parts suppliers than in Michigan's or Ohio's un-ionized auto plants. "In 2015 the chances of losing a finger or limb in an Alabama parts factory was double the amputation risk nationally for the industry, 65 percent higher than in Michigan and 33 percent about the rate in Ohio" (Waldman 2017). The Korean-owned plants have greater safety violations than other foreign-owned facilities, accounting for "36 percent of all infractions and 52 percent of total fines from 2012–2016."

POLICY CHANGES AS A RESULT OF FOCUSING EVENTS

Focusing events can be used as tools to make changes in policy. Because focusing events are sudden, they have not become commonplace like crime, disease, or pollution. Communities have not been acculturated to dealing with the long-term effects of sudden disasters and tragedies, so focusing events tend to galvanize support for changing the conditions which precipitated the disaster or tragedy. Focusing events are generally geographically concentrated in one community, so their impact is acutely felt by the local population. Policy change advocates will look for ways to expand and advance the local impact of tragedies to broader communities of interest who may be situated in similar environments and work proactively to prevent future disasters from occurring in those geographies. Birkland (1998) writes that focusing events "serve as important opportunities for politically disadvantaged groups to champion messages that had been effectively suppressed by dominant groups and advocacy coalitions" (54). The greater the sustained negative attention on the harm done to workers and communities as a result of a focusing event, the greater the chances of attracting attention from change agents, those who have the efficacy to affect policy and who can alter dominant or monopoly policy toward safer and healthier environments for workers.

Opponents of policy changes to protect workers, which decrease corporations' profit margins, do not sit on the sidelines while advocates for workers attempt to move the needle toward more worker protections. Business interests attempt to maintain the status quo through efforts to block policy changes by political lobbying, increased financial support to office holders who support corporate agendas, and stronger public relations campaigns which assure the public of their genuine concern for their workers and their well-being. Pro-business groups will attempt to create a narrative which downplays the focusing event as less detrimental to the lives of workers and their families than originally labeled and describe how policy changes would create unnecessary and burdensome regulations requiring more corporate money to be spent on environmental and safety compliance and less money on wages and benefits. Opponents of policy changes to protect workers downplay the severity of the focusing event and claim existing policy is strong enough to deal with any current or future problem.

History is replete with such tragedies in which subcontracting leads to inhumane working conditions and wage theft. In 1938, the Fair Labor Standards Act was passed in order to provide some stability in the free exchange of commerce by introducing some standards in labor conditions which had been determined detrimental to the long-term best interest of workers and their well-being.[1] The Act provided for a minimum wage of $0.25 per hour, a guaranteed 150 percent per hour wage for hours worked in excess of forty hours per week with one employer, established record-keeping and reporting requirements, and prohibitions against some forms of child labor. The mechanism to adjudicate violations of the Act was to sue in federal court; aggrieved workers individually or through class action suits or the Secretary of Labor could kick start the adjudication process. The crux of the Act is as follows:

> (a) The Congress finds that the existence, in industries engaged in commerce or in the production of goods for commerce, of labor conditions detrimental to the maintenance of the minimum standard of living necessary for health, efficiency, and general well-being of workers (1) causes commerce and the channels and instrumentalities of commerce to be used to spread and perpetuate such labor conditions among the workers of the several States; (2) burdens commerce and the free flow of goods in commerce; (3) constitutes an unfair method of competition in commerce; (4) leads to labor disputes burdening and obstructing commerce and the free flow of goods in commerce; and (5) interferes with the orderly and fair marketing of goods in commerce. That Congress further finds that the employment of persons in domestic service in households affects commerce.
>
> (b) It is declared to be the policy of this chapter, through the exercise by Congress of its power to regulate commerce among the several States and with foreign nations, to correct and as rapidly as practicable to eliminate the conditions above referred to in such industries without substantially curtailing employment or earning power. (Enrollment 2012)

The April 2013 Rena Plaza building collapse marked a "turning point from the failed auditing model of CSR toward a GSC industrial relations model and made possible the Bangladesh Accord on Fire and Building Safety, a groundbreaking legally-binding agreement between global unions and among 200 garment MNCs" (Holdcroft 2016, 4). Previous factory workplace tragedies in Bangladesh resulting in many workplace fatalities and structural damage to buildings had not moved the needle toward workplace safety even though countless efforts of worker rights organizations had pushed for some type of binding agreement under which "brands and retailers would be contractually required to make their factories safe" (Nova 2016, 27). The sheer numbers of lost lives and the magnitude of the building devastation at Rena Plaza coupled with the public scrutiny and humanitarian needs forced corporations to implement a safety plan shoring up worker protections and reshaping their public world image as cognizant of workers' rights. The Bangladesh Accord on Fire and Building Safety, known as the Accord, moved voluntary compliance for workers' health and safety to an enforceable contract between major corporations who designed apparel supplied from Bangladesh workers and their representatives and covers "over half of all apparel production in Bangladesh" (Nova 2016, 27).

The Accord stipulates MNCs maintain financial responsibility to upgrade working environments and conditions within their GSCs. If suppliers do not comply, the MNC can end its relationship with the supplier. Based on this model, Industriall created and signed a memorandum of understanding (MoU) known as ACT which establishes "systems of industry-wide collective agreements supported by brand purchasing practices as the primary means of wage-fixing in the global garment industry" (Holdcroft 2016, 4). Holdcroft (2016) writes:

> By linking national industry-level collective bargaining between unions and employers to the purchasing practices of brands, the ACT process creates a framework for genuine supply chain industrial relations. Through industry bargaining, workers can get a wage that is enough to properly support themselves and their families, and at the same time the specific nature of the industry, working hours, productivity and other issues that have bearing on wages, can be addressed. (4)

Though over one hundred major corporations became signatories to the Accord, US-based firms, whose relationships with labor unions remains contentious, did not become signatories, but rather formed the Alliance for Bangladesh Worker Safety, which weakened the contract by rejecting its enforceability and replacing it with voluntary compliance.

Anner, Bair, and Blasi (2016) explain there exists some historical precedence for contractual relationships between retailers/brands and unions/workers in jobber's agreements. Jobber's agreements first surfaced as contractual relationships in the apparel industry between the jobber, the corporation/firm which designed and sold apparel, and the supplier/worker who actually produced the apparel. Early twentieth-century apparel firms outsourced their production to suppliers or home-based sewing workers in order to skirt labor unions, drive down costs, and manage fluctuating production demands by hiring/firing workers at will. The jobber's agreement was an enforceable mechanism to control the relationship between jobber and worker in order to "regularize the flow of work into sub-manufacturing shops . . . cause closer relations between jobbers and manufacturers, and stabilize working conditions in the shop" (Stein 1977, 280–280 in Anner 2016). The jobber's agreement never took root because firms simply moved their manufacturing processes to "nonorganized factories, or 'runaway' shops, in lower-cost regions" (Anner 2016, 244); this continued until passage of federal laws codified labor management relationships in the New Deal of 1935. This same structural situation exists currently on a global scale between corporations and workers. Superimposing legacy contractual relationships on corporations has little traction, but, according to Anner, Bair, and Blasi (2016), the Accord does have elements of a jobber's agreement which include that signatories ensure financial liability of compliance with applicable labor laws, worker representatives have equal rights with corporations in agreement implementation, obligations are legally enforceable, and signatory density strengthens worker safety. Final evaluations of the strength of the Accord are yet to be accessed, but its existence is one step forward in protecting workers' rights.

Business interests attempt to prevent focusing events from outraging the public who might push for policy changes. They wish to modify the negativity associated with corporate policy which promotes and ensures the existence of the hidden or informal economy and deflect attention from the real reasons for workplace tragedies, corporate profit seeking and the dehumanization of their workforce.

Equity-seeking groups such as vulnerable and exploited populations rely on advocates to "gain a hearing [through legislative means] or see their preferences translated into policy [who] must overcome the sometimes aggressive blocking action of their political opponents" (Bachrach and Baratz 1962; Gaventa 1980 in Birkland 1998, 56). The suddenness of the disaster or tragedy gives to equity-seeking groups political advantage because they are on the offensive against the status-quo which must now defend its negative anti-worker agenda.

In 2011, the Special Representative of the United Nations Secretary-General, Professor John Ruggie, presented to the United Nations Human Rights Council a six-year compilation of standard global business practices with regard to human rights. This document, known as the Guiding Principle on Business and Human Rights, provides a blueprint for governments and businesses concerning existing standards and practices based on a threefold approach. The Council endorsed the Guiding Principles and, though not a legally binding document, recommends the "Protect, Respect and Remedy" framework promoted by the Principles. These principles are:

- The state duty to protect human rights
- The corporate responsibility to respect human rights
- The need for greater access to remedy for victims of business-related abuse

This framework sets

> clear benchmarks and represents an important milestone in the evolving understanding of human rights in our societies. . . . Clarity about the baseline expectations of business with regard to human rights is a first important step towards developing appropriate and effective responses to such problems. (Pillay 2009 in Corporate responsibility 2012, 1)

The Guiding Principles comprise thirty-one principles which outline processes for governments to respect human rights, provides a blueprint for firms to manage risks which have an adverse impact on human rights, and sets benchmarks to measure the respect businesses have for all stakeholders (Poverty 2012). The hope is that businesses will voluntarily comply with the standards which provide a foundation for building best practices.

The European Coalition for Corporate Justice (ECCJ) was organized in 2006 in response to corporate overreach and human rights abuses occurring within the European Unions' GSCs. Their vision and mission is "of a sustainable work in which corporations' drive for profit is balanced by the interest of society at large and respect for human, social and environmental rights" (ILO 2013, 1). The ECCJ seeks to bring corporate accountability focused on three main issues: access to justice, corporate liability, and corporate transparency. These goals are outlined as follows:

1. Corporate liability: Introduce legislation holding companies accountable for adverse social, environmental, and human rights impact that result from their own activities and those linked to them via their business relationships including supply chains.
2. Corporate transparency: Require mandatory disclosure of key information on companies' activities and their relationships; major risks and impacts these activities have on society and how firms plan on mitigating these risks; and ensure stakeholder have access to information useful in asserting their rights.
3. Access to justice: Ensure affordable and effective access to remedy for those affected by human rights and environmental abuse by European companies or their business relationships.

The ECCJ believes voluntary efforts by corporations to ensure corporate social responsibility are not effective because they do not have legal standing for enforcement; the complex structure of MNCs and their subsidiaries bear little to no responsibility for human rights abuses because these harms are not committed by them directly and only the existence of a legal framework for accountability will hold corporations responsible for these injustices.

CONCLUSION

It doesn't have to be this way. There are countless layers to unpack in determining how to construct policies beneficial to firms and their workers. Though all workers want firms for whom they work to be successful in order to provide decent wages, benefits, and working conditions, that success should not be predicated on disparaging, disadvantaging, and discounting workers' health, safety, and dignity. Surely there is some common ground to be found in maintaining adequate profit margins while protecting workers' rights. States such as Alabama, the nation's fifth poorest state, should never be held hostage to agreements requiring tax credits and incentives to corporations in exchange for the privilege of hosting low paying jobs. Distancing owners of production from workers through subcontracting and temporary agencies in order to avoid culpability for workers injuries and death is a nefarious strategy which only serves corporations and not workers. Disengaging from global standards which would provide a baseline for global workers' rights sets up conditions for exploration and abuse. This is the modus operandi of MNCs seeking profits at all costs. The costs, though, are human injury and life.

Industrial disasters and tragedies as focusing events can engender policy changes beneficial to workers and the working environments if groups, organizations, and coalitions who push for changes in health and safety legislation are joined by MNCs and governments to resolve long-standing inequities in wages, benefits, and working environments. But the track record for improving worker protections is far from perfect. Overall, the number of major industrial accidents in higher in developed countries than in developing countries though the number of deaths and injuries is less. This may be the result of some improved safety regulations and enforcement in developed countries as well as a decreasing number of accidents in general (Mihailidou 2008), but there is still a long way to go.

NOTE

1. 29 U.S.C. §§ 201–216 (2006). Section 206 requires payment of minimum wages; Section 207 requires time-and-a-half for hours worked in excess of forty per week.

Chapter Six

Corporate Social Responsibility

LEARNING OBJECTIVES

By the end of this chapter, students will be able to:

1. Identify three ways in which trade union representation is a barrier to corporate profits.
2. Define "creative destruction."
3. Identify why corporate codes of conduct are ineffectual.
4. Discuss how global framework agreements (GFAs) are trying to shore up corporate codes of conduct.

Key terms: Corporate social responsibility, Codes of conduct, Brand engagement, Creative destruction, Global framework agreements

This chapter explores how and why unilateral, voluntary, and non-binding corporate social responsibility (CSR) models have failed, the ineffectual auditing processes used in identifying and addressing the causes and barriers to success, examples of failed CSR efforts, and steps which could be taken to increase CSR within multinational companies (MNCs).

WHY CORPORATE SOCIAL RESPONSIBILITY MODELS FAIL

Corporate social responsibility, sometimes called corporate societal responsibility, is framed as a three-pronged approach to society which concerns people, the planet, and profit. This triple-bottom-line theory either directly or indirectly affects the ways employees are treated, how activity affects the environment, and how profits are made (Clavet 2008). The controversy over whether voluntary efforts or binding laws are the best way to enforce CRS is at the core of the discussion concerning CSR codes. Most of society agrees that "resort[ing] to social dumping, sacrificing workers' rights and the world around us in a sort of global, no-holds-barred race for maximum profit" (Clavet 2008, 11) is detrimental to people, the planet, and profits. This issue of whether CSR is more or less effective than binding law is sometimes seen as black or white and an either/or issue. Taking a look at a soft law or a binding law approach will help sort out the theoretical and practical applications of CSR.

The concept of CSR results from the internal and external push and pull of actors who want/need "to monitor and control the consequences of corporate and economic activities" (Bair 2015, 6) in order to achieve some desired outcome. Some actors make a business case for CSR because they believe putting measures in place during the production and delivery processes speaks to a "market for virtue" (Vogel 2005 in Bair 2015, 6) which will encourage consumers to more actively engage with a firm and buy more product. This perspective is called the internal or instrumentalist approach and speaks to a firm's ability to create competitive advantage or shared value, making their product more attractive to consumers through better quality or lower cost (Porter 2006).

A second perspective, the external or environmental approach, believes the behaviors of the firm are shaped by outside institutional forces, domestic and international, such as social demands, forms of capitalism, and politics. The vacuum of international governance in GSCs creates a space in which actors, NGOs, social movements, state governments, and others exert pressure on firms to conform to their particular set of interests such as protecting workers within a capitalist marketplace or protecting regional market shares. The difficulty in creating an overarching structure responsive to all stakeholders lies in satisfying the concerns of these competing interests. This situation attempts to blend political/state interests with private firms' interests which has resulted in voluntary codes of conduct, an alternative to binding law.

CSR models are attractive to firms because they do not involve behavioral obligation, entail legal liability when breaching obligations, or require damages as a remedy for noncompliance. CSR codes fall under the category of *soft law*, a voluntary, non-enforceable recommendation or suggestion which strives to act as a shield against unwanted sanctions for violations and a public relations cover in case untoward behavior is discovered within working environments. The argument is that soft law, not amenable to the court system, "overturns the age-old views of legal norms as hierarchical commands and of laws as a coercive order" (Clavet 2008, 12). Proponents of soft law argue such a non-authoritarian method of directing behaviors is preferable to binding law because it sets forth guidelines which provide wiggle room for firms to be flexible in the organization of work and allows them to remain competitive in a harsh market. They claim soft recommendations can be considered legal and cite the ILO recommendations as examples.

Binding law, enforceable by penalties or sanctions if violated, is usually thought of as coercive because public authority, such as a court system, provides a framework for activities and actions, can force certain behaviors of conduct within some organization or group, judges whether there is compliance with the rules, and exacts penalties for violations. Clavet (2008) writes, binding laws "formulate[s] how things should be, reduces the scope of what is possible, stabilizes the actor's expectations and thus perpetuates the social order" (12). In the current decentralized society, there doesn't exist one international legislative authority which "has [a] hierarchical command and operates on the principle of the sovereign equality of states" (Clavet 2008, 13). The complexity of socioeconomic issues involved in trying to conduct a one-size-fits-all international law which would govern all involved states presents challenges to its very existence; soft law, on the other hand, allows some system suited to the diversity of multiple players and is the firm's preferred technique for global governance.

THE EFFECTIVENESS OF CSR

As firms struggle to remain competitive, MNCs attempt to eradicate all barriers to profit maximization, one of which is the trade union. They find trade union representation a barrier to their ability to direct and manage their workforces in profit-oriented ways. The representation trade unions affords to workers has a cost to firms because is wrests some control in the production process away from the firm and into the hands of workers. Adhering to labor standards, protecting human and worker rights, and remaining socially responsible incurs cost for firms, so they make grand efforts to avoid the impact of these components through voluntary compliance with internally constructed codes of CSR which gives MNCs cover to exhort their compliance with best practices and basic standards while continuing to push for profits at all costs. According to Gregoratti (2011), compliance with voluntary codes of CSR "raises serious questions about the overall effectiveness and long-term sustainability of such an approach, which the economic crisis has served only to bring into much sharper focus" (Gregoratti 2011, 85). An overall view on the impact of CSR codes is "code compliance remains weak and monitoring largely ineffective" although there is some "evidence of improved code compliance among first-tier suppliers" (Wells 2007, 86). Some firms believe trade union rights are not the purview of corporations but rather belong in the political arena. Therefore, they believe the freedom of association and right to collectively bargain are state issues and carry no weight in the computation of MNCs' relations with their suppliers.

THE CONCEPT OF CREATIVE DESTRUCTION

The underlying tension between MNCs who want complete control of the work processes and global trade unions who protect workers' rights through freedom of association and the right to collectively bargain is based on the capitalist idea of *creative destruction.* In order for workers to make a living wage in a capitalist economic system, there must be triangulation between wage growth, productivity, and competition. Wages rise when productivity rises, and productivity rises when new technologies make production more efficient, new forms of work organization are instituted, and new products or management methods are created (Hoffer 2016). Classical economic theory says competition drives efficiencies in production as each firm must be more innovative, creative, and ingenious than its counterparts to remain competitive in the market. This means firms are constantly on the lookout for ways to streamline production, lower costs, and produce more goods or services at a lower cost per unit.

Joseph Schumpeter, an Austrian-born economist, created the term "creative destruction" which epitomizes the competitiveness of firms to produce and sell more goods to consumers at the lowest cost. He explains the nature of capitalism is never static and constantly evolves because the "fundamental impulse that sets and keeps the capitalist engine in motion comes from new consumers, goods, and the new methods of production or transportation, the new markets, [and] the new forms of industrial organization that capitalist enterprise creates" (82). The textbook explanations of competition, he writes, usually thought of when discussing the wage component in production, are not nearly as important in formulaic computations of cost reductions as are the new innovations made possible by technology or the reorganization of work. Competition acts as "an ever-present threat. It disciplines before it attacks" (Schumpeter 1975 [orig. pub. 1942]) because management subconsciously operates on the assumption they must remain competitive even when no competitive threat is apparent. Also known as *Schumpeter's gale,* this economic concept reflects the constant restructuring of old economic orders which must be destroyed, either through war, economic crisis, or dereliction, so new wealth can be created.

This pro-capitalist economic approach is the basis for MNCs push to produce more and better goods and services even at the expense of their most precious input, their workers. MNCs are powerful interests seeking ways to "weaken the potential for collective bargaining and collective actions, notably the capacity of workers to withhold their labor at the point of production through strikes" (Anner 2016). Yet workers are not without some forms of resistance and are finding ways of counterattacking these powerful forces through well-timed *wildcat strikes,* an unauthorized work stoppage which disables firms from meeting production deadlines and *natural soldiering*, the tendency to slow down or otherwise interrupt the work flow. This gives workers leverage in meeting some of their demands.

GLOBAL FRAMEWORK AGREEMENTS: A POTENTIAL COMPROMISE

Global framework agreements (GFAs), also known as international framework agreements (IFAs), are global arrangements between a *global union federation* (GUF), an international organization of trade unions representing specific industries, and a MNC in which ubiquitous standards for health, safety, and environmental practices, quality of work principles, and trade union rights, regardless of a country's stance on human, civil, or worker rights, are negotiated. The GFA is sometimes seen as a way to shore up CSR codes and often compels management, who generally discount interaction with unionism at any cost, to engage unions in negotiations as a way to mitigate risk across international borders (Fichter 2015). IFAs are replacing industry-specific frameworks in attempts to introduce a new model of industrial relations between global trade unions and MNCs.

GFAs act as "overarching instruments towards securing and maintaining international standards and workers' rights" (Fichter 2015, 1). GFAs are not CSR codes of ethics and are not legally enforceable but try to move beyond specific corporate codes of conduct by drawing on global minimum standards and encouraging MNCs to shoulder some of the responsibility for labor rights in GSCs. After the end of the Cold War, GUFs constructed GFAs as an alternative to CSR codes of conduct in order to gain a foothold in negotiating some balance between workers and management. The idea was through GFAs, trade unionism could be made stronger and global human resource practices could be influenced (Fichter 2015). According to Fichter (2015), all attempts prior to 1990 at international unions to become legitimate representatives of workers had failed, and by 2014, there existed over 100 GFAs between MNCs and at least one GUF. In principle, a GFA is a contract which included the following:

- Mutual recognition of labor and management
- Process for conflict resolution
- Basic standards which recognize workers' rights based on ILO core labor standards

- Geographic delineation of MNCs boundaries which include suppliers, subcontractors, business partners in its GSC

Attempts to use IFAs as mechanisms for global social compliance which positions freedom of association and collective bargaining as the centerpiece of MNCs and trade unions are based on four characteristics:

1. Establishing a platform for defining GUFs as legitimate business partners with MNCs
2. Setting global minimum standards where government interventions fail
3. Encouraging MNCs to accept responsibility throughout supply chains for labor rights violations
4. Including labor in implementation and monitoring processes of labor rights violations (Hammer 2005, 218)

IFAs are often couched within corporate codes of conduct so trade unions are generally excluded from their implementation and enforcement. Although all IFAs uphold International Labor Organization (ILO) Conventions to freely associate (ILO Convention, n. 87) and to collectively bargain (ILO Convention, n. 98), they are considered "soft accountability mechanisms under the banner of corporate social responsibility" (Papadakis 2008, 2) and, therefore, trade unions are at a disadvantage when trying to use IFAs to enforce workers rights violations. Global trade unions make efforts to strengthen their position in relationships with MNCs by using the IFA as a tool to uphold the fundamental rights of workers and organize workers into trade unions as well as in urgent appeal cases where "victimization, retrenchments of union officials and the use of compensation sums to fend off the return of reinstated union officials" occurs (Gregoratti 2011, 87).

EFFORTS BY THE ILO TO INCORPORATE LABOR RIGHTS INTO IFAS

ILO Convention number 87 is all workers have the right to free association which means all workers have the right to organize into trade unions through collective bargaining. IFAs seek to incorporate this right into specific agreements with MNCs. The first international framework agreement to apply to an outsourced apparel supply chain was a test case between Inditex SA, the Spanish fashion retailer and the International Textile, Garment and Leather Workers Federation (ITGLWF) which sought to resolve longstanding trade union recognition disputes was unsuccessful. The underlying issues for the trade union was exploitation and denial of fundamental rights at work, the acceleration of mass production relocation seeking cheaper labor, and competition between buyers/retailers for the lowest cost goods among Asian, African, and Latin American suppliers (Barrientos 2008; Gregoratti 2011) in the Cambodian knitwear factory. The basis of the agreement is rooted in the "promotion of freedom of association, dialogue and collective bargaining" (Gregoratti 2011, 1). As a result of foreign direct investment, the River Rich garment factory located in Khandal province, Cambodian, which produces knitted goods for the European market, was purchased in 2005 by Hong Kong–based group Addchance Holding Limited. Hong Kong and Taiwan now own more than half the factories in the Cambodian garment industry. The firm hired 1,748 workers, 90 percent of whom are women and 70 to 80 percent of whom work under *fixed duration contracts* (FDCs), a contractual relationship between an employer and an employee for a set amount of time (Gregoratti 2011).

Unionization efforts at the River Rich factory were unsuccessful primarily because of the temporary nature of FDCs which, in practice, cede freedom of association rights to employers. Workers who didn't meet quotas, took sick leave, or spoke about forming a union were simply terminated or their contacts were not renewed. Legal challenges brought against Addchance Holding Limited were decided in favor of River Rich, recommendations were made against the reinstatement of union leaders, and 117 union members and leaders were fired.

ORGANIZATIONS WHICH SEEK TO SHORE UP WORKER POWER

Industriall

Industriall, founded in 2012, is a federation of global trade union federations which brings together GUFs such as the International Metalworkers' Federation (IMF), International Federation of Chemical, Energy, Mine and General Workers' Unions (ICEM), and the International Textiles, Garment and Leather Workers' Federation (ITGLWF) and has GFAs with many firms (Industriall 2018a). Their mission is to establish stronger unions through organization and mobilization, fight against precarious work, promote industrial policy and sustainability, promote social justice, democracy, and inclusiveness, ensure equal rights for all workers, and create safer workplaces. After negotiations with many MNCs, Industriall secured over forty agreements which reflect basic human rights, social responsibility, and core labor standards as defined by the ILO and the Declaration of Human Rights (Industriall 2018a).

Because GFAs are not backed by the force of law, some MNCs simply choose not to honor their agreement with a global trade union. Such is the case when the LafargeHolcim firm, producers of glass, cement, ceramic, and associated industries, unilaterally refused to sign a GFA at the headquarters of the ILO in Geneva, Switzerland, on January 10, 2018, which had successfully been negotiated between the firm and the Building and Wood Workers' International Global Union (BWI). LafargeHolcim's new CEO simply said their "current internal arrangements meet the requirements of the company without any need to make further additions" (Industriall 2018b, n.p.). The GFA would have established a social dialogue between LafargeHolcim and BWI, ended subcontracted and temporary work, and improved occupational health and safety thus lessening injuries and deaths among workers. Larage-Holcim has an atrocious health and safety performance record, and their refusal to engage with BWI to protect workers and their rights is an example of the fragility of these agreements and just how powerful are MNCs forces.

ACT

Action, Collaboration, Transformation (ACT) is the first GFA which seeks to support a living wage in the garment sector "in a scaled up, sustainable, industry-wide approach" through the collaboration of all stakeholders. It is apparent that raising wages cannot be implemented and sustained by simply organizing retailers and brands alone, so exploring ways to increase wages fairly across the board by "establishing industry-wide collective bargaining supported by world class manufacturing standards and responsible purchasing practices" (ACT 2017b) is ACT's goal. Establishing global unions of all textile workers who can negotiate wages and working conditions on a global scale is no small task; each country will have its own rules and policies regarding collectives and how they interact with governments, non-governmental organizations (NGOs), trade unions, and corporations. Yet, the power of MNCs to set agendas and fix wages and working conditions through GSCs necessitates a counter force to level the playing field for workers. *Industry-wide collective bargaining* in the form of collective bargaining agreements (CBAs) moves the locus of representation from an industry-specific site to an international level which brings together national representatives of firms, workers, unions, and governments to negotiate and settle on wages and working conditions applicable to whole industrial sectors within a country in a CBA, the results of which are legally binding and enforceable (ACT 2017b). These industrial scale agreements between workers' representatives and employers build on establishing industry appropriate wage mechanisms and other conditions of employment. Only enforceable agreements have the power of law behind them to orchestrate change in the bargaining relationships between workers and employers.

Industry-wide collective bargaining can be more effective than site-specific industry bargaining because it introduces certainty into the worker/employer relationship by

- Ensuring labor costs are predicated on innovation and quality instead of wages
- Requiring all workers, including migrants and contract workers, within a specific industry such as textile or metal, to be covered by collective bargaining
- Reducing labor costs of enforcement and leveling the playing field because all manufacturers must play by the same rules
- Creating more efficiency through reduction in proscriptive decisions in reductions in the workforce, hiring/firing/classification systems, and movements within the firm
- Requiring all industry-wide factories adhere to the same labor standards
- Reducing workplace conflict because everyone is playing by the same rules
- Increasing compliance between employers by diminishing competition so all workers who make garments, regardless of the brand, are paid at a fair level (ACT 2017a; ACT 2017b)

The Hague Institute for Innovation of Law

The Hague Institute for Innovation of Law (HIIL) is an international not-for-profit social organization which collects and makes available to policy makers data reflecting the needs and satisfaction of users of justice systems. Their goal is to give 150 million people the ability to "prevent or resolve their most pressing justice problems" (Hague Institute 2018) by 2030 by giving to decision makers information on specific problems in an effort to find new ways of solving those problems. HIIL works with ACT as a neutral third party to help establish industry-wide collective bargaining in the global garment and textile supply chains. They helped ACT bring together fourteen major suppliers in a supportive sphere which encouraged trust and participation. Toward this end, these participants agreed on Enabling Principles, have signed a Memorandum of Understanding (MOU), and began their first program in Cambodia (Russell 2015).

NOT ALL GFAS ARE CREATED EQUAL

The evolution of GFAs over the last two decades suggests there is still much work to do as no mandatory components of GFAs has been internationally embraced though the trend seems to be in the direction of including ILO principles such as conventions on freedom of association and collective bargaining (Hadwiger 2015). The content of GFAs depends on the negotiations between the employer, usually a multinational enterprise (MNE), and the workers' representative, usually a GUF. The strength of the GFA lies in the inclusion of text referencing the reach of the GFA to the entire supplier chain including subcontractors and contract work, the ability of the MNE to honor contracts without unilateral termination, and some mechanism to inform subsidiaries of the entire supply chain of the content of the GFA. According to Hadwiger (2015), about 20 percent of GFAs do not include any reference to subcontractors at supplier firms which potentially exonerates them from responsibility from liabilities, 40 percent do not include any obligation to inform downstream suppliers and subcontractors of the content of the GFA, weakening their ability to respond to grievous injustices, and 25 percent include arbitrary wording which makes it unclear if, when, and how sanctions apply and to what extent the severity of those sanctions is administered.

There exists some agreement that the way forward for GFA should include some best practices to shore up implementation and enforcement mechanisms. These include establishing a continuous dialogue between MNEs and GUFs about working conditions and relationships throughout the entire supplier chain, establishing a compliance mechanism, such as an audit, site visits or review, by which violations within the supply chain are addressed and appropriate actions taken, committing to police violators through a system of warnings and punitive measures, and fully disclosing supplier information to GUFs and trade unions which are usually not privy to company information.

Though best practices are in the interest of all workers worldwide, let us be clear that GFAs have, to date, a very limited impact on the actual and practical day-to-day work lives of the majority of workers in GSCs. When violations in supply chains are brought to light, there may be some public relations fallout if these events are egregious enough to alert consumers to exploitative and abusive practices, but MNEs have deep pockets and use the power of the media, well-paid attorneys, and public relation campaigns to counter any major upheaval to the usual way of doing business which is putting profits before people. Regardless, it behooves MNEs and GUFs to continue working to find commonalities in their relationships which support both workers and the continual existence of good paying jobs.

OTHER STRATEGIES TO PROTECT WORKERS' RIGHTS

Brand Engagement

Brand engagement is a strategy for brand management which encourages brand buyers, unilaterally or in coalitions, to form an emotional or rational relationship between the consumer and the brand to encourage loyalty to the brand and consequently further sales of the brand. This strategy, long used by the automobile industry to develop loyalty ties between consumers and dealers who pushed increased car sales by giving discounts for frequent trade-ins, is now used as a tactic to protect workers' rights through public relations campaigns which expose to the world workers' human and labor rights violations in order to force MNCs to pursue standards of decency and best practices within their GSCs. Major brands, and sometimes minor brands such as "Hanes, Fruit of the Loom, and Gildan Activewear" (What do we mean 2016, 2), are susceptible to public forces who care about how and by whom the products they purchase are made. After exhausting other legal means to resolve human and labor rights abuses, trade unions, labor rights organizations, and women's auxiliaries often turn to brand engagement (What do we mean 2016) which increases the public's exposure to the human rights violations involved in the production and delivery of goods and services as well as strengthens the chances of forming alliances with other like-minded groups who, through solidified efforts, might compromise a brand's ability to sell its product in certain markets.

One example to level the playing field between workers and management through brand engagement was orchestrated by the Maquila Solidarity Network (MSN) with support from the American Federation of Labor and Congress of Industrial Relations (AFL-CIO). The MSN is an organization formed to support women's and labor rights in the Central American and Mexican garment factories. They work to improve wages and working conditions as well as to secure dignity and voice in the workplace. This workshop, the materials of which are available online, was created to help participants "understand the power relationship in the global garment industry, the role of the international brands in this industry, and the possibilities and challenges in attempting to engage with or campaign against international brands" (Network 2015, n.p.). Held in 2013 to 2014 in San Salvador, El Salvador, and San Pedro Sula, Honduras, women leaders came together to discuss and formulate plans to put pressure on apparel brands to respect labor rights in regional supplier factories.

These workshops sometimes focus on popular brands, such as Nike, Gap, and Adidas, whose market share is often based on consumers' loyalty to their brand name and are particularly vulnerable to these public relations campaigns. University students have sometimes engaged in these campaigns with some success against sportswear and food service supplies for their campuses. Some MNCs are surprised when suppliers in their GSCs are targeted for these abuses and violations because they have so distanced themselves from their actual workers that they have little knowledge of working conditions in their supply chains. This is a good example of how little control they exercise over the production of goods and services for which they are ultimately responsible. These public relations campaigns reveal how ineffective CSR codes are and how much MNCs are willing to spend in legal defense of their brands against trade unions, women's groups, labor rights organizations, and civil society groups who collectively join together to expose worker exploitation and labor violations.

Strategy of Co-Determination

Another approach to level the playing field between workers and employers is the German *strategy of co-determination*. Established through the Codetermination Act of 1976, the legislation seeks to induce loyalty from workers by extending to them the firm's decision-making power. The idea is that an investment in human capital is made profitable by rewarding workers with more participation rights. Practically, co-determination is facilitated by mediating conflicts through the establishment of work councils, an intermediary between labor and management and consisting of employee representatives. Independent of the German Trade Union Confederation, work councils can be established in firms with more than five employees and meet with employers monthly to resolve disputes. Work councils have jurisdiction over matters not regulated by legislation and a collective bargaining contract; their existence is ensured by the Works Council Constitution Act (1952, 1972, 2001). Although work councils exist in eighteen of the twenty-five European member countries, "Germany has one of the most highly developed systems of board-level co-determination" (Page 2011, 38). Though co-determination requires the interests of workers must be taken into account by management, Page (2011) reports:

> Nowadays it is the demands of global investors for a high return on their capital that determines the way companies are run, and this raises anew the question of their role and social obligations. The latest European initiatives on "corporate social responsibility," largely triggered by and directed at the financial markets and stock exchanges, demonstrate the relevance of this question. (41)

The power of co-determination as a "democratic project" (Page 2011, 41) could play a bigger role in MNCs' and global investors' success if launched on a broader European scale.

CONCLUSION

It doesn't have to be this way. The last several decades have witnessed the use of voluntary CSR as one method firms use to convince buyers their product is ethically produced under enforced environmental and human rights standards. This way firms represent themselves (or misrepresent themselves) as good corporate citizens. Corporations create codes of conduct which tout voluntary compliance of all regulations ensuring human, worker, and environmental standards. This self-regulation has proven to be lax and "leads to lower degrees of stringency and incomplete implementation" (Fichter 2016b, 2).

The use of GFAs is currently considered the best path forward for MNEs and GUFs to ensure workers in downstream supplier chains, subcontractors, and contract workers are treated with respect, paid a living wage, and work in safe conditions. GFAs which provide for continued social dialogue, mechanisms for information flow throughout the entire supply chain, and sanctions and/or penalties for noncompliance are best practices which allow both parties to contribute to the social and economic well-being of workers, the corporations' greatest asset. Yet, the implementation and enforcement power of GFAs continues to predominantly lie with MNEs who fear sharing their power with GUFs and the workers they represent will structurally weaken their profit-oriented ability. Until MNEs voluntarily or by force cede some of that power to their workers, difficulties will continue throughout GSCs as workers struggle to survive.

According to Luc Fransen (2012), the most successful way of forcing MNCs to comply with regulation is through the use of union participation which leads to labor standards conforming to ILO conventions. Many MNCs engage in the self-promotion of ethically induced behaviors which might lead to the safety of workers and the protection of the environment if put into practice, but the primary focus of MNCs is shareholder profits and committing to regulations has a cost, so their rhetoric often doesn't match their actions (Fransen 2012).

Chapter Seven

Political and Legal Strategies to Regulate Global Supply Chains

LEARNING OBJECTIVES

At the end of this chapter, students will be able to:

1. Identify three plans/efforts by various countries to protect workers' and environmental rights
2. Identify three negative consequences of compensation claims for accountability
3. Define export processing zone
4. Discuss the implications of "due diligence" for corporations and workers

Key terms: Export processing zone, Due diligence, Strategic litigation

This chapter describes the arguments and challenges employers face concerning regulations within the global supply chain (GSC) and how they attempt to mediate workers' concerns through voluntary measures.

TRANSNATIONAL CORPORATIONS AREN'T HELD ACCOUNTABLE FOR HUMAN RIGHTS ABUSES

In a global economy which generates around $150 billion each year in the private sector alone, firms exploit gaps in international labor and migration law and enforcement in order to remain profitable. In order to do this, firms use every tool at their disposal to avoid, circumvent, and thwart laws and policies which protect workers' rights and prevent exploitation of the environment. All consumers have a right to know and understand by whom, how, and from where the products they purchase are made. Consumers also have a responsibility to purchase products which are ethically sourced and manufactured. Sharron Burrow (2017), General Secretary of the International Trade Union Confederation, notes:

> We all have a responsibility to the women forced to mine for minerals in Eastern [Democratic Republic of the Congo] DRC for our smart phones, migrants on Thai fishing boats fishing for seafood, low-wage workers in Malaysia making our TVS and washing machines, and the Gulf States relying on a workforce enslaved by the kafala system [a system monitoring construction and domestic workers in Middle Eastern countries] to staff international hotel chains, department stores and construction companies. (3)

It is ironic that the very laws originally designed to protect workers from slavery and abuse are now being used to exploit these same workers. Burrow (2017) explains that as consumers of goods and services, we have an obligation to police unscrupulous employers who build their profit mechanism system on the backs of workers victimized by modern slavery and human trafficking due to outdated or non-existent laws which should protect these workers.

Trust in transnational corporations (TNCs) to voluntarily "fix" these issues is low and international and national treaties to hold multinational corporations (MNCs) and GSCs accountable are necessary to hold owners of production accountable for their suppliers' and subcontractors' actions. (ITUC 2016). Corporate greed, which has superseded corporate responsibility, will continue to exploit workers' rights and engage in environmental degradation as long as they are allowed to do so. The only stop gap measure in light of lax or non-existent international law to govern TNC activities and behaviors across the board is through open and transparent international governance structures which force corporate compliance. All stakeholders, even TNCs themselves, know the current approach taken is wrong-headed, but finding solutions for multi-player stakeholders in different countries who construct laws for self-protection in the market is a difficult task. Organizations external to the corporation such as governments, NGOs, labor and civic rights groups, and others are leading the way in establishing laws and policies to protect workers in the formal and informal economies against human rights abuses and environmental exploitation (Kinley 2006).

TNCS DISTANCE THEMSELVES FROM CULPABILITY

TNCs, in general, are not liable for violating their workers' rights in GSCs. International law says only states are subject to international conventions or treaties, therefore, TNCs cannot be held accountable for human rights abuses or human trafficking violations. So the TNC remains free to increase profits at the expense of its labor force but can't legally be held accountable for doing so (Zimmer 2016). A second avenue used by TNCs in skirting culpability for workers' rights violations is the distance or space created between the corporation and its suppliers who actually create and deliver goods and services. The supplier can be held liable for workers' rights violations under a specific countries' laws, but suppliers exist at the end of the production chain removing responsibility from the TNC and shifting it to the supplier.

TNCs generate networks which create a complex organizational structure through decentralization strategies and fragmentation of their legal obligations among "subsidiaries, contractors, suppliers or licensees and adopting several legal forms through many different links of commercial character" (OEIGWG 2016, 16). This decentralization strategy results in the dissolution of the parent company's liability within the GSC while encouraging the international nature of commercial activity in different countries. This allows the TNC to leverage each state's legislation against other states in order to achieve competitive advantage in social, labor, environment, and cultural arenas. For this monopoly of power to be dissolved within TNCs, there must exist some form of treaty, an international binding agreement, enforceable through some international tribunal which dissolves the parent company's liability protections in its GSC.

ATTEMPTS TO HOLD TNCS ACCOUNTABLE

The issue at hand is how to hold TNCs accountable for human rights and environmental degradation when there is no legal or enforcement mechanism to do so. The debate centers around creating a top-down approach through an international mechanism which binds corporations to respect and enforce laws protecting human rights and sanctions corporate misbehavior versus a bottom-up approach which focuses on soft laws allowing industry-specific voluntary measures, such as corporate ethical codes, in which corporations police themselves. Those in favor of binding international law propose the need for an international law to fill a legal void where currently only soft law or no law exists. The debate continues today with TNCs pushing back against any legal requirement mandating their inclusion in protecting human and workers' rights. Those in opposition to binding international law adjudicated through an international court or tribunal believe the enforcement of human rights violations is the purview of individual states and putting the onus of compliance and enforcement "'privatizes human rights'" (Kinley 2007, 36) by shifting the obligation to non-elected and non-qualified third-party representatives such as TNCs.

In 1947, the United Nations Human Rights Commission created the Subcommission on the Prevention of Discrimination and Protection of Minorities, which later came to be known as the Sub-Commission on the Promotion and Protection of Human Rights, consisting of experts from various countries charged with developing new international standards to address human rights violations and protections (Kinley 2006). The Sub-Commission was to act as a think tank for combatting human rights abuses. As deregulation and trade liberalization became the custom in the following decades, an increased concern over the number of human rights abuse cases was the catalyst for further action concerning how best to prevent human exploitation and trafficking.

In 1970, the United Nations, at the behest of developing countries, created the Centre for Transnational Corporations (CTC). Throughout the next two decades, CTC drafted compliance codes for TNCs focusing on TNCs' acquiescence with host countries' laws in relationship to foreign direct investment (FDI). Globalization's need for increased investment in developing countries during the early 1990s shifted attention from compliance with host countries' needs to shore up their economic abilities for their own protection to structural adjustment policies (SAPs) which benefited developed countries rather than developing host countries. The idea was to create a "set of human rights obligations directed at companies, but which would be imposed upon them by way of the usual means of international law, namely, the domestic laws of individual states" (Kinley 2007, 31). The next serious effort to create and strengthen recommendations against human rights abuses took place in 2003 (Kinley 2006; Ruggie 2014).

Moving recommendations from third parties such as the UN into legal status is an arduous process which fosters mistrust and deal making on both sides. In 2003, spurred by increased incidents of sweatshop labor, environmental ruin, and declining worker protections, and after much debate within the working group of the Sub-Committee to produce a document reflecting the connections between TNCs and human rights, the Sub-Committee proposed a set of regulations called the Norms on the Responsibilities of Transnational Corporations and Other Business Enterprises with Regard to Human Rights (Norms) which acknowledged "the undoubted capacity of corporations 'to foster economic well-being, development, technological improvement and wealth'" as well as corporations' capacity "'to cause harmful impacts on the human rights and lives of individuals through their core business practices and operations, including employment practices, environmental policies, relationship with suppliers and consumers, interactions with

Governments and other activities'" (Kinley 2006, 449). The main thrust of the Norms imposed corporate liability for human rights abuses occurring in suppliers, but didn't extend those protections to third-party suppliers. Expected to become binding, the Norms obligated firms to "'promote, secure the fulfillment of, respect, ensure respect of and protect' human rights" (Ruggie 2014, 6). Corporations strongly opposed the Norms, as did the Commission on Human Rights, because compliance would mean possible liability for violations and translate into impediments to corporations' decision-making power, monetary sanctions, and the need for further clarity to avoid lawsuits. The Norms, abandoned as corporations fought against them, left a vacuum in international adjudication of human rights abuses.

One outcome of the Norms' demise was a United Nation's mandate for a "special procedure" (Ruggie 2014, 7) to flesh out existing standards and best practices, clarify controversial concepts, and make recommendations on how to proceed. John Ruggie, appointed by the Secretary General of the United Nations in 2005, responded with the Protect, Respect, and Remedy Framework based on the state's duty to protect against human rights abuses by intermediates, corporate responsibility to respect human rights, and victims' access to remedy in and out of the courts. "The Protect, Respect, and Remedy Framework addresses *what* should be done to move in this direction; the Guiding Principles [on Business and Human Rights, a polycentric approach to developing an overarching international system of global governance] show *how*" (Ruggie 2014, 9). To date, the Guiding Principles are just that: a framework on which to further build an enforceable strategy for worker protections through global governance.

Ruggie (2014) contends "constructing an authoritative framework for business and human rights inevitably was an exercise in polycentric governance" (9) because states alone cannot meet all the international challenges, conceptually or practically, of an overarching framework for global governance. According to Ruggie (2014), three types of governance are at play here: a system of public laws and governance as administered by states, a system of civil governance involving consumers and their advocates, and a system of corporate governance which oversees its own business dealings. The challenge is creating and administering an alliance which is complimentary but yet allows each governance system to maintain some autonomy. The Protect, Respect, and Remedy Framework responds to these challenges and is embedding in the Guiding Principles, yet the result is "a patchwork of uncoordinated schemes competing vigorously for adherents, resources, legitimacy, and public notice" (Ruggie 2014, 10). Though the Guiding Principles are supported by the Human Rights Council, previously the United Nations Human Rights Commission, the UN has no enforcement power, so the actual practice of ensuring measures to avoid and eliminate human rights abuses remains unsettled, as does remedies for those affected by the abuses.

The International Labour Organization (ILO), which sets standards for human rights abuses and human trafficking, engages in treaties with states/ governments and not companies, so their reach is limited. Efforts to protect workers' rights in global supply chains were a major topic at the International Labour Conferences, 2016 and 2017, in which ways to strengthen existing provisions as well as ways to create new provisions were discussed. The topic drew high expectations from workers and low expectations from employers (Busser 2016). The conferences recognized GSCs are "diverse, complex, fragmented, and present in many sectors" and "power relations between capital and labour have become more unequal due to the increase in global supply chains" (Busser 2016, 1). Further recognition included the acknowledgment that women and workers in *export processing zones* (EPZs) are problem areas. EPZs are special economic zones created by developing countries from which goods can be exported, stored, handled, manufactured, reconfigured, or re-exported without the obligations of customs regulations or duties/tariffs. Sometimes these spaces are called free trade zones. Since specific state governments can't enforce legislation other than in their own country, state governments' cross-border reach is restricted. This creates work and government gaps, a sort of no-man's land, neither serviced by governments nor employers (Kinley 2006). There is a huge need for some sort of overarching policy, a "global binding instrument" (Busser 2016, 3) with enforcement mechanisms to be created and given authority by participating governments.

In October 2016, the Human Rights Council of the United Nations entertained proposals from the Global Campaign to Reclaim Peoples Sovereignty, Dismantle Corporate Power and Stop Impunity to promote "the protection and fulfilment of human rights in the long-term and on a global scale [in order to] contribute to ending the impunity that TNCs routinely enjoy for their human rights violations" (OEIGWG 2016, 2). Launched in 2012, the Global Campaign is

> a network of 200 social movements, networks, organizations, and affected communities resisting the land grabs, extractive mining, exploitative wages and environmental destructions of transnational corporations (TNCs) in different global regions particularly in Africa, Asia and Latin America. It is a peoples' global response to unaccountable corporate power which provides for facilitation for dialogue, strategizing, exchanging information and experiences, acting as a space for visibility of resistance and deepening of solidarity. (OEIGWG 2016, 2)

This Global Compact proposal includes points which, in their diversity, would form a legally binding instrument to "end corporate impunity and address the systemic power of TNCs which has reached unprecedented impacts on the daily lives of affected communities" (OEIGWG 2016, 2). The proposals are

1. To close the legal gap in international human rights law which allows TNCs impunity for human rights violations by giving TNCs legal status as persons under international law as does state and interstate law. This way TNCs would be subject to the same scrutiny under the Declaration of Human Rights which says no person, state, or group can engage in any activity or perform any act aimed at the destruction of any of the rights and freedoms set forth within the Declaration (Article 30).
2. To consider the scope of TNCs' extraterritorial obligations as one economic unit instead of a "home" base free of culpability for its supplier chains' human rights abuses/violations of workers' rights. The 2011 Maastricht Principles on Extraterritorial Obligations in the Area of Economic, Social, and Cultural Rights clearly reflect the obligation of states to take necessary measures to "ensure economic, social and cultural rights relat[ing] to non-state actors that are subject to States' regulatory powers" (OEIGWG 2016, 8), so it is justifiable to consider actions performed by subsidiaries are the responsibility of the parent company.
3. To create an autonomous international tribunal as an enforcement mechanism triggered when states violate their duties to "protect, respect, and remedy" (2011, 5), "operate[s] as a complement to national, regional and universal mechanisms and guarantees access to an independent judicial forum for affected people and communities to obtain justice for violations of their civil, political, social, economic, cultural and environmental rights" (OEIGWG 2016, 12), has the authority to sanction TNCs for noncompliance, and has the force of international law to make its actions binding in contrast to the current state which reflects a "glaring asymmetry and imbalance in terms of rights and obligation of TNCs with regards to human rights" (OEIGWG 2016, 12).
4. To require and enforce transparency throughout the TNC concerning the origins of capital, nationality of board members, commercial decisions, profits destination, product externalization, and the identification of the parent company (OEIGWG 2016) by requiring compliance with the International Law of Human Rights, International Framework Agreements (IFAs), ILO conventions, and criminal and civil rules of all state governments involved.
5. To require the International Monetary Fund (IMF) and World Bank (WB), subject to international law and responsible for structural adjustment policies and neoliberalism particularly in the Global South,

accountable for human rights violations resulting from their complicity in forcing states to open their economics to TNCs, meet international/national obligations related to human rights, and stop promoting policies which threaten the very existence of countries they claim they are helping, conduct evaluations of their policies' effect on human rights and repatriate any damages they own, refrain from and monitor loans to private firms which damage environmental and human rights, and submit to international/national courts their violations and pay for negative actions they have caused.

6. To establish a reciprocity agreement between TNCs and states which places human rights and environmental protections above the rights of TNCs and their investors and "end the investor-to-state dispute settlement (ISDS) regime, and reclaim state sovereignty over public policy and state priorities" (OEIGWG 2016, 24–25). The trade and investment regime in the form of the World Trade Organization (WTO), free trade agreements (FTAs), international investment agreements (IIAs), and bilateral investment treaties (BITS) have "rolled back the economic, social, cultural, and environmental rights of people across the Global South . . . and these Agreements also aim for a similar rollback of peoples' rights in the Global North" (OEIGWG 2016, 22). These actions facilitated an "unprecedented regulatory asymmetry that functions as an architecture of legitimation and impunity for the operations of TNCs" (OEIGWG 2016, 22). This allows TNCs to sue states, under the investor-state dispute settlement mechanism, but does not allow states to sue TNCs. TNCs have been able to win these disputes and siphon huge sums of money from states which weakens states' ability to pay for needed infrastructure and social payments for their citizens.
7. To make more equitable the power relationship between TNCs and equity-seeking people through "regulation and remedy" (OEIGWG 2016, 27). That includes rejecting the ability of TNCs to sue states without reciprocity, broadening the definition of "persons affected by corporations" (OEIGWG 2016, 28) through linking the obligations of states to include human rights, limiting or eliminating court costs for victims seeking redress in the courts, engaging in class action lawsuits, encouraging prompt/reasonable time frames for court case/settlements, and limiting transactional remedies or out of court settlements to protect people against TNCs.

As of December 17, 2017, a delegation from the European Union to the United Nations General Assembly's Fifth Committee, which represents TNCs, is attempting to eliminate funding from the Human Rights Council's intergovernmental working group (IGWG), the group charged with drafting contractual language to protect human rights within TNCs by creating an international access mechanism for affected people seeking justice for human rights violations (2017). This compliments the strategy of TNCs who attempt to thwart every effort toward more equitable power relationships between themselves and workers. As of this writing, the delegation is still unsuccessful in eliminating the funding from this working group.

TRYING TO FIND A BALANCE

No one is suggesting that firms should not make a profit or that GSCs are not an efficient way to logistically move products from conception to delivery, but I am suggesting these same outcomes could be achieved while still protecting workers' rights. The ILO's provisional record of the 2016 conference states:

> The positive impact of global supply chains on job creation is important in view of demographic changes in terms of aging, population growth and the increase of women's participation in the labour market. Across the world, millions of young women and men are looking for opportunities to enter the labour market. Participation in global supply chains increases their chances of getting a foothold in the world of formal work, doing well for themselves and their families, and succeeding in life.

At the same time, failures at all levels within global supply chains have contributed to decent work deficits for working conditions such as in the areas of occupational safety and health, wages, and working time which impacts the employment relationship and the protections it can offer. Such failures have also contributed to the undermining of labor rights, particularly freedom of association and collective bargaining. Informality, non-standard forms of employment and the use of intermediaries are common. The presence of child labor and forced labor in some global supply chains is acute in the lower segments of the chain. Migrant workers and homeworkers are found in many global supply chains and may face various forms of discrimination and limited or no legal protection (n.p.).

Within the current structure, GSCs are treating workers as simply a disposable commodity in the production process. This fosters two main problems. First, workers, as creative and intelligent humans, are the most prized asset a firm has to make its business more competitive and lucrative; humans hold the ingenuity and knowledge to make GSCs work. Tapping into the potential of the human brain is one of the most efficient strategies a firm can use to promote, secure, and broaden its reach. Secondly, it is never in the long-term best interest of the firm, their workers, or the broader community to ill equip workers to buy goods, contribute to the social, cultural, or political environment through starvation wages and benefits, or create a glut of automaton workers whose creativity and ingenuity is stifled through repetitive and monotonous motions. Firms have power to change this dynamic by uplifting their workers through decent wages and working conditions, education and training, and dignity and voice in the workplace. Strategies to include workers in decision-making processes, provide living wages and benefits, and treat workers with respect and dignity are in the long-term best interest of the firm.

HUMAN RIGHTS DUE DILIGENCE

Firms have a responsibility to "respect human rights, and human rights due diligence (HRDD) is now widely recognized as an efficient way to put this principle into practice" (ECCJ 2017b, 1). HRDD is a means by which firms can identify gaps in their global supply chains in order to protect workers' rights, make available to the public their efforts to correct the injustices, and strengthen their relationship with their workers by improving their "risks assessment and management, helping state authorities meet their duty to protect human rights, and improving access to justice for victims of corporate abuse in and outside Europe" (ECCJ 2017b, 1). The operational principle enshrined in the United Nations Guiding Principles on Business and Human Rights (UNGPs) to put firms' responsibility to protect human rights into practice is known as *due diligence*. Due diligence is recognized as a "set of useful practical steps to address companies' human rights and environmental impacts and promote responsible business behavior" (ECCJ 2017b, 1). The process of due diligence begins with identifying the adverse impacts of human and environment concerns, preventing and mitigating those concerns, and finding remedies for the concerns. Though not yet a legal obligation, parts of HRDD such as assessment impacts and reporting are included in some national and international frameworks involving human and labor rights, environmental and consumer protections, and fights against corruption. As of yet, though, HRDD obligations do not extend beyond European borders.

EFFORTS TO PROTECT WORKERS' AND ENVIRONMENTAL RIGHTS AND HOLD CORPORATIONS ACCOUNTABLE

Busser (2016) states there are "a number of actions governments, business enterprises, and social partners should undertake, as well as action from the ILO" (2) in order to strengthen workers' rights and hold corporations accountable in GSCs. These include:

- Actively promoting social dialogue, freedom of association, and collective bargaining
- Using public procurement to advance decent work in GSCs
- Ensuring that non-standard forms of employment are not used to undermine labor rights and decent work

In order for workers' rights to be protected, social partners should take part in dialogue with other countries and continue to work for international framework agreements and collective bargaining while businesses should work toward establishing some mechanisms for grievance handling and the promotion of human rights, and the ILO should promote cross-border dialogue, decent work in EPZs, and bring together experts who could devise measures to promote decent work in GSCs (Busser 2016).

There begins to be a crack in this TNC armor in the effort to protect workers. The United States modernized a 1930s law, the Trade Facilitation and Trade Enforcement Act of 2015, which now prohibits entry into US ports goods produced by forced labor including "indentured child labor" (Trade 2015, 1). The goods are subject to seizure, and their confiscation may lead to criminal charges against the importers. The law is now considered an important human rights tools and not just a trade law (Burrow 2017; Trade 2015).

In February 2017, the French National Assembly adopted *a duty of vigilance bill* which was the first historical step toward better human rights and environmental protections. The central objective of the bill requires large companies to carry out a vigilance plan to identify and publish the adverse impacts of their activities throughout their supply chains, and if they fail to do so, the law "empowers victims and other concerned parties to bring the issue before a judge" (ECCJ 2017a) who can fine the companies. Originally the bill included civil penalties for noncompliance, but the French Constitutional Council struck down civil penalties for firms who failed to comply. Civil society organizations argue the bill doesn't go far enough because it only applies to about 100 large companies, and the burden of proof still falls on victims who may be ill equipped to seek justice. Importantly, the offending company only has to prove it has done its best to avoid damaging human rights and the environment to be found innocent of the charges. These first important steps should now be followed by national and international binding agreements to ensure the laws work for everyone (ECCJ 2017a).

Various countries' attempts to comply with or incorporate the Respect, Protect, and Remedy Framework as embedded in the GP have met with mediocre success. Though no country suggests the GPs are unimportant as a framework in which state, civic, and corporate actions could reach agreement, the hesitancy to incorporate stronger protections for human rights into law is robust. The United Kingdom (UK) developed a National Action Plan (NAP) in 2013 to implement the GPs. A 2016 analysis of the NAP's progress suggests "the enforcement of human rights obligations *vis-à-vis* corporations still depends on mechanisms of protection activated within national legal systems" (Fasciglione 2016, 635). Additionally, the UK, in 2015, passed the Modern UK Slavery Act (MSA), a broad coalition of business, labor, and non-governmental organizations (NGOs) to address issues of *supply chain transparency*, readily available information for end users of a good or service about its source, production, and delivery, *extraterritoriality*, exempting a territory from the legal jurisdiction of local law, and due diligence and civil remedies for supply chain violations.

Supply chain transparency asks British firms with an annual turnover of three million pounds to publicly disclose efforts at combatting human trafficking and publish the information on their websites. The government contends firms will then compete with each other to provide the best and most viable information which will eventually lead to changed behavior. The fallacy with this thinking is the unlikeliness of firms to provide accurate information if that information could lead to stringent and legal liabilities. In reality, firms only provide annual statements for public relations purposes because governments do not compel them to provide other pertinent information and do not require UK subsidiarity firms to report because they are outside the scope of the agreement.

Extraterritoriality should hold accountable UK firms who engage in the slavery of a non-British persons. Yet the MSA gives short shrift to this offense unless the offense is a criminal act covered under another law such as the Trafficking Victims Protection Act 18 USC 1596 which prohibits torture or child sexual slavery. Due diligence and civil remedies for supply chain violations, publicly disclosing a firm's process for complying with the UN's Guiding Principles on Business and Human Rights, are also non-existent in the MSA. Though these are good first steps in combating human slavery and trafficking, there exists no enforcement mechanisms to force a firm to comply with these recommendations. At this point, the recommendations function merely as suggestions. Though the language in these pieces of legislation would have to be fleshed out to include subsidiaries, the general principle of workers' protection seems to be taking hold at least in some countries (Zimmer 2016).

Germany, the fourth largest economy in the world and Europe's economic engine, continues to distance itself from incorporating mechanisms to ensure protections from human rights abuses by stating their belief that the international obligation to protect human rights lies with the state and not with the corporation (Bauer 2013). The Netherlands, Italy, Sweden, and Switzerland are discussing similar legislative measures addressing child labor, duty of care, and due diligence. The EU member states, who have yet to legislatively participate in human rights due diligence, do so to maintain their status quo as low-regulation business environments which makes them attractive to foreign direct investment and protects their internal markets. "This creates a two-tier system of corporate governance within the EU" (ECCJ 2017b, 3) which prevents the implementation of the GPs. The European Parliament encourages member nations to adopt the French model of HRDD suggesting that respect for human rights is an EU obligation and should be incorporated into European law, state, civil, and corporate, as soon as possible.

STRATEGIC APPROACHES FOR COMPENSATION AND CORPORATE ACCOUNTABILITY

The power TNCs have to affect people's lives, communities, living standards, infrastructure, the environment, and job security has both positive and negative effects. Sometimes TNCs offer jobs which are better than those available in local businesses or in areas where no jobs previously existed. But the negative impacts often outweigh the positive impacts. When TNCs ignore environments regulations simply because the cost of compliance is too high or when workers' organizing efforts are met with disdain and punitive repercussions, entire communities suffer. Muller-Hoff (2011) writes:

> The contamination of water and soil, loss of land, destruction of sacred sites, unemployment, security issues, displacement and the destruction of social and economic networks are some of the consequences which lead to destruction of livelihoods and constitute grave violations of basic human rights. (5)

It is in the long-term best interest of all parties to strategically pre-design, investigate, and implement plans to correct these imbalances and establish, restore, and/or strengthen social justice for all stakeholders.

How to resolve these issues continues to be debated within the ILO. The Protect, Respect, and Remedy Framework strongly recommends governments, workers, and trade unions keep open a dialogue concerning best practices within GSCs which are in compliance with international labor standards (Ryder 2016). Another proposal resulted from a series of workshops sponsored by the European Center for Constitutional and Human Rights in 2011 at Douala, Cameroon, which proposed compensation for harm such as loss of livelihood which throws people into poverty and "limits their possibilities to act, to mobilize and to articulate themselves in order to defend their rights and interests" (Muller-Hoff 2011, 4). The problem with a compensation strategy is the length of time, resources, and strategizing expended by both parties to mediate or negotiate settlements whether the "compensation agreement is defined by law, by contract, or by individual or collective negotiations" (Muller-Hoff 2011, 4). Sometimes the outcomes lead to "counter actions/claims for defamation or libel" (Muller-Hoff 2011, 4).

Compensation claims often have negative results for workers filing the claims. Women and other equity-seeking groups are disadvantaged because of the lack of information about the investment projects and "opportunities for participation and development" are often excluded from the "consultation and negotiation processes" (Muller-Hoff 2011, 5). Monetary compensation is unfairly distributed by corrupt power structures exacerbating existing inequalities within the local context such that workers have less control over their own existence. Workers are dissuaded from filing or pursuing compensations claims through harassment, physical or sexual assault, or detention, and conflict is sown among workers representing various factions, such as whites against black, or women against men, to encourage division and weaken organizational strength.

For example, TNCs interested in mining, extractive operations, or industrial agricultural must acquire property rights to land areas which are held by families/communities who are asked to sign contracts to rent/sell their land to the TNC. Often these families/communities are indigenous people or women who do not have enough information to knowingly negotiate a fair price for their land use and often suffer negative long-term income because of their diminished negotiating power. Often these groups are displaced or evicted from their land and find they have no source of income, access to housing, jobs, food, clean water, or healthcare. This has a dilatory effect on their ability to socially connect with others who might be able to provide assistance; consequently they suffer social isolation and discrimination. Resettlement efforts are minimal and insufficient at best so entire communities are dispersed, divided, and destroyed. Entire populations, searching for new places to live, often travel long distances on foot, placing them at peril for hunger, thirst, lack of shelter, and "physical and sexual violence" (Muller-Hoff 2011, 9).

To achieve positive results from compensation claims against TNCs requires concerted and strategic planning, financial and human resources, and long-term tenacity because it is very likely the claim will take several years to make its way through the court system and incur counter-claims along the way. Mediation, negotiation, and the courts all provide avenues to establish international models for just compensation. Though perseverance is the key, the result could be case law for corporate accountability which builds toward establishing base line rights for workers. The Douala conference concluded there are common components of any successful compensation claim: solidarity among workers who defend their rights, a clear goal, concrete, detailed information about the claim, a strategic plan for achieving the claim, recommendations, and access to relevant, vetted, and corroborative material (Muller-Hoff 2011).

OPTIONS FOR COMPENSATION CLAIMS

Corporations have carte blanc in violating human rights because there are few mechanisms in place to stop them unless there is some state legislation, such as anti-discrimination law; corporations also frustrate environmental rules because of lax state enforcement. There could be some blowback to corporations if state laws prevent torture or cruel and unusual punishment and a case could be made the physical harms to their workers is a human rights violation (Muller-Hoff 2011, 18). According to Muller-Hoff (2011), several options exist for pursuing a compensation claim against a TNC and choosing the right one is important. One compensation avenue is *soft law*, a non-enforceable though significant recommendation or suggestion which refers to guidelines, policy declarations, or codes of conduct. Soft laws include corporate codes of conduct, the Human Declaration of Human Rights, and the Organization of Economic Co-Operation and Development (OECD). Though soft law doesn't carry the impact of binding law, it sometimes forms the basis for emerging law or morphs into binding law. Filed by aggrieved workers, NGOs, or states, soft laws usually result in mediation, agreements, or recommendations and are strongly guided by the TNC.

A second compensation option is *civil action*, a collective lawsuit filed by multiple plaintiffs with a shared concern. Civil actions can be filed against a subsidiary of the TNC or the TNC itself in the local host country or the country in which the firm is headquartered and are used when compensation is the goal. One deterrent in filing a compensation civil case is the "rule that the party who loses a claim must pay the costs of the winning party" (Muller-Hoff 2011, 22).

Criminal complaints, a third compensation option, penalize illegal corporate or individual behavior so when a TNC loses a criminal case, they may be economically sanctioned or incur negative public relations. Consequently, prosecutions are taken seriously. Convictions may occur, but even if they don't, the dialogue leading up to the conviction showcases the issues and problems of concern.

The fourth compensation option involved filing claims based on a specific country's national legislation and sovereignty so a workers' rights claim or an environmental claim can be prosecuted only within the country in which the offense occurs. Extraterritorial legislation doesn't apply in these cases.

A final compensation claim option against TNCs and individuals within those companies is to file an appeals case in an international court because lower state court efforts have failed. Certain parameters must be in place such as inadequate access to justice provided by the lower court. Though international court decisions are binding, those decisions are only enforced if there exists some state mechanism for enforcement or political pressure for enforcement emanated from the will of the people.

There is no one best approach for pursuing compensation claims. Each case should be evaluated on the expected reason for the compensation (loss of income, dignity in the workplace, exploitation of human/worker rights, and so forth) as well as multiple strategies for settling the claim (mediation, negotiation, out-of-court settlements, and/or litigation). Both parties involved use what is known as *strategic litigation* or *impact litigation*, presenting carefully selected victims' rights cases to the courts in order to make broader societal changes, "which aims at setting precedents and advancing policies that strengthen the legal framework for global human rights accountability and achieving greater social justice" (Muller-Hoff 2011, 31). Strategic litigation designed for building a defense against compensation claims is beyond the scope of this chapter but you should know that "key issues to be addressed and planned in advance such as the objectives, foreseeable risk and challenges and the consolidation and strengthening of the group that pursues the claims" hold the distinct possibility of "success without victory" meaning there is a considerable chance that such cases will lose before a court of law. In order to avoid this risk, both parties are open to having a case settled out of court to avoid the risk of losing the case, receiving zero compensation, and instead having to pay all the costs (Muller-Hoff 2011, 31).

CONCLUSION

It doesn't have to be this way. No firm, employer, TNC, business, or other profit-seeking entity should benefit directly or indirectly from human slavery, trafficking, or environmental degradation. The international community has long held that forced labor is a human rights crime and "slave traders, the antecedents to today's human traffickers" (Burrow 2017, 9) are enemies of all mankind. Slave traders should have no legal protections and should not be allowed to hide within the confines of MNCs and GSCs. Industry-based initiatives like corporate codes or multilateral initiatives such as the Global Compact have not yielded the necessary restraints on "corporate misbehavior" in the arenas of human and workers' rights or environmental and labor concerns (Kinley 2007, 30).

The challenge of constructing a top-down international framework under which public, civic, and corporate governance work together is embedded in the Guiding Principles on Business and Human Rights as the Protect, Respect, and Remedy Framework, a set of "practical ways of integrating human rights concerns within enterprise risk management systems" (Ruggie 2014, 14). Though no international enforcement mechanism exists as yet to police violations and apply remedies, some progress has been made through efforts toward human rights due diligence and remedies in the form of grievance mechanisms; advocacy campaigns, civic engagements, and collectives in the form of labor and trade unions continue to push for fairness and equity in this unbalanced tripartite.

Chapter Eight

Strategies and Tools to Promote Workers' Rights in Global Supply Chains

LEARNING OBJECTIVES

By the end of the chapter, students will be able to:

1. Identify three approaches which help strengthen workers' rights
2. Identify five ways in which social media can be used to organize/ mobilize workers
3. Define the term shock doctrine
4. Discuss how corporate campaign strategies can orchestrate a resurgence of the trade unions

Key terms: Shock doctrine, Multi-stakeholder initiatives, Cross-border networks, Cross-border unions

Let's begin this chapter with a wrap-up of what we know so far about the status of workers' rights worldwide. In an increasingly competitive global climate, multinational corporations (MNCs) seek to remove all barriers in their global supply chains (GSCs) which prevent them from making the greatest profits. MNCs disengage with workers through offshoring, outsourcing, temporary or precariat labor, and subcontracting which allows them to skirt liability issues for workers' welfare. Corporations distance themselves from culpability from legal action by promoting policies of deregulation (because complying with regulations costs money), deunionization (because unions contractually have a say in the decision-making process), privatization (because corporations, which hold the status of personhood, adhere to the philosophy of free market capitalism), and dehumanization (which strips workers of their dignity and voice in the workplace). These neoliberal policies have increased the GSC of production which fueled the "growth of an immense information economy around the world, allowing companies to rapidly adjust supply to demand" (Center 2008, 19). These neoliberal trends push for economic reform in developing countries toward open markets and export economics which devastate local and regional poor economics by implementing austerity measures. The only winners here are MNCs.

Workers have absorbed the brunt of corporate strong arming. The majority of workers in the informal economy have no health/pension benefits, no sick/annual leave, or even the assurance their job will last through the day. They work for poverty wages. These workers face the uncertainty of maintaining any sort of living standard which could support them or their families. They have few resources, if any, on which to rely, so there is constant ambiguity and apprehension about the future. This uncertainty has created a generation of mobile migrant workers, particularly in the Global South, as well as "an array of complex immigration, infrastructure, and security issues for host-country governments" (Center 2008, 19). Workers in the formal economy aren't faring much better. The dismantling of workers' protections due to legislative and court decisions places these workers in precarious situations as well.

CHANGING THE DYNAMICS BETWEEN MNCS AND LABOR

Changing the dynamic between MNCs and labor is a monumental task. Pantland (2015) writes:

> Unions face unprecedented attacks from employers and right wing governments across the world. We face our biggest challenge for a generation. There is a concerted assault on all the conditions we have won, especially the social democratic reforms won after the Second World War. The global financial crisis unleased *shock doctrine*[1] capitalism that aims to fundamentally undermine the rights and conclusions of working people, and oversee a massive transfer of wealth and power to the elite. There is an ideological attack on trade unions and the public sector. The right has managed to shift the blame for the financial crisis from the banks to public sector workers and welfare programs. The result is that even people who were sympathetic to unions will often say we need to be "realistic" in the current economic climate. To challenge this, we need to take the union narrative to the public, and tell our story in clear, simple language. (9)

The theory of *shock doctrine*, as explained by Naomi Klein in her book, *The Shock Doctrine: The Rise of Disaster Capitalism* (2007), is an approach taken by orthodox free market capitalists who see privatization in the ownership and allocation of all goods and services as the one and only viable economic system to sustain a global economy. These hyperglobalists seize on natural and man-made disasters, which leave citizens homeless, jobless, and desperate, to impose austerity measures in the form of cuts to social welfare payments, privatization of state-owned resources, and anti-trade union rhetoric and the elimination of trade barriers. Popular movements to oppose these draconian measures are met with the appointment of free-marketers to official state decision-making positions, state force, torture, and the disappearances of protestors.

Articulating the connection between capitalizing on disasters to further the free market agenda, Klein (2007) expounds on three decades of fundamental changes in which "neoliberals have been 'perfecting this very strategy: waiting for a major crisis, then selling off pieces of the state to private players while citizens were still reeling from the shock, then quickly making the "reforms" permanent'" (Engler 2008, 119). Implementing this strategy at a national or global level victimizes a country's population three times: once when the disaster strikes; secondly when the neoliberal policies of privatization, deregulation, deunionization, and dehumanization are insidiously embedded in the policies and laws which are supposed to protect the citizenry; and lastly when the population is in survival mode and their resistance and dissent is met with torture and repression.

The history of this strategy provides many examples of state intervention to protect hyperglobalism through austerity measures, dismantling worker protections, and placing the burden of proof for violations on workers as individuals. Examples can be drawn from countries across the globe: the former Eastern Bloc countries following the collapse of the Soviet Union; the end of apartheid in South Africa; the Falkland War in 1982; Tiananmen Square Massacre in 1989; Asian Financial Crisis in 1997; Hurricane Mitch in 1998; collapse of the Soviet Union in 1991; and Great Recession in United States in 2007 to 2008. Let's look at three examples which represent different regional world blocs, have very different cultures, have far-reaching consequences for workers and consumers, solidified a global neoliberal agenda, and yet have yielded to shock doctrine as a means to ensure approaches to free market capitalism.

During the 1950s, the nationalist or socialist bent taken by the third world countries of Latin America proved problematic for European and American economics who often encountered barriers to trade with these countries. Western and European corporations, attuned to developing countries' cries for nationalization as a way to shore up their economies, began a public relations campaign touting nationalism as the first step toward communism, and, after WWII, railed against any country who would want that type of government. In the early 1950s, precursory efforts to squelch nationalism surfaced during the Eisenhower administration and the CIA who colluded to overthrow Mohammad Mossadegh in Iran and President Jacob Arbenz Guzman in Guatemala because of their nationalist tendencies. The fear was developmentalism and nationalism would root itself permanently in third world countries and disadvantage developed countries' corporate power. Thus began an effort by US free market thinkers to undermine developmentalism in Latin America. The preening of protégés to infiltrate Chile's institutions of higher learning during the 1960s by the Chicago School of Economics was an attempt to make Chile the poster child for free market reform in southern Latin America, sometimes known as the Southern Cone. When this effort at discounting nationalism as so left-leaning was rejected by Chile's democratically elected socialist president, Salvador Allendre, in 1973, the Nixon administration, fearful that Allendre's election would lead to decreased profits from US mining and other investments, devised a plan to undermine and speed the economic collapse of the Allendre government.

Insidiously, the United States propped up the overthrow of Allendre by introducing economic sanctions which crippled Allendre's ability to receive foreign direct investment and adequately supply the transfer of social payments to Chile's citizenry. The result was escalating unemployment, inflation, and increases in poverty. As jobless and starving citizens demanded reform, a bloody coup headed by General August Pinochet swept Allendre and government officials who supported him from office. Pinochet, supported by the United States, not only imposed sweeping economic reforms in Chile but quieted dissent through decades of torture and disappearances. Those who dissented were mostly workers and consumers who simply couldn't survive on poverty wages in an authoritarian regime, yet they were classified as terrorists, shot with water cannons when gathered together, yanked from their homes and job sites under the pretense of being subversives, and shot and butchered in the streets. The Pinochet regime sought to cleanse Chile of a culture of socialism and replace it with a culture of neoliberalism. This was nothing more than corporate-sponsored torture in an effort to open up markets in Chile and the Southern Cone to international trade and investment by developed economies. The coup in Chile was followed by a coup in Argentina.

The second example of shock doctrine application occurs in the aftermath of Hurricane Katrina, which left thousands of New Orleanians homeless and jobless. This natural disaster was seized as an opportunity by free-marketers, followers of the Freidman School of laissez-faire economics, to reshape devastated New Orleans communities as an oasis of private education, shored up by public funds in the form of government vouchers, to remake the landscape in a permanent image of free market capitalism at its best. Instead of funding the rebuilding of levees, homes, and communities through public infrastructure or public education, the Bush administration channeled millions of dollars into charter schools, a publicly-funded private institution of learning which privatizes public assets. This shift from providing free public education to all Americans to privatizing education to only those who could afford it is seen as an attempt to undo civil rights gains. The efficiency with which the transfer was achieved is notable as compared to the lengthy process of infrastructure rebuilding. Klein (2007) reflects New Orleans's public school teachers called this "an educational land grab" (6), and the American Enterprise Institute, an ultra-conservative think tank, noted, "Katrina accomplished in a day . . . what Louisiana school reformers couldn't do after years of trying" (de Rugy 2006).

A 2012–2013 study reflects the effectiveness of New Orleans's transition from private to public education has mixed results: indicators positively associated with student achievement were the addition of kindergarten as an entry grade, extended school years, and more experienced teachers while negative associations were more support services, higher percentages of teachers with graduate degrees, and higher student-teacher ratios (Wolf 2018). It seems proponents and opponents of New Orleans's charter schools claim victory here.

A third example of shock doctrine follows the fall of the Berlin Wall in 1989 and Lech Walesa's surge to power in Gdarisk, Poland which set off a wave of democratic and political reforms fomenting the possibility of worldwide political freedom and economic security. Frightened by urges and surges toward democratic reform, the People's Republic of China, a country trying to maintain a communist political form of government while engaging in capitalist economic reforms, saw hundreds of thousands of young people and workers roil into the streets in protests of lowered wages, job insecurity, and rising inequality between the rich and the poor. President Deng tore a page from Friedman's playbook and moved full force ahead, crushing what he deemed insurrection and dissidence against anything other than free market liberalism, by rolling tanks through Tiananmen Square in Beijing, China, and squelching any hopes for political democracy. The number of workers (and it was mostly workers who took to the streets) killed that day, June 3, 1989, by the People's Liberation Army is unclear but estimates range from "two thousand and seven thousand and the number of injured as high as thirty thousand" (Klein 2007, 237). Following weeks saw thousands of workers jailed and tortured and hundreds executed. The free market was then alive and well in China under the regime of Deng Xiaoping who claimed a victory for capitalism at the expense of political reform, and it only took a massacre of his own people to solidify capitalism.

THE SHOCK DOCTRINE'S APPLICATION PRODUCES FALLOUT FOR WORKERS AND CONSUMERS

Public disasters have always been focusing events which begat positive and negative changes for workers. The Great Depression birthed the New Deal, stalwart legislation which introduced a new era of labor-management relations and strengthened the middle class by shifting the balance of power to collectives and away from corporations: 9/11 witnessed the development of the Department of Homeland Security's preventative measures against further terrorists attacks designed to protect the citizenry at the expense of civil liberties; the 2007–2008 worldwide financial crisis beginning in the United States under the Bush administration, the domino effect of which saw global financial markets crash and left millions of workers jobless. The fallout to human life and survival from these disasters filters into the everyday life of workers worldwide through statutory and common law decisions. For instance, in May 2018, the US Supreme Court, in *Epic Systems Corp. v. Lewis*, handed a major blow to workers when they ruled workers can no longer collectively address work issues through class action lawsuits but only through arbitration suits brought by individuals (Gorsuch 2018). This so disadvantages individual workers who are unable to financially incur the cost of arbitration and advantages corporations who can now force workers to sign arbitration agreements as a condition of employment.

Another example of disadvantaging workers is the May 2018 ruling in Phnom Penh, Cambodia, which reclassifies workplace fainting/passing out resulting from "low levels of essential minerals in workers' blood" (Arenco 2018, n.p.) as accidents rather than a result of workplace conditions. The Cambodian Confederation of Unions (CCU) claims the decision to reclassify fainting as an individual health issue and not a workplace condition is an effort by the National Social Security Fund (NSSF) to slough off their responsibility for workers on the job and diminish workers' claims for fair compensation when falling ill at work. The CCU claims any incident occurring in the workplace during working hours is considered a workplace accident and therefore not the worker's fault (Arenco 2018). The small smattering of focusing events and their fallout on which I can focus in this text is but a microcosm of a broader strategy which uses natural and man-made disasters as catapults to further promote neoliberalism and supersize the inequality already in existence between corporations and their workers.

A POSITIVE STEP TO ADDRESS LIABILITY ISSUES IN THE EUROPEAN UNION (MAYBE)

By 2019, the European Commission, the executive arm of the European Union (EU) charged with promoting the interest of each EU country through proposing, implementing, and enforcing EU policies and legislation, will evaluate the current applicability of and determine how to interpret certain terms such as "'produce,' 'defect' or 'damage'" (Leadley 2018, n.p.) within the Product Liability Directive, a three-decades-old law designed to protect workers and consumers from accidents and faulty products respectively. The original intent of the Directive was to allow "the single market for goods to function smoothly and to reduce administrative burden" (European Commission 2018, n.p.) by giving consumers a conduit to address defective products should the product cause them harm or injury. Consumers remain at a disadvantage because they must still bear the cost of litigation and provide the causal link between injury and product defect, but at least there exists some redress for consumers.

Though the Directive tries to provide a balanced framework within the EU's legal system between corporations' abilities to produce new and innovative products for the market and the worker/consumer who is injured/harmed during the manufacture or use of the product, the burden of proof continues to lie with the worker who suffered the injury or the consumer harmed by a defective product. Constructing rules related to the manufacture and distribution of a product, such as artificial intelligence or pharmaceuticals, add complexity to the equation because various EU member states subscribe to different liability formulas.

The current and future Directive discussions involve addressing the challenges of new digital technologies such as robotics, artificial intelligence, and cybersecurity, the complexity of pharmaceuticals, and the upcycling or refurbishing of products. These discussions have the potential to move in two different directions. First, the discussions could further increase the gaps between corporate liability for production of faulty goods and services and workers' and consumers' ability to seek and receive compensation by moving in the direction of nonbinding policy instead of passing legislation to protect workers. This approach harmonizes with a global trend toward nonculpability for corporations who distance themselves from workers and workplaces within global supply chains. Secondly, the tension between corporations and workers is unlikely to weaken as the Directives undergo scrutiny, but, at this point, the Directives seem to provide an overarching international EU framework within which debate among member states can occur. A comprehensive liability framework should be constructed so that

> At the end of the day, a producer is and needs to be responsible for the product it puts into circulation, while injured persons need to be able to prove that damage has been caused by a defect. Both producers and consumers need to know what to expect from products in terms of safety through a clear safety frame work. (European Commission 2018, n.p.)

This might be the best opportunity for the European Commission to do what's right in equating the power balance between corporations and workers' rights and providing stability between producer and consumer. If the decisions lead to non-binding suggestions instead of obligatory remedy for workers, then the gap between corporations and workers within global supply chains will widen and worker protections and recourse will be weakened.

SETTING THE STAGE FOR RECOVERY IN A SHIFTING POLITICAL AND ECONOMIC LANDSCAPE

The economic and political environment resulting from three decades of a push for neoliberalism is an entrenched free market system upheld and promoted by most developed countries. The result reflects underdeveloped and undeveloped countries' dismal outlooks given they are held hostage to corporations by structural adjustment policies which cripple their economies, increase poverty and unemployment for their populations, and place workers in untenable positions when trying to negotiate wages, better working conditions, or dignity in the workplace with MNCs. There was a brief period from the late 1990s to early 2000s when resistance to neoliberalism took hold as evidenced by demonstrations and protests against the World Trade Organization (WTO) in Seattle, Washington, which came to be known as the Battle at Seattle, and against the World Bank's and the IMF's annual meeting in Washington, DC. This movement's resistance emanated from workers' and consumers' opposition to gutting the public sphere of money and self-worth to fatten the coffers of the elite, those few individuals and families who own 90 percent of the world's wealth. Klein (2017) writes, "We objected to the way transnational institutions were using trade deals to globalize pro-corporate policies that were extremely profitable for a small group of players but which were steadily devouring so much of what used to be public and commonly held: seeds, water rights public health care, and much more" (109).

The resistance to neoliberalism primarily focused on global trade deals which have grave economic consequences for workers' well-being and environmental concerns. The push-back seemed to be gaining ground when the World Trade Center Towers in Manhattan, New York, the United States's center of financial control, were hit by jets hijacked by terrorists. On September 11, 2001, everything then changed. Demonstrations and protests against neoliberalism stopped and were replaced by collective anger against terrorism. This turning point in our economic and political landscape signaled a regression away from the meta-movement against the free market and tamped down the world's resistance against Friedman's policy of neoliberalism. The Bush administration's response to 9/11 offered two messages to the world's population, both of which had free trade at the core. Standing in the rubble of the fallen World Trade Center Towers and speaking through a megaphone, President Bush said, "You are either with us or against us," forcing people to choose one side over the other, and when asked what people should do to help with recovery efforts, he responded, "Go shopping."

Nothing screams of a neoliberal agenda like urging citizens experiencing a disaster and fearing the future unknown to buy products or polarizing the population into two camps, those who support free market ideology and those who don't. Categorizing those who do not support neoliberal policies as "other" places them in a disposable category. This well-known strategy was successfully used in Nazi Germany's eradication of Jewish people because Jews were equated with disease-ridden rats, vermin, and lice. Certainly it is okay to eradicate that which will harm, infect, or kill you. Otherwise rational people can be moved to engage in horrific behaviors when fearful for their lives. It is not a far reach then to associate others different than the status quo of white, Anglo-Saxon, and protestant, whether they are Jewish, Muslim, Hispanic, Black, women, disabled, aged, or gay, as threats to one's survival simply because they are different.

The hope that filled the space during episodes of resistance, demonstrations, and protests in the late 1990s was subsumed by dread after 9/11 as populations feared they lacked control over their own safety from terrorists. Because most of the 9/11 terrorists were of Saudi descent, neoliberalists capitalized on this fear and discontent by equating terrorism with "other" and making Muslims the scapegoat for all things terrorist. It then was not a giant leap to equate immigrants, legal and undocumented, as a major problem during the 2007–2008 Great Recession, which saw 15,000 million workers in the United States alone lose their livelihoods and led to global social and institutional economic repercussions.

The 2008 presidential election of Barack Obama began a slow and steady economic recovery from the Great Recession and resulted in improved financial conditions, a reduced deficit, and lowered unemployment rates only to be undone in 2017 by the Trump administration which promotes capitalism on steroids by negating worker protection legislation, decimating the Environmental Protection Agency by undoing environmental protections, pushing for restrictions on immigration, threatening public dissent through divisive social media Tweets and public gatherings, sowing public distrust of governmental institutions like the Federal Bureau of Investigation and the Department of Justice, and providing examples of immoral and indecent behavior unbefitting the office of the president of the United States.

The inauguration of the Trump administration in 2017 embodied the malcontent primarily felt by white middle class Americans who had seen their jobs disappear and prospects for the future vanish. The rallying cry of the Trump campaign, "Make America Great Again," was really code for "make America white again," a time and feeling when "other" was subordinated to white privilege and immediately squelched when it reared its ugly head. This became and is currently the polarized "us against them" culture in which we live. It is the "illusion of control through bashing immigrants, vilifying Muslims, and degrading women" (Klein 2017, 113) that emboldens neoconservatives and white supremacists to feel they have the blessing of the supreme leader sitting in the White House.

Resistance to Trump's xenophobic, homophobic, anti-immigrant, anti-women, and anti-union policies takes the form of street marches, counter-demonstrations at rallies, and voter registration drives in hopes of organizing a protracted backlash against Trumpism at the ballot box. Yet, for all the countless protests with millions of people taking to the streets, Trump has successfully moved the needle supporting neoliberalism to the far right by dismantling worker protections via the courts and statutory legislation, deregulating environmental protections, and fostering job growth abroad instead of in the United States.

POTENTIAL AVENUES OF HOPE TO PROTECT WORKERS

Changing business as usual is no small task. The job calls for restructuring a global power arrangement from one where all power resides with the corporation to one which shares power with and values workers and their labor. This means predicating the global economic structure on values and not profits. Our current system is based on transitioning resources from the public to the private, extracting and depleting natural resources from the land, and sucking labor and dignity from workers. This is unstainable. Capitalism is an economic system which implodes upon itself. The nature of capitalism is based on consumption which requires the endless use of resources, a finite commodity. Once the resources are gone, the entire economy crashes. We, as global citizens, must rethink our use of resources and move toward a sustainable system which is in the best long-term interest of the populations and the planet. This requires overturning laws favoring corporate power through grassroots, bottom-up activism which translates into worker protection legislation and enforcement. All the laws on the books mean little if unaccompanied by enforcement practices. There are three approaches to making changes which hold out some hope of workers recovering their rights in the global market place and translating those changes into law. These are corporate campaigns, soft law agreements, and technology.

Corporate Campaigns

Unions struggle to maintain power within a globalized world in which MNCs have unprecedented power (Juravich 2007). Old methods of bargaining and organizing have been compromised through legislation and court decisions empowering the economic power structure to shift toward management; unions have been weakened, and workers' rights have systematically been destroyed through common and statutory law. In this new globalization environment of MNCs, labor must find some way of recouping resources, increasing membership, and regaining power through unions and the collective if workers and the planet are to survive.

The labor movement has been pondering how best to orchestrate this resurgence for decades. The current trend to regain power is through strategic comprehensive campaigns, sometimes known as corporate research, corporate campaigns, strategic campaigns, or coordinated campaigns. Juravich (2007) writes that to be successful, "unions need to gain a comprehensive understanding of the firm and the industry in which it is situated" (1). They can then use this information to strategize on the best way to counter the employer's diversified and multi-faceted approach to maintain power. This could be achieved through collectives of cross-border networks and cross-border unions (Coe 2008; Helfen 2013).

Cross-border networks are multi-unions representing workers in different countries who join together to form a network of workers sharing common interests such as health and safety standards and respect for organizing and bargaining rights (Lee 2016). More participation from workers including contractors, precariat workers, and upstream/downstream workers in the supply chains in these networks means power is generated from the bottom up and can have a significant effect on the balance of power between labor and management.

Cross-border unions are composed of global unions or national unions who band together to represent workers worldwide. Generally the union with the most members or the union in the multinational corporation's home country takes on the leadership position for the cross-border union. The communication between these unions, their meeting times, and their governance varies depending on their needs. Cross-border unions may meet periodically or on a need-to-meet basis, may or may not have good relationships with the corporations in which they work, and may or may not meet face to face. The power of cross-border unions is their ability to "build solidarity, exchange information and develop programs of action" (Lee 2016, 2). They can identify common concerns which can form a common global bargaining strategy which could include a corporate campaign against the corporation and its suppliers, plan and carry out a coordinated day(s) of action(s) at companies' worksites, organize solidarity in response to violations of human/

environmental rights, and put pressure on the company through protests at shareholders' meetings (Lee 2016). To be effective, cross-border unions need resources. That means they must have funding which can be gleaned from union members, support groups, or from the multinational corporation itself.

Ron Oswald, General Secretary of the Global Union Federation that organizes the United Food, Farm and Hotel Workers Worldwide (IUF), writes that the most important recognition union members need is the right to organize, form a union, and negotiate. Without these rights, workers have no voice in their work life and remain at the mercy of their employer. The Global Union Federation is then an organization which works toward securing a worker's fundamental right to organize, join a union, and bargain. He explains the campaign is a useful tool in opening up a "space to exercise and access rights" (Oswald 2016, 1) and the absence of the campaign suggests acquiesce/acceptance that workers' rights should be denied. Oswald (2016) continues:

> The wider agenda for us is essentially to force companies to recognize that unions are organized internationally and to sit down with those unions at an international level through a global union federation and essentially negotiate how the workers access the rights that they have, that are often denied. Normally we prefer to do that through a negotiation across the table, but there are of course many companies who refuse to negotiate, who refuse to open that conversation and that means very often that a campaign is often designed to change that position. A campaign is often to get a company to the bargaining table at the international level so that we can exercise influence over their local management to allow our members to access the rights that they obviously have. (1)
>
> The Global Union Federation then acts as an organization to which members who choose to belong receive the benefits of the organization.

Kate Bronfenbrenner (2016), an expert in how workers and unions win comprehensive campaigns against transnational corporations, concludes there is a greater likelihood of success when corporate strategy encompasses three elements:

1. Strategic corporate research
2. Escalating, multifaceted campaigns that build on research
3. Involvement of rank-and-file workers and their allies in every aspect of the campaign

Bronfenbrenner (2016) gives examples of successfully using corporate strategy in the "victories of rubber workers at Bridgestone plantations in Liberia, UPS workers in Turkey, and security guards at GS4 in South Africa" (1).

These campaigns created a SWOT analysis (strengths/weaknesses/opportunities/threats) which readies the union to develop a comprehensive view of the company including the firms' profit centers, growth strategies, decision makers, key relationships, and supply chains (Bronfenbrenner 2016). Information gathering kick starts the process by a research team who talks to all involved stakeholders and then completes a critique of the company focusing on five areas where union power has the greatest potential for impact: profit centers, segments of the company that generate the highest profits; growth strategies, the firm's plans for increasing future sales and market share through acquisitions, e-commerce, regional expansion, new product lines, and new businesses; supply chains, the vulnerability of a firm because of its placement within the supply chain; decision makers, internal/external individuals essential to the firm's ability to make profit, execute growth strategies, and recognize/settle with the union; and key relationships, which impact the firm's business strategy and can resolve issues with the union. The success or failure of the corporate campaign lies in the strength of these assessments and the union's ability to maintain solidarity throughout the campaign. Though not an easy task, if done well, comprehensive campaigns can take on and win against TNCs (Bronfenbrenner 2016).

Conducting a comprehensive campaign is difficult. There is much publicly available information about firms, but there is scant information on how to design a useful framework for accessing that information. One resource for data concerning the structure and design of a comprehensive strategy is the Strategic Corporate Research website. Another resource is the Solidarity Center, a nonprofit organization providing assistance to workers building democratic and independent trade unions around the world.

Soft Law Agreements

The pressure on MNCs to protect and respect workers' rights in a growing global economy leads to new strategies which promote accountability. Known as *soft law agreements*, these mechanisms include international human rights law, international framework agreements, multi-lateral government instruments for companies, multi-stakeholder cooperation, global trade union initiatives (GUF), declarations of principles, codes of conduct, and mission statements. These non-binding, unenforceable voluntary approaches used by corporations are, in theory, promising methods for worker protections. In reality, though, they have no enforcement power, and, for the most part, serve as public relations campaigns to shore up a company's brand. The most popular form of public relations has been *corporate social responsibility* (CSR). Voluntary in nature, "it has serious shortcoming as a tool to improve the conditions of workers worldwide" (Center 2008, 187), yet has the potential to influence broader coalitions pushing for human and environmental rights.

Emerging in the 1970s, corporate social responsibility developed as a result of multilateral government efforts, concerns of international trade unions, companies, non-governmental organizations (NGOs), and organizations outside of corporations such as civil society groups and social auditors who were concerned about the way workers, especially in the Global South, were being treated. This was a departure from the traditional ways in which concerns were being raised about workers' welfare and their rights which were usually in the purview of trade unions. Trade unions are/were "the first line of defense against violations of worker rights and the primary advocates for freedom of association for workers throughout the world" (Center 2008, 187).

Corporate codes multiplied in the 1990s and were seen as ineffective because corporations' efforts to police themselves were ineffective; new codes called *multi-stakeholder initiatives* (MSIs) proliferated. MSIs involve multiple parties, governments, the private section, and civil society, participating in the formulation of policy which holds corporations accountable, allows collective bargaining to be protected and enforced, and strengthens the ability of workers to freely associate with unions. "Different ways of assessing compliance emerged in the form of monitoring, verification, and certification systems" (Center 2008, 202). The lack of universal standards, terms, and agreements complicated the way these initiatives were monitored and verified. Stiffer auditing and transparency mechanisms were demanded. As a result of ineffective corporate social responsibility, various organizations have joined together to demand corporations treat workers fairly and humanely.

CSR, intended to moderate corporate greed, is only effective as a complement to binding law because it cannot be enforced. Corporations use CSR as a façade to promote their compliance with and loyalty to the protection of workers' rights, but, in reality, CSR is little more than a cover. Countries should first and foremost work to put enforceable legislative and regulatory policies in place which protect workers and then work with corporations who espouse CSR. Though CSR is unenforceable within the law, it does have the power in the court of public opinion to put pressure on corporations to treat workers more humanely.

The idea of CSR is not all negative. International human rights law is becoming more robust. Though not always enforceable, the idea of treating workers fairly is getting traction. There currently are three regional treaty-based human rights systems—European, Inter-American (both North and South America), and African, in which member nations seek to address workers' rights issues and are enforced by each country's government. When violations of workers' rights occur, the worker(s) seek remedy from the government and not a corporation. These foundational rights include the right to humane treatment, personal liberty, a fair trial, privacy, property, freedom of conscience, religion, thought, and expressions, the right to assembly, and equal protection under the law.

Submitting complaints and receiving resolution for complaints in these regional treaty-based human rights systems is still very difficult, but at least their existence suggests a recognition that protecting workers' rights is important as a long-term solution for continued growth in the market. For a fuller discussion on CSR, see chapter 5 of this text.

Technology

Trade union activists are front line change agents in the battle to protect workers' rights. In an interconnected world in which much communication is digital, social media is one tool which can inform/reach people with little outside interference. Incorporating social media as a tool for strategizing change allows diverse and grassroots voices, which might otherwise not be heard, to provide input for solutions. Social media "gives us the space to tell our own stories in our own words, and also learn about other people's struggles without the mediation of the mainstream media" (Pantland 2015).

Having said that, it is important for union members to use social media responsibly when presenting a different picture of the workplace than that espoused by their union. The official line espoused by the union might be different than that of the picket line, yet social media comments which counter the official stance of the union may be considered inauthentic, so it is worth noting the importance of presenting a united front when dealing with external organizations. The first line of defense for union members is to be safe at work, and the prying eyes of employers who monitor their employees' social media pages strongly suggests union members should never identify their employer by name or nuance. Also following company policy against unauthorized computer use at work or internet and social media policies against posting online about work-related issues may have consequences for employees, so be aware of these policies, and post nothing which could jeopardize one's job.

Creating decent work in global supply chains requires a deep understanding of the way in which workers' stories are presented. Most people used to receive their news about the world through established media (TV, newspapers, and/or radio) which may, depending upon the source of the funding, present a slanted picture of workers' plight. The trend now is for people to receive their news through social networks. The proliferation of mobile devices provides a new/different conduit through which information is disseminated. According to Cherisse Gasana from Industriall Global Union (2016), there are five things to know when using social media: know your audience, learn by doing, catch people's attention, use hashtags, and build networks.

One of the first things we're taught in all writing and public speaking courses is to know one's audience. The goal of the written or spoken word is to impart some information, sway an opinion, or convince your audience to take some action. So each written or oral message should be tailored to a specific group, using jargon, language, and level of complexity commensurate with the audience's educational, career-oriented, political, geographical, and age-appropriate level.

Secondly, instant communication via social media allows instant feedback. No longer do organizers or researchers have to wait days or weeks to know if their messages are resonating with their audience. If the message is generating negative comments, tweak the message until positive response is generated. Social media success can be knowable in a heartbeat.

Thirdly, it is important to catch people's attention. The first sentence in Tony Morrison's book, *Paradise,* is "They shot the white girl first." Who wouldn't want to continue reading this novel to find out why this happened, to whom did it happen, and what caused this to happen? Often known as the "hook," the initial sentence or word in written or oral communication draws in the audience and allows the writer to share power stories of abuse and exploitation, which capitalize on those stories by using words or images (the hook) which portray workers' substandard/hazardous working conditions, tell a specific worker's story to emphasize the plight (engage), and then encourage the audience to do something like contribute to a fund, send an email, etc. to correct a horrible situation (action). This way the audience is invested in the outcome of the situation and has some closure. Though Morrison's 800-page novel is a long way from a tweet or an instant message on Snapchat or Instagram, the theory behind the hook is the same.

Also maintain a social presence portal through which all information can be accessed such as an organizational website which maintains current and credible information. Pay particular attention to the drivers to the website such as Twitter, Facebook, Instagram, and/or Snapchat (or other social media accounts). It is important to remember that in the current media frenzy, fake news is everywhere, so finding credible information from reliable sources is paramount. Being consistent, engaging, and informative is essential to maintain credibility (Gasana 2016). The best, most informative, well-designed website on the planet does little good if no one visits it, so a multi-pronged approach moving people to the website is important.

Fourth, use hashtags as a way to silo or organize information so users can easily track topics. Keep the hashtag short and to the point. #Blacklivesmatter or #FastFoodGlobal. It is cleaner for the organization to coordinate the use of the same hashtag for clarity.

Lastly, build networks and coalitions of like-minded people who share concern over similar causes to get together (digitally or in person) and broaden their listserves through sharing data.

There are several good recommendations for union-affiliated persons when using social media as a platform for communication. Pantland (2015) cautions users of social media within a unionized context to follow some rules for union activism. Remember, your post doesn't recede into a black hole and remain visible forever. The goal is to convince others your message is in the long-term best interest of workers and the environment and your best chance of doing this requires tact, patience, and diplomacy. This means not airing grievances (though there are many grievances to be aired), and building a case from facts, not opinions. Always comply with Netiquette (the internet's acceptable communication style) and never be defamatory. Rules for Standard English use apply when posting online just as they do when writing for hard copy. Think before posting: social media posts can be copied and reposted so always be conscious of how posts might be shared by others for good or nefarious purposes. Use words and images carefully. One can be legally accountable for one's posts. Post wisely.

The ability to use the internet in working environments presents the ever present challenges of misuse at work. Never use company property for personal gain even if the property (computers, mobile devises, and so forth) is readily available; using social media at work while on company time has no positive results for workers. Using social media to insinuate negativity about the firm when "not on the clock" may have serious consequences for workers as well because workers are often considered representatives of the firm. Know and adhere to the workplace policy on social media.

CONCLUSION

It doesn't have to be this way. I once heard Carl Bernstein, a political commentator and journalist who broke open the Watergate scandal in the 1970s, in an appearance on the Bill Maher show say, "The hope is in the resistance." I have since thought long and hard about that statement and believe it sums up the approach and action necessary to counter corporate power's immense hold over workers. I include that phrase (with credit to Mr. Bernstein of course) in my email signature. The hope for workers worldwide whether economic, social, or political is from the bottom up, a groundswell of grassroots activism which encompasses the collective and becomes a movement of mass solidarity as strong and powerful as any corporate force in existence.

Though the power dynamic between workers and corporations is extremely slanted toward MNCs, workers are not without some ability to change the equation. Corporate campaigns, soft law agreements, and technology, strategically used, can move toward altering a free market capitalist economic system which only recognizes and gives credence to corporate greed and replace it with corporate responsibility. The predilection for our world in the last three decades has been to focus on short-term fixes which increase profits for corporations and disadvantage workers and the environment. This approach requires a global reliance on past experiences and institutional memories based on a "we've always done it that way" mentality. It is a lopsided, zero-sum, winner-take-all method which advantages the few and disadvantages the many. Though the power structure is greatly tilted toward MNCs, workers are not without some leverage if they join together in solidarity through a collective, find common ground on which to build their resistance, and work through an international framework which supports human and environmental rights for all workers. As collectives of workers and consumers join together in workplaces, villages, states, and regional blocks, power can shift, corporations can be tamed, and workers' lives can be changed for the better.

NOTE

1. The "shock doctrine" is a term coined by Naomi Klein in her book by the same term. It refers to using crisis—wars, recessions, and natural disasters—to force through extremist neoliberal policies that would not be accepted in normal times. She theorizes that in crisis, the population is too bewildered to mount an effective opposition, and politicians take advantage of this (Pantland 2015, 9).

Glossary

ACT (Action, Collaboration, Transformation): a global framework consisting of relevant stakeholders who support living wages in the garment industry with a scaled up, sustainable, industry-wide approach

Agenda 21: a voluntary action plan for sustainable environmental development created during the Earth Summit, United Nations Conference on Environment and Development (UNCED) in Rio de Janeiro, Brazil, in 1992 and signed by 178 countries

American Federation of Labor and Congress of Industrial Organization (AFL-CIO): a federation of national and international trade unions which seeks to improve workers' wages, job security, and dignity in the workplace

Arab Spring: a series of antigovernment and anti-corruption protests beginning in 2010 in the Middle East and North African countries

associational power: the capacity to effect change via connections with other groups or organizations such as coalitions

at-will employment contract: an unwritten contract between labor and management in which management can be hired/fired for any reason and in which labor can quit at will

Bangladesh Accord on Fire and Building Safety: a legally-binding agreement between global unions and brands to work for safety and health in the garment industry

Bangladesh Rena Plaza collapse: a structural failure of the Rena Plaza building in Savar Upazila, Bangladesh, on April 24, 2013, which killed 1,134 workers and injured thousands more

bespoke goods: products made to consumer specifications

Big Labor: the term applied to large labor unions or labor unions as a collective who wield economic, political, or social clout

binding laws: a legal phrase which means a conscious decision made by parties who agree to comply with the terms of a contract with sanctions for non-compliance

bonded labor: see economic debt bondage

brand engagement: an aspect of brand management which attempts to form an emotional/rational bond between a consumer and a brand in order to extract loyalty from the consumer

branding: associating an image or design with a controlling interest such as a corporation

Business for Social Compliance Initiative: an international business-driven initiative proposed in 2003 by the European Union Commission to govern working and environmental conditions in global supply chains

Business for Social Compliance Initiative Code of Conduct: worker and environmental protections built on the ILO conventions and recommendations

buyer-driven commodity chain(s): a global value chain in which the buyer has the power to affect decisions made by producers through design and marketing functions

capitalism: an economic/political system based on private ownership and private allocation of goods and services

captive governance: a control system utilized by major buyers to compel small firms to compete against each other in order to lower major buyers' costs

capture fisheries: an area associated with fish/aquatic life harvested for commercial value

certiorari: a higher court's order which reviews a lower court's order

Channel Industries Mutual Aid Association: a coalition of emergency responders, firefighters, and rescue personnel which provides mutual assistance to man-made, natural, or war emergencies along the Houston Ship Channel near Pasadena, Texas

charter school: a publicly funded private institution of learning which operates independently of public schooling; an example of privatization of public assets

circular obligation: a form of debt bondage used to keep workers in forced labor situations requiring payment of fees/charges to third-party intermediaries for procuring work

civil action: a non-criminal lawsuit entered into by plaintiffs to protect or enforce their private rights

classical liberalism: a political ideology which emphasizes freedom from government interference in religion, speech, assembly, and press

collective bargaining agreement: a contract between labor and management which stipulates the terms and conditions under which they will work for some specified period of time

commons: a legal term for common or shared land or space

comparative advantage: the ability to produce a good/service at the lowest opportunity cost (the value of what is given up)

competitive advantage: the superiority or leverage of a firm over its competitor through producing one unit of product or service at the least cost

compulsion by necessity: the illusion of choice workers face when their prospects for economic and social mobility are limited or nonexistent

consumer-driven commodity chains: see buyer-driven commodity chains(s)

contract at will: a contractual relationship between an employee and an employer in which an employee can be terminated for any reason and without warning or can quit without warning

convention: a pact or agreement between two or more countries stipulating a rule or policy

core labor standards: a basic set of principles agreed to by international actors which protect basic worker rights, enhance job security, and improve the terms of employment

corporate campaigns: a comprehensive strategy to explore/investigate/assess every facet of a corporation in order to obtain strategic advantage in negotiating a collective bargaining contract

corporate codes of conduct: a set of rules created by a corporation which sets parameters for employee behavior in and outside the workplace

corporate governance: the internal rules and policies which guide a corporations' day-to-day activities

corporate social responsibility: a firm's effort to assess and take responsibility for the effects the firm has on society and the environment

craft production: a specialized form of work organization in a pre-industrialized world in which master craftsmen had control of the work process in producing goods and services

creative destruction: an economic concept in which the competitiveness of firms must destroy old economic orders (either through war, economic crisis, or dereliction) in order to create new wealth (also known as Schumpeter's gale)

cross-border networks: linkages between various multi-unions in different countries who share a common interest in protecting workers' rights through collectives

cross-border unions: global or national unions who band together to support workers worldwide

culpability: responsibility or accountability, guilt, or blame for an illegal action

cultural hegemony: the domination of the ruling over society through manipulation of culture via institutions, values, and norms

debt bondage: a financial obligation to keep workers in forced labor situations requiring some form of payment in return for job security

dependency theory: the concept that underdeveloped countries feed developed countries resources to their own detriment

deregulation: the removal of government barriers to the operation of an organization

digital revolution: a shift from analogue technology to digital technology thought to have begun during the 1950s with the invention of the transistor allowing firms to compete on a global scale

disaster: a sudden event, an accident, or a natural occurrence which causes enormous damage, injury, or loss of life

domination by consent: the working classes' identification with elite powerbrokers who use ideology to maintain control over values and norms in the lives of working people

downstream suppliers: firms in the supply chain which distribute, ship, or sell a product after it is manufactured

due diligence: reasonable steps taken to address a firm's human and environmental impacts and promote responsible firm behavior

duty of vigilance bill: a French law requiring French companies to establish and implement due diligence measures to identify and prevent human rights violations and environmental damages in connection with their operations

economic debt bondage: the unwritten contract between an employee and an employer in which the workers are compelled to work for some period of time to repay a debt or for their freedom

economics of scale: the cost advantages firms use to produce more goods at the lowest price point

embedded liberalism: an ideology held from WWII to 1970 in which the legitimacy of international markets was reconciled to social values and shared institutional practices

endogeneity: a problem in a statistical model when there is a correlation between an x variable and an error term in the model

environmental degradation: deterioration of natural resources and destruction of the eco-systems including habitat, wildlife, and pollution

European Coalition for Corporate Justice: a platform which advocates for European guarantees of corporate accountability and transparency in global supply chains to ensure justice for victims of corporate malpractice

European Commission: a politically independent executive arm of the EU consisting of commissioners from each EU member state who promotes EU interest by proposing, implementing, and enforcing legislation

European Corporate Social Responsibility Framework: a non-binding self-policing framework allowing firms to monitor and enforce their own environmental and working conditions

European Union: an international collection of political and economic member states which govern common economic, social, and security policies created by the Maastricht Treaty in 1993 to enhance Europe's political and economic integration

export processing zone: (also known as free trade zones) a special economic area in a developing country created to offer incentives such as reduced tariffs in order to promote economic growth and attract foreign investment

expropriation: the action of an authority or a state to take property away from an owner and give it to the state

extractiavism: the large-scale removal of natural resources for the purpose of exporting raw material

extraterritoriality: the state of exemption from local law jurisdiction as a result of diplomatic negotiations

fair trade: a social movement to help Global South producers gain access to markets, promote sustainable farming, and receive better prices for their products through better trading conditions and sustainable farming

federal direct investment: an investment of a firm in one country into the firm of another country in order to influence or control the foreign firm's profits.

fixed duration contract: a contractual relationship between employer/employee for a fixed or set amount of time

flag ships: fishing vessels operating under a country's flag

Flexible Specialization theory: the term, coined by Adam Smith in his *Wealth of Nations*, is the idea that breaking apart large jobs into smaller components allows workers to perform based on their skills, abilities, and knowledge and contributes to the efficiency of the production process and, therefore, economies of scale

focusing event: an unexpected, uncommon, harmful occurrence which imperils workers' health and safety, is geographically concentrated, and attention grabbing

forced labor: any work/service in which humans are conscripted, receive little to no pay, and for which punishment is meted for noncompliance

Fordism: a system of mass production, pioneered in the early 1900s by Henry Ford, which introduced the assembly line into production methods

formal economy: all jobs which have standardized hours, wages, and benefits subject to taxation

Foxconn: Taiwanese multinational electronics corporation; also known as Hon Hai Precision Industry Co. Ltc.; world's largest electronics manufacture

free trade zones: see export processing zone

freedom of association: the right to join or leave a union and collective bargaining

Friedman, Milton: an American conservative economist who promoted free market capitalism at all costs

G20: an international forum of the leading industrialized and emerging economics formed in 1999 for the purpose of promoting international financial stability

General Agreement on Tariffs and Trade: trade agreement signed in 1947 by twenty-three countries to reduce trade barriers in order to increase global trade; it was replaced in 1995 by the World Trade Organization

German strategy of co-determination: a strategy to comingle the economic and social purposes of a firm by broadening the firm's decision-making scope to include all stakeholders such as workers, investors, management, and consumers; the goal is to make human capital investments profitable and reward employee loyalty with decision-making power

Glass-Steagall Act of 1933: legislation signed into law during the Franklin Roosevelt administration known as the Banking Act of 1933 which prohibited banks from speculative investments thought to be a cause of the Stock Market Crash of 1929; the Act separated investment banking from commercial banking and diverted investments into agriculture, industry, and commerce; it was repealed with the passage of the Gramm-Leachy-Bliley Act of 1999

global capital theory: the concept of a flexible global system which allows corporations to dictate financial operations across borders

global framework agreement: an instrument negotiated between multinational corporation(s) and a global union federation in which they agree to respect the labor standards of the countries in which they do business (also known as international framework agreements)

global governance: rule making on a global scale orchestrated by transnational actors managing transnational processes

global production network: a worldwide web of interconnected functions, operations, and transactions necessary to produce, deliver, and consume goods and services

global supply chain: a network of local, regional, national, and international firms who produce and distribute goods and services worldwide (also see global value chain and global production networks)

Global Union Federation: an international federation of trade unions organizing in specific industrial sectors or occupational groups

global value chain: a set of interrelated activities a specific firm uses to create a competitive advantage (often used interchangeably with global supply chain and global production network)

Golden Age of Labor: a period between 1935's passage of the National Labor Relations Act and 1947's passage of the Taft Hartley Act when labor's power was greater than corporate power

governance: the power to allow/constrain behavior and activity of stakeholders to set/enforce implicit or explicit rules

Gramsci, Antonio: an Italian Marxist, philosopher, and politician credited with the theory of cultural hegemony which says the capitalist ruling class maintains power through cultural institutions rather than through violence and economic force

gray economy: see informal economy

Great Recession of 2007–2008: a period of economic decline caused by toxic mortgage lending, lax government oversight of financial institutions, and financial firms incurring too much debt; it is considered the biggest financial crisis since the Great Depression of 1929

gross domestic product: the total value of all goods/services produced in a country

Guiding Principles on Business and Human Rights: the United Nation's strategy for implementing the Protect, Respect, and Remedy Framework through state, corporate, and access remedy foundational and operational principles

Hague Institute for Innovation of Law (HiiL): an international not-for-profit social enterprise which collects and makes available data relating to the needs and satisfaction of justice system users

hidden economy: see informal economy

hierarchy value chain: top to bottom chain of command characterized by vertical integration in-house; firms control their own inputs and outputs within their own structure

homeworkers: subcontracted workers, primarily in the informal economies of electronics, textiles, and piece-rate goods, who have no legal status, no assurance of pay, and no social/legal protections

horizontal foreign direct investment: the arrangement of investments into duplicate firms within two or more countries in which sales occur domestically

human bondage: see human slavery

Human Rights Council: a United Nations international body charged with strengthening the protection and promotion of human rights (formerly known as the United Nations Commission on Human Rights)

human slavery: the conscription of humans into work for which they receive no/little pay, have no benefits, and continue the work for fear of repercussions

human trafficking: modern-day slavery involving the use of force, fraud, or coercion to obtain some type of labor or commercial sexual exploitation

hyperglobalist: individuals who support unfettered free market capitalism

impact litigation: see strategic litigation

industrial governance: an umbrella structure coordinated by stakeholders in global value chains which guides and directs international economic behaviors in an effort to coordinate transactions between buyers and sellers

industrial policy: a country's strategic effort to increase its manufacturing efforts

Industrial Revolution: a period of time between 1820 and 1870 in which the production of goods and services moved from the home to the factory and was brought about by technological innovations like steam power and mass goods production

Industriall: an international trade union to defend workers' rights, build union power, confront global capital, fight precarious work, and promote sustainable industrial policy

industry-wide collective bargaining: an industrial scale agreement between workers' representatives and employers built on establishing industry-appropriate wage mechanisms and other conditions of employment

informal economy: all jobs which operate outside formal contracts, have no set hours or benefits, and untaxed wages not counted in the gross domestic product

insecurity-and-risk-transfer: the shift of employment obligations and liabilities from the corporation to various lower points with workers as the endpoint in global supply chains

institutional power: the capacity to effect change in institutions such as governments, corporations, or other entities through elections, rule or policy making, or legislation

institutional vitality: the capacity of an organization's flexibility to adjust to new contexts and situations

International Chamber of Commerce: an international organization of businesses which seeks to promote international trade and investment as vehicles of growth and prosperity

international framework agreements: see global framework agreement

international investment agreements: an agreement between countries to invest internationally in order to diversify, spread risk, and shore up investment portfolios which protect, promote, and liberalize investments; cross-border treaties protecting, promoting, and liberalizing cross-border investments

International Labour Organization: a tripartite United Nations agency founded in 1919 which collaborates with governments, workers, and employers of 187 member states to set labor standards and develop policies and programs which promote decent work for everyone

International Labour Organization's Core Labor Standards: five minimum standards set by the ILO that should be a right for every worker: freedom of association, the right to collective bargaining, elimination of forced and compulsory labor, abolition of child labor, and elimination of discrimination in employment and occupation

International Ladies Garment Workers' Union: the largest union representing the US/Canadian women's garment industry as a result of the merger of New York City garment workers unions in 1900; it merged with the Amalgamated Clothing and Textile Workers Union to form UNITE in 1995

International Monetary Fund: an international financial institution created after WWII which fosters monetary cooperation and makes loans to developing countries in order to create financial stability in the global market

International Trade Union Confederation: an international organization which promotes and defends workers' rights and interests and seeks to strengthen workers' power through advocacy campaigns among major global institutions and trade unions

Interstate Commerce Act: legislation signed into law by the Cleveland administration in 1887 to control railroads and their unfair business practices

Interstate Commerce Commission: a five-member regulatory agency enforcement board charged with regulating railroad operations

investor: an individual or organization which puts money into some project which will provide a monetary return in the form of profits

Jobber's agreement: a contractual relationship in the apparel industry between a firm who designs and sells apparel (known as a jobber) and those unions/workers who produce the apparel; the contract stipulates the jobber use only union workers, provide safe working conditions, and decent wages

Just in Time model: a work organization model of manufacturing which aims at reducing production time and warehouse inventory

Kafala system: a system of monitoring migrant workers in construction and domestic industries in Middle Eastern countries

Keynesian economics: an economic theory developed by Keynes in 1936 which posits government intervention in the market is necessary to shore up demand for goods, the driving economic force; it supports expansionary fiscal policy and government spending

Kondratieff, Nickolai: a Soviet economist, author of *The Major Economic Cycles* (1925), first observed long wave theory as an explanation of changes in economies

Kondratieff theory: an approach suggesting economies go through four long cycles or waves from forty to sixty years in length which are influenced by natural events, inequity, opportunity, and social freedoms (inflation, stagflation, beneficial deflation, and deflation)

labor process theory: a way of thinking about work organization under capitalism and how labor is used to add value to a good or service

laissez-faire market: an economic approach which fosters the free market minus government intervention

lean manufacturing: a production method focusing on efficiency and waste minimization

least developed country: a low-income country with low levels of human assets/capital representing the poorest/weakest segment of the international community, unable to embrace sustainable development because of structural impediments, and highly vulnerable to economic and environmental shocks

living wage: a wage which supports an adequate living standard

long wave theory: an idea credited to Kondratieff, a Russian economics professor, that developments in technology rule fifty to sixty year economic cycles

Maquila Solidarity Network: a women's and labor organization formed to support the rights of workers in GSCs to improve wages, working conditions, and voice in the workplace

market: place where buyers and sellers come together

market governance: external institutions which guide and direct exchanges between buyers and sellers in local, regional, and international markets

minimum wage: the lowest wage legally permitted by a government and generally lower than a living wage

modernization theory: a concept which describes the progressive transition from a traditional society to a modern society

modular governance: a control system using standardized machinery in which firms take responsibility for the products made to customers' specification

multilateralism: principle of alliances between three or more governments seeking to achieve a goal

multinational corporation: an international corporation with assets in at least two countries which focuses on adapting products/services to an individual local market/consumer such as McDonalds, Proctor & Gamble, Seven-Eleven, or Unilever

multinational initiatives: efforts to bring governments, civil society, and private firms together to address challenging problems which one party alone cannot solve

natural soldiering: the tendency to slow down or otherwise interrupt the work flow process

netiquette: the Internet's acceptable and correct communication style

New Deal: a series of programs and government intervention under the Franklin Roosevelt administration to restore the US economy after the Great Depression of 1929

new international division of labor: the geographic reorganization or shift of production in the division of labor from hierarchical to horizontal and from developed countries to developing or undeveloped countries

non-culpability: not guilty or free of blame

non-governmental organization: a local, national, or international non-profit organization founded to effect some change in government, social, civic, or cultural institutions

Office of Economic and Cooperative Development: an intergovernmental organization created to stimulate world economic progress and trade

offshore financial centers: small, lower-taxed jurisdictions attractive to off-shore corporate and commercial investors

planned obsolescence: producing goods and products which quickly become obsolete through design changes, use of non-durable inputs, or termination of replacement parts, requiring frequent replacement

point of equilibrium: the point at which a buyer and seller in the market conclude a transaction

positive transition effect: the switch for workers who move from an informal economy to a formal economy with worker protections in the form of trade unions

post-Fordism: a period between the 1940s and 1970s characterized by changes in the labor-management dyad, power shifts away from workers and into management hands, elimination and revision of worker protections, and increased flexibility in production and distribution as a result of digital technology

power: the capacity to effect change, influence, or control behaviors or outcomes

Process Safety Management of Highly Hazardous Chemicals: an OSHA standard set of choreographed approaches requiring the management of hazards associated with process industries using highly hazardous chemicals and intended to reduce the frequency and severity of incidents resulting from chemical releases and other sources

production-driven commodity chains: a global value chain in which the producer has the power to affect decisions dependent on the capacity of the firm and its ability to deliver product

Protect, Respect, and Remedy Framework: a 2005 document presented to the UN Human Rights Council by John Ruggie which proposed a three-core approach against human rights abuses through policy, regulation, and adjudication

public good: a concept in which goods/services are non-excludable and non-rivalrous so the use/consumption of one good/service by an individual does not interfere with its use/consumption by another individual

public utility commissions: a governing body regulating rates and services for public utilities which can be privately or publicly owned

purchasing practices: the interaction between global retailers and brands with manufacturers who produce their products; the practices include strategic planning and development and values, principles and behaviors which affect workers

Pure Food and Drug Act of 1906: legislation passed during Theodore Roosevelt's administration which prevented the manufacture, sale, or distribution of unsafe food, drugs, medicine, or liquor

regulation theory: the idea that capitalism must have rules and policies in place to stabilize market fluctuations

relational governance: a control system which builds relationships through reliance on the reputation of firms and family/ethnic ties

remunicipalisation: returning services from private control to public control

return on investment: the percentage of a firm's profitability in relationship to its cost

run-away insurance: a form of debt bondage used to keep workers in forced labor situations by requiring them to pay an insurance fee mitigating the risk should they abscond

SARA Title III: the Superfund Amendments and Reauthorization Act is a change in the 1980 Comprehensive Environmental Response, Compensation, and Liability Act (CERCLA), which is enforced by the Environmental Protection Agency (EPA), also known as the Superfund, which establishes the Emergency Planning and Community Right-To-Know Act (EPCRA); commonly known as SARA Title III, it sets requirements for local and state emergency planning around hazardous chemicals, the right of the public to access information on chemical hazards in their community, and the reporting responsibilities for facilities that use, store, and/or release hazardous chemicals

Schumpeter, Joseph: Austrian-born political economist and Harvard professor known for the concept "creative destruction," the idea that old ways of doing must be destroyed before new ways of doing can be created

Schumpeter's gale: another term for creative destruction which reflects the constant restructuring of old economic orders destroyed by war, economic crisis, or dereliction into new avenues for wealth creation

second industrial divide: a term coined by Piore (1984) which designated a period of time around the 1970s which focused on economies of scope rather than economies of scale

Sherman Act: 1890 federal antitrust legislation prohibiting any contract, conspiracy, or combination of business interests in restraint of foreign or interstate trade; the act effectively prohibited firms from fixing prices or any single organization from becoming a monopoly; it was created to counter the rising power of Standard Oil and US Steel and was hailed as the working people's Magna Carter

shock doctrine: the theory of capitalizing on a man-made or natural disaster which forces people and/or the environment into precarious circumstances and imposes austerity measures as a remedy in order to promote free market ideology

social power: the capacity to effect change by framing discourse through expertise, skill, knowledge, and information

social wastefulness: the idea that replacing a new product when the old product still has value is uneconomical activity

soft law: a voluntary, non-enforceable recommendation shielding violators of obligations from unwanted sanctions

special purpose entities: a legal unit, such as a limited partnership with outside parties, used by firms to protect the firm from financial risk

speed up: a management tactic to produce more units within the same time frame without accompanying pay increases

strategic litigation: (also known as impact litigation) presenting carefully selected human rights' cases to a court in order to affect broader societal changes

strategy of co-determination: legislation designed to elicit loyalty from employees by sharing decision-making power

structural adjustment policy: economic policy in the form of credit from the World Bank or the International Monetary Fund extended to developing and underdeveloped countries in order for these countries to repay debts owed to creditors

structural power: the capacity to effect change through a position within a structure such as an organization, market, government, or community

supply chain: a conduit through which goods and services are produced and distributed

supply chain transparency: readily available information to end users about sourcing, production, and delivery of a good or service

SWOT analysis: a study by an organization to identify its strengths, weaknesses, opportunities, and threats

Taft-Hartley Act of 1947: legislation passed during the Truman administration which allowed business to file unfair labor practices against labor unions and planted the seeds for right-to-work legislation; it passed over Truman's veto

Taylorism: a form of work organization which breaks down every job/action into its smallest segments in an effort to increase efficiency with a production system

trade agreement: a pact between two countries which set terms for the exchange of goods and services

Trade Facilitation and Trade Enforcement Act of 2015: US legislation to ensure a fair and competitive trade environment through enforcement by Customs and Border Patrol (CBP) which prohibits the entry of goods, subject to seizure, made by forced/conscripted labor into any US port

trade unions: an group of workers forming a solidarity bond to protect their wages, benefits, working condition, workplace voice, and social/political status

tragedy: a sudden event, accident, crime, or natural occurrence which causes enormous suffering, destruction, and pain

tragedy of the commons: an economic theory which says individuals choose to work in their own self-interest and deplete the resources available to everyone

transition economy: an economy moving from a command-centered economic system, characterized by state ownership and allocation of resources of goods and services, to a market-based economy, characterized by private ownership and allocation of goods and services

transnational corporation: a complex type of multi national corporation which has assets in at least two countries and gives decision-making power to individual foreign markets; examples are pharmaceuticals, petroleum, and information technology such as Shell, Deloitte, Glaxo-Smith Klein, and Roche

transnational interest blocs: a group of transnational firms based in market economies of the US, Japan, and the European Union who control GSCs by disproportionately influencing regional and global trade and investment agreements through business and trade negotiation linkages

Transpacific Partnership: a trade agreement between twelve countries in the Pacific Rim and North America to lower trade barriers and establish a dispute settlement process

Triangle Shirtwaist factory fire (1911): New York City's worst industrial disaster in which 146 garment workers died from fire and smoke inhalation

triangular employment: an employment arrangement in which the worker is separated from the employer through a third party

UK Modern Slavery Act of 2015: legislation enacted by the UK parliament requiring any commercial organization in an sector with a global annual turnover of 36 million pounds to disclose, in an annual Slavery and Human Trafficking Statement, the steps taken to address modern slavery in their business and supply chains

UN Human Development Report: an annual report published by the United Nations which gauges countries' sustainability in environmental, economic, and social arenas

UNCTAD: United National Conference on Trade and Development is the principle arm of the United National General Assembly responsible for trade, investment, and development in developing countries

UN-ICC Global Compact: a partnership, formed in 2016, between the United Nations and the International Chamber of Commerce to improve and promote private enterprise through awareness, opportunities and participation which supports the United Nations 2030 Agenda for Sustainable Development and its goals

Union Solidarity International: an organization based in the United Kingdom which uses media to train and support international trade union solidarity

United Nations 2030 Agenda for Sustainable Development: a set of seventeen sustainable development goals for peace and prosperity situated in the UN 2030 Agenda, an action plan for eliminating extreme poverty

United Nations Commission on Human Rights: a United Nations international commission concerned with protection and promotion of human rights in existence until 2006 when it became the Human Rights Council

United Nations Global Compact: a corporate sustainability initiative encouraging firms to align strategies/operations with the universal principles on human rights, labor and environment laws, and take action again corruption and for advancing societal goals

United Nations Human Rights Council: an inter-governmental organization within the United Nations responsible for promoting and protecting global human rights

upstream suppliers: firms in the supply chain who provide raw material for production

value chain governance: an umbrella term for different types of governance within global value chains including market, modular, relational, captive, and relational

vertical foreign direct investment: the arrangement of investments in upstream/downstream suppliers/distributors in different countries for the purpose of creating efficiencies in logistics, wages, skills, and availability of inputs

vertical integration: a strategic arrangement of suppliers and distributors owned or subcontracted by a firm in order to control production and distribution of a product

Washington Consensus: a group of free market economic ideas supported by the World Bank, the International Monetary Fund, developed industrialized countries, trade agreements, the World Trade Organization, and international organizations

welfare capitalism: the idea that management take responsibility for labor's well-being thus negating the need for labor to be represented by a union

wildcat strike: an unauthorized work stoppage

Women's Trade Union League: a coalition of working and professional women who joined together in 1930 to help organize low wage women workers into trade unions

Workers' Rights Consortium: an independent labor rights organization which monitors factories producing university apparel and logos in an effort to protect workers' rights and introduce transparency into the production system

World Bank: an international financial institution created after WWII to help reduce or alleviate poverty in developing countries

world system theory: a macro-concept which divides the world into core, periphery and semi-periphery countries focusing on the differences in high-skill, capital-intensive production and low-skill, labor-intensive production

World Trade Organization: an international organization created in 1995 to ensure smooth and predictable trade flows by enforcing the rules of trade between nations

Bibliography

ACT: Action, collaboration, transformation. 2017a. Geneva, Switzerland: IndustriALL Global Union. Accessed 01.25.2019. https://www.hiil.org/wp-content/uploads/2018/08/ACT_COMMS_Factsheet_2017_Final_Web.pdf.

ACT: Towards living wages in global supply chains. 2017b. The Hague, Netherlands: Hiil Innovating Justice. Accessed 01.25.2019. https://www.hiil.org/projects/act-towards-living-wages-in-global-supply-chains/.

Allen, B. 2011. Phillips 66: A lesson learned late. Health and Safety at Work. Surrey, UK: Lexisnexis. https://www.healthandsafetyatwork.com/content/phillips-66-lesson-learned-late.

Amin, S. 1976. *Unequal development*. New York: Monthly Review Press.

Andrees, B. 2016. Forced and child labour in the global supply chain. Penn State: Global Labour University.

Anner, M. 2015. Labor control regimes and worker resistance in global supply chains. *Labor History, 56*(3): 292–307.

Anner, M. 2016. Workers' strategies in a global economy. Penn State: Global Labour University.

Anner, M. 2017. Decent work in global supply chains. In *Script for video lecture: Pricing and sourcing dynamics in Global Supply Chains*. Pittsburgh, PA: Penn State.

Anner, M., Bair, J., & Blasi, J. 2013. Toward joint liability in global supply chains: Addressing the root causes of labor violations in international subcontracting networks. *Comparative Labor Law and Policy Journal, 35*(1): 1–44.

Anner, M., Bair, J., & Blasi, J. 2016. Learning from the past: The relevance of twentieth-century New York jobbers' agreements for twenty-first century global supply chains. In *Achieving Workers' Rights in the Global Economy*. Edited by R. Appelbaum & N. Lichtenstein. 239–258. Ithaca, NY: Cornell University Press.

Anner, M. & Caraway, T. 2010. International institutions and workers' rights: Between labor standards and market flexibility. *Studies in Comparative International Developments, 45*(2): 151–169. doi: 10.1007/s12116-010-9064-x.

Appelbaum, R. 2008. Giant transnational contractors in East Asia: Emergent trends in global supply chains. *Competition & Change, 12*(1): 69–87.

Appelbaum, R. & Lichtenstein, N. 2006. A new world of retail supremacy: Supply chains and workers' chains in the age of Wal-Mart. *International Labor and Working-Class History, 70*(1): 106–125. doi: 10.1017/S0147547906000184.

Arenco, E. 2018. Brand responsibility for mass fainting in Cambodian garment factories. Washington, DC, International Labor Rights Forum Blog. Accessed 01.25.2019. https://labor

rights.org/blog/201806/brand-responsibility-mass-faintings-cambodian-garment-factories.

Arrighi, G. 2009. China's market economy in the long run. In *China and the Transformation of Global Capitalism*. Edited by H. Hung. 22–49. Baltimore, MD: The John Hopkins University Press.

Bachrach, P. & Baratz, M. 1963. Decisions and nondecisions: An analytical framework. *American Political Science Review, 57*(3), 632–642. doi:10.2307/1952568.

Bair, J., Miller, D., & Dickson, M., ed. 2013. *Workers' rights and labor compliance in global supply chains: Is a social label the answer?* New York: Routledge.

Bair, J. & Palpacuer, F. 2015. CRS beyond the corporation: Contested governance in global value chains. *Global Networks, 15*(1): 1–19.

Bakvis, P. 2006. How the World Bank & IMF use the *Doing Business Report* to promote labour market deregulation in developing countries. Washington, DC: ICFTU/Global Unions.

Baldwin, R. 2012. Global supply chains: Why they emerged, why they matter, and where they are going. The Graduate Institute: Centre for Economic Policy Research, Geneva.

Barrett, J. 2016. Decent work in global supply chains. Global Labour University.

Barrientos, A. 2008. Financing social problems. Manchester, England: Brooks World Poverty Institute, University of Manchester.

Barrientos, S., Kothari, U., Phillips, N. 2013. Dynamics of unfree labour in the contemporary global economy. *The Journal of Development Studies, 49*(8): 1037–1041. doi: 10.1080/00220388.2013.780043.

Barrientos, S. & Smith, S. 2007. Do workers benefit from ethical trade? Assessing codes of labour practice in global production systems. *Third World Quarterly, 28*(4): 713–729.

Bauer, J. 2013. Where is business and human rights in Germany. Northampton, MA: CRSwire. Accessed 01.25.2019. http://www.csrwire.com/blog/posts/1139-where-is-business-and-human-rights-in-germany.

Birkbeck, C. D. & Botwright, K. 2015. The future of the global trade and investment architecture: Pursuing sustainable development in the global economy. The E15 Initiative. Geneva, Switzerland: International Centre for Trade and Sustainable Development. https://www.researchgate.net/profile/Carolyn_Birkbeck/publication/299997721_The_Future_of_the_Global_Trade_and_Investment_Architecture_Pursuing_Sustainable_Development_in_the_Global_Economy-Overview_of_Issues_Challenges_and_Debates/links/5708fe4e08ae2eb9421e2904/The-Future-of-the-Global-Trade-and-Investment-Architecture-Pursuing-Sustainable-Development-in-the-Global-Economy-Overview-of-Issues-Challenges-and-Debates.pdf.

Birkland, T. 1998. Focusing events, mobilization, and agenda setting. *Journal of Public Policy, 18*(1): 53–74.

Blanton, S., & Blanton, R. 2007. What attracts foreign investors? An examination of human rights and foreign investors? *Journal of Politics, 69*(1): 143–155.

Bolman, L. & Deal, T. 2013. *Reframing organizations: Artistry, choice, and leadership*. San Francisco, CA: Wiley.

Briquelet, K. 2017. Bride-to-be crushed to death by car-factory robot. The Daily Beast, January 3. https://www.thedailybeast.com/bride-to-be-crushed-to-death-by-car-factory-robot.

Bronfenbrenner, K. 2016. Strategic corporate research. Penn State: Global Labour University.

Burrow, S. 2016. The realities of work in global supply chains. Penn State: Global Labour University.

Burrow, S. 2017. Closing the loopholes: How legislators can build on the UK Modern Slavery Act. Brussels, Belgium: International Trade Union Confederation.

Busser, E. 2016. Decent work in global supply chains: the way forward. Penn State: Global Labour University.

Büthe, T. & Milner, H. 2008. The politics of foreign direct investment into developing countries: Increasing FDI through international trade agreements. *American Journal of Political Science, 52*(4): 741–762. doi: 10.1111/j.1540–5907.2008.00340.x. Cambridge, MA: Harvard University Press.

Caught at sea: Forced labour and trafficking in fisheries. 2013. Geneva, Switzerland: Governance and Tripartism Department-Special Action Programme to Combat Forced Labour (SAP-FL).

Center, Solidarity. 2008. Justice for all: A guide to worker rights in the global economy. Washington, DC: American Center for International Labor Solidarity.

Centre Medico International. 2017. Factory fire at KiK supplier. Frankfort, Germany: Medico International. Accessed 01.25.2019. https://www.medico.de/minor-fire-safety-improvements-could-have-saved-lives-16961/.

Chan, A. 2011. *Walmart in China*. Edited by A. Chan. Ithaca, NY: Cornell University Press.

Chan, J., Pun, N., & Selden, M. 2013. The politics of global production: China's new working class. *New Technology, Work, and Employment, 28*(2).

Chandler, A. 1990. *Scale and scope: The dynamics of industrial capitalism*. Cambridge, MA: Belknap Press of Harvard University Press.

Chirot, D. & Hall, T. 1982. World-system theory. *Annual Review of Sociology* 8: 81–106.

Clark, T. 1972. Structural-functionalism, exchange theory, and the new political economy: Institutionalization as a theoretical linkage. *Sociological Inquiry, 42*(3–4): 275–298.

Clavet, R., de Castro, G., Duagareilh, I., Duplessis, I., Gravel, E., Henry, H., Javillier, J., Linnik, M., Thorsen, S., Gao, Y., & Zack, A. 2008. Governance, international law & corporate social responsibility. Research Series. Geneva, Switzerland: International Institute for Labour Studies.

Coe, N., Dicken, P., & Hess, M. 2008. Global production networks: Realizing the potential. *Journal of Economic Geography, 8*(3): 271–295. https://doi.org/10.1093/jeg/lbn002.

Conference, International Labour. 2014. Transitioning from the informal to the formal economy.

Connections, Microlinks. 2016. 2.6.2. Types of value chain governance. USAID.

Corporate responsibility to respect human rights: An interpretive guide. 2012. New York and Geneva: United Nations Human Rights Office of the High Commissioner.

Cottle, E. 2016. The impact on development: Extractive industries. Penn State: Global Labour University.

Cox, R. 2013. Transnational capital and the politics of global supply chains. *Class, Race, and Corporate Power, 1*(1). doi: 10.25148/CRCP.1.1.16092153.

Cunningham, D. 2017. Alabama auto plants' horrific safety record reads "like Upton Sinclair or even Dickens." New York: Bloomberg Business News.

de Rugy, V. & Newmark, K. 2006. Hope after Katrina: Will New Orleans become the new city of choice? *Education Next, 6*, 4 (fall): 12–21.

Decent work in global supply chains. 2016. Geneva, Switzerland: International Labour Office.

Dole, E. 1990. Phillips Company Houston Chemical Complex Explosion and Fire. Washington, DC: Occupational Safety and Health Administration.

Duhigg, C. & Barboza, D. 2012. In China, human costs are built into an iPad. *New York Times*, January 25. https://www.nytimes.com/2012/01/26/business/ieconomy-apples-ipad-and-the-human-costs-for-workers-in-china.html.

Efrat, A. 2012. *Governing guns, preventing plunder: International cooperation against illicit trade*. Cambridge, MA: Oxford University Press.

Engler, M. 2008. Capitalism as catastrophe: A review of Naomi Klein's *The Shock Doctrine: The Rise of Disaster Capitalism*. *Dissent, 55*(2): 118–123.

Enrollment status of the population 3 years old and over by sex, age, race, Hispanic origin, foreign born, and foreign-born parentage: Table 1. 2012. Washington, D.C.: US Census Bureau.

Environmental Protection Agency. 2000. Amendments for testing and monitoring provisions. In *CFR > Title 29 > Subtitle B > Chapter XVII > Part 1910 > Subpart H > Section 1910.119*. Washington, DC: Federal Registry.

European Center for Constitutional and Human Rights. 2015. Fire in Akistani factory supplying European Companies kills over 260 people. Brussels, Belgium. Accessed 01.25.2019. http://corporatejustice.org/case-album/19-fire-in-akistani-factory-supplying-european-companies-kills-over-260-people.

European Coalition for Corporate Justice (ECCJ). 2017a. France adopts corporate duty of vigilance law. Retrieved June 2017. http://corporatejustice.org/news/393-france-adopts-corporate-duty-of-vigilance-law-a-first-historic-step-towards-better-human-rights-and-environmental-protection.

European Coalition for Corporate Justice (ECCJ). 2017b. Human rights due diligence. Brussels, Belgium: European Coalition for Corporate Justice.

European Commission. 2018. Report from the Commission to the European Parliament, the Council, and the European Economic and Social Committee on the application of the Council Directive on the approximation of the laws, regulations, and administrative provisions of the member states concerning liability for defective products (8/374/EEC). Brussels, Belgium: European Commission. Human Rights Treaties Division.

Fasciglione, M. 2016. Corporate human rights responsibility, states' duty to protect and UN GPs' National Action Plans: Some thoughts after the UK 2016 NAP update. *European Papers Insight, 1*(2): 621–635. doi: 10.15166/2499-2449/68.

Feasley, A. 2015. Deploying disclosure laws to eliminate forced labour: Supply chain transparency efforts of Brazil and the United States of America. *Anti-Trafficking Review* (5): 30–49. doi: 10:14197/atr.20121553.

Fichter, M. 2015. Fact sheet on global framework agreements (GFAs). Penn State: Global Labour University.

Fichter, M. 2016a. TNCs and labour: The contested terrain. In *Decent work in global supply chains*. Penn State: Global Labour University.

Fichter, M. 2016b. Transnational corporations as actors. Pittsburgh, PA: Global Labour University.

Flecker, J. 2010. Fragmenting labour: Organizational restructuring, employment relations and the dynamics of national regulatory frameworks. *Pluto Journals: Work Organization, Labour & Globalisation, 4*(1): 8–23.

Frank, A. 1984. The unequal and uneven historical development of the world economy. *Contemporary Marxism, 9*: 71–98.

Fransen, L. 2012. Corporate social responsibility and global labor standards: Firms and activists in the making of private regulation. New York: Routledge.

Frontlines. 2016. Scandal: Inside the global supply chains of 50 top companies. Brussels, Belgium: International Trade Union Confederation. GEHandbook-FINAL-FULL-WEB.pdf. Geneva: International Labour Office.

Gasana, C. 2016. Using technology to win. Penn State: Global Labour University.

Gereffi, G., Humphrey, J., & Sturgeon, T. 2005. The governance of global value chains. *Review of International Political Economy, 12*(1): 78–104.

Gereffi, G., Humphrey, J., & Sturgeon, T. 2013. Global value chain-oriented industrial policy: The role of emerging economies. In *Global value chains in a changing world*. Edited by D. L. Elms & P. Low. 329–360. Geneva: World Trade Organization.

Gereffi, G. & Lee, J. 2012. Why the world suddenly cares about global supply chains. *Journal of Supply Chain Management, 48*(3): 24–32. doi: 10.1111/j.1745-493X.2012.03271.x.

Gorsuch, J. 2018. *Epic Systems Corp. v. Lewis*. Edited by US Supreme Court. Washington, DC: US Supreme Court.

Graham, L. 1995. *On the line at Subaru-Isuzu*. Ithaca, NY: ILR/Cornell.

Gregoratti, C. & Miller, D. 2011. International framework agreements for workers' rights? Insights from River Rich Cambodia. *Global Labour Journal, 2*(2): 84–105. doi:http://dx.doi.org/10.15173/glj.v2i2.1098.

Grenier, Guillermo. 1988. *Inhuman relations: Quality circles and anti-unionism in American industry*. Philadelphia: Temple University Press.

Hadwiger, F. 2015. Global framework agreements: Achieving decent work in global supply chains? In *International Journal of Labour Research*: Decent work in global supply chains. Geneva: International Labour Office.

Hague Institute for Innovation of Law. 2018. Netherlands: The Hague. Accessed 01.25.2019. http://www.haguejusticeportal.net/index.php?id=2211.

Hale. T. & Held, D. 2011. *Handbook of transnational governance: Institutions and innovations*. Cambridge, UK: Polity.

Hammer, N. 2005. International framework agreements: Global industrial relations between rights and bargaining. *Transfer, 11*(4): 510–530.

Harris, K. 2015. The California Transparency in Supply Chains Act. California Department of Justice.

Helfen, M. & Fichter, M. 2013. Building transnational union networks across global production networks: Conceptualising a new arena of labor-management relations. *British Journal of Industrial Relations, 51*(3): 553–576.

Hirst, P. & Zeitlin, J. 1991. Flexible specialization versus post-Fordism: theory, evidence and policy implications. *Economy and Society, 20*(1): 1–56. doi: 10.1080/03085149100000001.

Holdcroft, J. & Lee, A. 2016. Workers' rights in global supply chains: Holding companies accountable. Geneva, Switzerland: IndustriALL Global Union. Last modified 02.14.2017. Accessed 02.14.2017. http://www.industriall-union.org/workers-rights-in-global-supply-chains-holding-companies-accountable.

Hoffer, F. 2016. Towards a living wage triangular industry-wide bargaining. Penn State: Global Labour University.

Horner, R. & Nadvi, K. 2017. Global value chains and the rise of the Global South: Unpacking twenty-first century polycentric trade. *Global Networks*. doi: 10.1111/glob.12180.

ILO domestic workers across the globe: Global and regional statistics and the extent of legal protections. 2013. Geneva, Switzerland: Department of Communication and Public Information.

Implications of global value chains for trade, investment, development and jobs. 2013. Saint Petersburg: G-20 Leaders Summit.

Industriall. 2018a. About us. Geneva, Switzerland: IndustriALL Global Union. Accessed 01.25.2019. http://www.industriall-union.org/about-us.

Industriall. 2018b. Unions outraged over LafargeHolcim's sudden u-turn on global commitments. Geneva, Switzerland: IndustriALL Global Union. Accessed 01.02.2019. http://www.industriall-union.org/unions-outraged-over-lafargeholcims-sudden-u-turn-on-global-commitments.

International Trade Union Confederation (ITUC). 2016. ITUC global rights index: Workers' rights weakened in most regions, worst year on record for attack on free speech and democracy. International Trade Union Confederation: Building Workers' Power. Accessed 02.16.2017. https://ituc-csi.org/ituc-global-rights-index-workers.

IUF. 2017. Uniting food, farm and hotel workers worldwide. The International Union of Food, Agricultural, Hotel, Restaurant, Catering, Tobacco and Allied Workers' Associations. Accessed 03.12.2017. http://www.iuf.org/w/.

Jeffress, C. 2000. Process safety management. Department of Labor. Washington, DC: Occupational Safety and Health Administration.

Jensen, Nathan M. 2003. Democratic governance and multinational corporations. *International Organization, 57*(3): 587–616.

Jha, P. 2016. Perpetuating dependency or climbing up the ladder. Penn State: Global Labour University.

Jha, P. & Chakraborty, A. 2014. Post-Fordism, global production networks and implications for labour: some case studies from National Capital Region, India. New Delhi: Institute for Studies in Industrial Development.

Juravich, T. 2007. Beating global capital: A framework and method for union strategic corporate research and campaigns. In K. Bronfenbrenner (Ed.), *Global unions: Challenging global capital through cross-border campaigns*. Ithaca, NY: Cornell University Press.

Kinley, D. & Chambers, R. 2006. The UN human rights norms for corporations: The private implications of public international law. *Human Rights Law Review, 6*: 447–497.

Kinley, D., Nolan, J., & Zerial, N. 2007. The politics of corporate social responsibility: Reflections on the United Nations Human Rights Norms for corporations. *Company and Securities Law Journal, 25*(1): 30–42.

Kilbourne, J. 2013. Brands must improve conditions for homeworkers in their supply chains. *The Guardian*, July 5. Cambridge, UK: Polity.

Klein, N. 2007. *The shock doctrine: The rise of disaster capitalism.* New York: Metropolitan.

Klein, N. 2017. No is not enough: Resisting Trump's shock politics and winning the world we need. Chicago: Haymarket.

Knudsen, J. 2013. The growth of private regulation of labor standards in global supply chains: Mission impossible for western small- and medium-sized firms? *Journal of Business Ethics, 117*(2): 387–398.

The Kondratieff theory. 2002. Accessed 02.15.2017. http://www.kwaves.com/kond_overview.htm.

Kucera, David. 2002. Core Labor Standards and Foreign Direct Investment. *International Labour Review, 141*(1): 31–70

Lamy, P. 2012. Governance of a multipolar world order. Singapore Global Dialogue Rajaratnam School of International Studies. Lanham, MD: Lexington.

Leadley, J., Corby, K., & Redmond, J. 2018. Update on the European Product Liability Directive—Still alive and kicking. *Global Compliance News*, May 24. https://globalcompliancenews.com/european-product-liability-directive-20180517/.

Lee, A. 2016. *Building cross-border trade union networks*. Penn State: Global Labour University.

Lichtenstein, N. 2009. *The retail revolution: How Wal-Mart created a brave new world of business*. New York: Metropolitan Books.

Lichtenstein, N., ed. 2005. *Wal-Mart: Template for 21st century capitalism?* New York: New York Press.

McDonough, T. 2003. What does long wave theory have to contribute to the debate on globalization. *Review of Radical Political Economics, 35*(3): 280–286.

Mikler, J. 2013. *Global companies as actors in global policy and governance, the handbook of global companies*. Malden, MA: Wiley-Blackwell.

Moore, G. 2004. The fair trade movement: Parameters, issues and future research. *Journal of Business Ethics, 53*(1–2): 73–86.

Moore, W. 1974. *Social change*. 2nd ed. Englewood Cliffs, NJ: Prentice-Hall.

Moran, T. 2002. *Beyond sweatshops*. Washington, DC: Brookings Institute.

Mote, H. 2016. Trade and development in Africa. Penn State: Global Labour University.

Muller-Hoff, C. 2011. Making corporations respond to the damage they cause: Strategic approaches to compensation and corporate accountability. Berlin: European Center for Constitutional and Human Rights.

Network, Maquila Solidarity. 2015. Brands and labour rights: How and when to engage with brands. http://www.maquilasolidarity.org/en/brands-and-labour-rights-how-and-when-engage-brands.

Nova, S. & Wegemer, C. 2016. Outsourcing horror. In *Achieving Workers' Rights in the Global Economy*. Edited by R. Appelbaum, & N. Lichtenstein. 17–31. Ithaca, NY: Cornell University Press.

Olson, M. 1971. *The logic of collective action: Public goods and the theory of groups*. Cambridge, MA: Harvard University Press.

Oman, C. 2000. Policy competition for foreign direct investment: A study of competition among governments to attract FDI. Paris: OECD.

Open Ended Intergovernmental Working Group (OEIGWG). 2016. Building a UN treaty on human rights and TNCs: A way forward to stop corporate impunity. Geneva: Global Campaign.

Organization, International Labour. 2017. Forced labour, modern slavery and human trafficking. International Labour Organization. Accessed 03.12.2017. http://www.ilo.org/global/topics/forced-labour/lang--en/index.htm.

Oswald, R. 2016. Using campaigns to make a difference. Penn State: Global Labour University.

Page, R. 2011. Co-determination in Germany—A beginner's guide. The Hans Bockler Foundation.

Painter, J. 1995. Regulation theory, post-Fordism and urban politics. In *Theories of Urban Politics*. Edited by D. Judge, G. Stoker, & H. Wolman. 276–315. Thousand Oaks, CA: Sage.

Pantland, W. 2015. Using technology to organise: A guide for trade union activists from Union Solidarity International (USI). 3rd ed. Manchester and Glasgow: Union Solidarity International.

Papadakis, K. 2008. Cross-border social dialogue and agreements: An emerging industrial relations framework? Geneva: International Institute for Labour Studies.

Piore, M. & Sable, C. 1984. *The second industrial divide: Possibilities for prosperity*. New York: Basic Books.

Porter, M. & Kramer, M. 2006. Strategy & society: The link between competitive advantage and corporate social responsibility. *Harvard Business Review, 84*(12): 78–92. https://www.comfama.com/contenidos/servicios/Gerenciasocial/html/Cursos/Columbia/Lecturas/Strategy-Society.pdf.

Porter, M. & Kramer, M. 2011. Creating shared value: How to reinvent capitalism. *Harvard Business Review, 89*(1/2): 62–77.

Poverty rates for selected detailed race and Hispanic groups by state and place: 2007–2011. 2012. Washington, D.C.: US Census Bureau.

Rana Plaza: A look back and forward. 2014. Institute for Global Labour and Human Rights. http://www.globallabourrights.org/campaigns/factory-collapse-in-bangladesh.

Richter, J. 2001. Regulation of transnational corporations: A historical perspective. In *Holding corporations accountable: Corporate conduct, international codes*. Edited by J. Richter. 6–27. London and New York: Zed.

Robinson, W. 2011. Globalization and the sociology of Immanuel Wallerstein: A critical appraisal. *International Sociology, 26*(6): 723–745. doi: 10.1177/0268580910393372.

Robinson, W. 2012. Global capitalism theory and the emergence of transnational elites. *Critical Sociology, 38*(3): 349–363. doi: 10.1177/089692051141159.

Ross, I. 1998. The invention of the transistor. *Proceedings of the IEEE, 86*(1): 7–28. doi: 10.1109/5.658752. San Francisco, CA: Wiley.

Ruggie, J. 2014. Just business: Multinational corporations and human rights. New York: W.W. Norton.

Russell, M. 2015. Brands back industry-wide wage bargaining Cambodia. just-style, September 25, n.p., News & Insights. https://www.just-style.com/analysis/brands-back-industry-wide-wage-bargaining-in-cambodia_id126265.aspx.

Scannell, G. 1991. Standard interpretations. Retrieved 3.5.2018. https://www.osha.gov/pls/oshaweb/owadisp.show_document?p_table=INTERPRETATIONS&p_id=20192

Scherer, A., Palazzo, G., & Baumann, D. 2006. Global rules and private actors: Toward a new role of the transnational corporation in global governance. *Business Ethics Quarterly, 16*(4): 505–532. doi: 10:5840/beq200616446.

Scherrer, C. 2016a. Introduction to the regulatory framework. Penn State: Global Labour University.

Scherrer, C. 2016b. Investment and dispute settlement. Penn State: Global Labour University.

Schumpeter, J. (1942) 1975. *Capitalism, socialism, and democracy*. New York: Harper.

Serrano, M. & Xhafa, E. 2016. From "precarious informal employment" to "protected employment": The "positive transitioning effect" of trade unions. Switzerland: International Labour Office. Services International and the Transnational Institute.

Shams, S. 2017. German retailer KiK compensates Pakistan's "industrial 9/11" families. Bonn, Germany: DW Akademie. Retrieved 09.02.2017. https://www.dw.com/en/german-retailer-kik-compensates-pakistans-industrial-9-11-families/a-37470138

Shannon, T. 2018. *An introduction to the world-system perspective*. 2nd ed. New York: Rutledge.

St-Onge, C. G. 2016. Forced labour: What investors need to know. United Kingdom: ShareAction.

Stuckler, D., McKee, M., Shaw, E., & Basu, S. 2012. Manufacturing epidemics: The role of global producers in increased consumption of unhealthy commodities including processed foods, alcohol, and tobacco. *PLoS Medicine, 9*(6): 695.

Suhong, L., Ragu-Nathan, B., Ragu-Nathan, T., & Rao, S. 2006. The impact of supply chain management practices on competitive advantage and organizational performance. *Omega, 34*(2).

Tokarski, E. 2013. *The safety professional's role: In support of industrial facilities, operations, and maintenance (O&M)*. Bloomington, IN: Xlibris.

Trade Facilitation and Trade Enforcement Act of 2015. 2015. Pub. L. No. 114–125, 19 U.S.C. 4301. Washington, DC: Government Publishing Office.

UNCTAD. 2013. Global value chains: Investment and trade for development. World Investment Report 2013, United National Conference on Trade and Development. New York and Geneva: United Nations Publication.

UNCTAD. 2015a. IIA issue notes: Recent trends in IIAs and ISDS. UNCTAD. http://unctad.org/en/PublicationsLibrary/webdiaepcb2015d1_en.pdf.

UNCTAD. 2015b. Information economy report 2015: Unlocking the potential of e-commerce for developing countries. UNCTAD. http://unctad.org/en/PublicationsLibrary/ier2015_en.pdf.

UNCTAD. 2017. World investment report: Investment and the digital economy. In *United Nations Conference on Trade and Development*. Geneva: United Nations.

UNEP year book 2014: Emerging issues in our global environment. 2015. Kenya: United Nations Publication.

United Nationals Environment Program. 2017. Trade and green economy: A handbook. International Institute for Sustainable Development. https://www.unenvironment.org/resources/report/trade-and-green-economy-handbook.

ur-Rehman, A., Walsh, D., & Massod, S. 2012. More than 300 killed in Pakistani factory fires. *New York Times*, p. A6. http://www.nytimes.com/2012/09/13/world/asia/hundreds-die-in-factory-fires-in-pakistan.html.

Utting, P. 2000. Codes in context: TNC regulation in an era of dialogues and partnerships. UK: The CornerHouse.

Vallas, S. 2003. The adventures of managerial hegemony: Teamwork, ideology, and worker resistance. *Social Problems, 50*(2): 204–225. doi: 10.1525/sp.2003.50.2.204.

Vitali, S., Glattfelder, J. & Battiston, S. 2011. The network of global corporate control. *PLOS One, 6*(10): 1–6. doi: 10.1371/journal.pone.0025995.

Wainwright, H. 2014. The tragedy of the private: The potential of the public. Amsterdam: Public Services International. http://world-psi.org/sites/default/files/documents/research/alternatives_to_privatization_en_booklet_web_april.pdf.

Waldman, P. 2017. Inside Alabama's auto jobs boom: Cheap wages, little training, crushed limbs. Bloomberg News, March 28. Retrieved 4.10.2018. https://www.bloomberg.com/news/features/2017-03-23/inside-alabama-s-auto-jobs-boom-cheap-wages-little-training-crushed-limbs.

Walker, M. 2015. *The daily grind: How workers navigate the employment relationship*. Lanham, MD: Lexington.

Wallerstein, I. 2011. *The modern world-system I: Capitalist agriculture and the origins of the European world-economy in the sixteenth century*. Berkeley and Los Angeles, CA: University of California Press.

Weil, D. 2014. *The fissured workplace: Why work became so bad for so many and what can be done to improve it*. Cambridge, MA: Harvard University Press.

Weiss, T. & Wilkinson, R., ed. 2014. *International organization and global governance*. New York: Routledge.

Wells, D. 2007. Too weak for the job: Corporate codes of conduct, non-governmental organization and the regulation of international labour standards. *Global Social Policy, 7*(1), 51–73.

What do we mean by "brand engagement?" 2016. Maquila Solidarity Network. Accessed 01.25.2019. http://www.maquilasolidarity.org/sites/maquilasolidarity.org/files/Brand_engagement_MSN_2016.pdf.

Wolf, P. J. & Lasserre-Cortez, S. 2018. An exploratory analysis of features of New Orleans charter schools associated with student achievement growth (REL 2018–287). Washington, DC: U.S. Department of Education, Institute of Education Sciences, National Center for Education Evaluation and Regional Assistance, Regional Educational Laboratory Southwest. http://ies.ed.gov/ncee/edlabs.

WTO. 2014. International Trade Statistics 2014. WTO. https://www.wto.org/english/res_e/statis_e/its2014_e/its2014_e.pdf.

WTO. 2015. Report on G-20 trade measures (mid-October 2014 to mid-May 2015). WTO. https://www.wto.org/english/res_e/statis_e/its2014_e/its2014_e.pdf.

Yates, J. 1989. Phillips Petroleum chemical plant explosion and fire (U. F. A. N. F. D. Center, Trans.). Washington, DC: Federal Emergency Management Agency.

Yeung, H. & Coe, N. 2015. Toward a dynamic theory of global production networks. *Economic Geography, 91*(1): 29–58.

Zimmer, R. 2016. Legal approaches to hold transnational corporations accountable. Penn State: Global Labour University.

Index

About the Author

Marquita R. Walker is an associate professor in the Department of Labor Studies, School of Social Work, at Indiana University Purdue University Indianapolis (IUPUI). She holds a PhD in educational leadership and policy analysis and an MS in public affairs from the University of Missouri, Columbia, and an MS and a BS in English from Missouri State University and Drury University respectively. Her scholarly research and career interests involve workers and their education, workers' (re)integration into the workforce, and gender roles as barriers to women in the workforce. Her previous publications include peer-reviewed articles, book chapters, and a book, *The Daily Grind: How Workers Navigate the Employment Relationship* (2015). Dr. Walker has been involved practically and theoretically with manufacturing, organized labor, and collective bargaining for over thirty-five years.